FOR WHOM THE DOGS SPY

FOR WHOM THE DOGS SPY

Haiti: From the Duvalier Dictatorships to the Earthquake, Four Presidents, and Beyond

Raymond A. Joseph

Arcade Publishing
New York

First Edition

Arcade Publishing books may be purchased in bulk at special discounts for sales promotion, corporate gifts, fund-raising, or educational purposes. Special editions can also be created to specifications. For details, contact the Special Sales Department, Arcade Publishing, 307 West 36th Street, 11th Floor, New York, NY 10018 or arcade@skyhorsepublishing.com.

Arcade Publishing® is a registered trademark of Skyhorse Publishing, Inc.®, a Delaware corporation.

Visit our website at www.arcadepub.com.

10 9 8 7 6 5 4 3 2 1

Library of Congress Cataloging-in-Publication Data is available on file.

Jacket design by Georgia Morrissey
Cover photographs: Thinkstock, Shutterstock, Associated Press

Print ISBN: 978-1-62872-540-7
Ebook ISBN: 978-1-62872-554-4

Printed in the United States of America

In sympathy with the families of the thousands of victims of the January 12, 2010, earthquake and in memory of my father Joseph Lemeuble Joseph and my mother Julienne Bonny.

CONTENTS

INTRODUCTION

Haiti, nicknamed the "Land of Voodoo," is full of mysteries. Even the 2010 devastating earthquake that razed Port-au-Prince and its surroundings was considered one of those mysteries. Some people tied it to the pact that the Haitian leaders supposedly made with the Devil to win independence more than two hundred years ago. Apparently God had been angry with Haitians ever since. That mystery is debunked in this book.

The book is titled *For Whom the Dogs Spy* because dictator François "Papa Doc" Duvalier used the mysteries of Voodoo to control the nation. Since inanimate objects and animals may have souls, Papa Doc convinced the people that certain animals, especially dogs, could spy for him and were in his service. In fact, he convinced the people that he himself could transform into a dog! And so as a result people, no matter how intelligent, would stop speaking whenever animals were around, especially when they were talking about politics. Fighting fire with fire, I managed to use the dogs against the dictator. But can dogs really spy? You will find out as you read this book.

Beyond superstition, there are the realities of Haiti. The ostracism of Haiti by the international powers was the price the country paid for its effrontery in challenging an economic system built on the backs of Black slaves. It took a major earthquake to make the world focus on Haiti.

Others have written about the history of Haiti going back to 1492 when Christopher Columbus "discovered" the jewel that he called Española (Little Spain) and to which he laid claim for the Crown of Spain. But I am concentrating here on an unique slice of history in which I participated from the late 1950s to the present. In having been involved with Haitian politics for decades and having worked under four presidents, I find it important to share a contemporary history of Haiti.

From 1967 – 1986, the struggle for democracy left about 30,000 dead by the Duvalier dictatorships of father-and-son. Thousands more were exiled. In a Cold War era, the dictators found favor with Washington, especially when the Republicans were in power. Yet, it was Republican President Ronald Reagan who finally severed ties with Jean-Claude "Baby Doc" Duvalier and pushed him out of office.

Then it was a bloody road to democracy which has yet to flourish in a land where most of the leaders identify democracy with their own interests. In their folly, they want to hold on to power for life, even if indirectly.

It is sad that a quarter century after the overthrow of Jean-Claude Duvalier's dictatorship, the specter of Duvalierism haunts us again. One would have thought that that doctrine died with the death of Jean-Claude Duvalier on October 4, 2014. But, by his actions, current President Michel Martelly shows that his model is François "Papa Doc" Duvalier.

Chapter 1

January 12, 2010: A Life Change

January 12, 2010, changed my life. Undoubtedly, many people, especially in Haiti, may make the same claim. In my case, the change was so profound it even surprised me. Instead of going into retirement after my second stint at the Embassy of Haiti in Washington, as I had envisioned, and concentrating on writing my memoirs, I decided to plunge into the internal politics of my country—for better or for worse.

Around 4:45 p.m. on that day, I was at the US Embassy when I received a telephone call from an official at the State Department who asked whether I had heard what happened to my country. I had not. He proceeded to tell me about an earthquake of a magnitude 7.0 on the Richter scale that destroyed the capital of Port-au-Prince and surrounding towns; that casualties, including the dead and wounded, were thought to be in the thousands.

"Really! Thank you," I said. "I will call you back." And I hung up.

Immediately, I picked up the phone to call Haiti and dialed the Foreign Ministry, my immediate boss. No answer. I tried the Prime Minister's office. No answer. And the President's office at the National Palace. No answer. I made a fourth call to the cell phone of the Secretary General. Ambassador Fritz Longchamp picked up and, in an anxious voice, asked: "How did you get to me, Ray? This is a miracle. I just parked my car, because there is no possibility of driving. I am walking on Bourdon, houses are falling, right and left. I don't know how I will get home, because there is a small bridge to cross to get to my house and I don't know whether it has not crumbled."

"Have you spoken to the president?" I asked.

"No!"

"To whom have you spoken? Any official?"

"To nobody."

And the telephone conversation went dead.

Then the images appeared on CNN. The National Palace, the seat of power, crumbled; the buildings housing various ministries, across from the Palace, flattened. It was desolation all around. I concluded that the officials were all dead! A feeling of helplessness engulfed me.

At that moment, alone in my office in Washington, I gave some weight to my title of "Ambassador Extraordinary and Plenipotentiary." I felt that I had to assume the responsibilities and accept the burden of the whole country, because my superiors were nowhere to be found. I was left without instructions. Yet, this was an emergency that required fast thinking and decisive action.

I began to call the authorities in the United States government and asked that certain actions be taken immediately. These included putting order and assuming control and security at the Port-au-Prince airport and setting up new communications towers. The major telephone networks were down. I asked the State Department to send the USNS *Comfort*, the 1,000-bed Navy hospital ship, to Haiti immediately. "Mr. Ambassador, the *Comfort* is more than twelve days away from Haitian shores," an official told me. "But we can give you four frigates. They will be there in the morning." Indeed they were.

Two days after the earthquake, order was restored at the Port-au-Prince airport by the US military and telephone service partially restored. The *Comfort*, which was docked in Baltimore at the time, was mobilized. It arrived in the bay off the capital on January 18, six days after the earthquake and six days earlier than previously promised.

At 5:15 p.m., the Dominican Ambassador to Washington, Roberto B. Saladin Selin arrived at my Embassy. He had walked from the Dominican Chancery on 21st Street, one block away from ours on Massachusetts Avenue. Ambassador Saladin expressed his condolences and those of the Dominican government and the Dominican people. Then, he told me that his Foreign Minister was in New York and wanted to talk to me. On his cell phone, Ambassador Saladin dialed Chancellor Carlos Morales Troncoso, who told me he needed an authorized signature to open the border crossings between the two nations. But he could not locate any of my superiors in Port-au-Prince. The Dominican Republic, however, was ready to take in as many of the wounded as possible and Dominican first responders were ready to cross into Haiti with equipment to help as soon as that could be authorized.

I told Chancellor Troncoso that I would sign the document his ambassador had presented me. And I did. By 6:00 p.m., the border crossings between the two countries sharing the island of Hispaniola were open. Aid started to flow in and the wounded began to arrive in Dominican hospitals—by ambulance, cars, trucks, and helicopters. The Dominican Republic became the gateway by which organizations and people streamed into Haiti.

By 5:30 p.m. Bernardo Alvarez Herrera, the Venezuelan ambassador in Washington, arrived at the Haitian Embassy, having walked from his residence on Massachusetts Avenue. After expressing his condolences and those of the Venezuelan government and people, he said he needed my signature to authorize delivery of 225,000 barrels of petroleum products—all grades comprised—to Haiti.

Shipments would have to come via the Dominican border, because the Port-au-Prince wharf was badly damaged. The ambassador said the shipments would meet Haiti's need for fuel for a full month. I signed. I also teamed up with Ambassador Alvarez in a program to have CITGO, the Venezuelan government-owned gasoline company in the United States, undertake help and rescue missions to Haiti.

That evening I was on CNN explaining the layout of the capital and the initial contacts that I had with several officials and diplomats, especially from the CARICOM countries. Then the other television networks descended on me or dispatched limousines to rush me to their studios. I was nearly 1,500 miles from the scene, what was I going to say? With no information from my superiors in Port-au-Prince, I felt stuck, so I decided to turn the tragedy into a platform to tell the world about Haiti's history, especially now that they were ready to listen. I wanted to reclaim the so-called "poorest country in the Western Hemisphere" as the "Fount of Freedom" for the Americas.

By 10 p.m. that day, I learned through our consul general in Miami that the President was alive. So were the Prime Minister and all the ministers. I was somewhat relieved, but still saddened, because we had lost several of our best cadres, including some at the Foreign Ministry with whom I used to communicate. That same evening, I also learned that Signal FM, a radio station in Pétionville, the former upscale suburb five miles east of Port-au-Prince, was operating. It was the main source of information via the Internet, especially for Haitians in the diaspora. Yet, no government official had gone to Signal FM to comfort and rally the people. Why?

On that day, I resolved that Haiti needed new leadership. I decided to return to Haiti to help provide new leadership at the top. I decided to run for the presidency.

I had always worked to bring people together, to create coalitions. The highest post to which I ever aspired was that of secretary general of the various opposition movements. I never craved the post of ambassador. But at critical times in recent Haitian history, when the country was undergoing major upheavals, I was called upon twice— in 1990 and 2004—to head Haiti's Embassy in Washington.

During the crisis, however, my urge for national leadership had to be put in abeyance. I threw myself totally into managing what I could from Washington. The Mayor of Washington, Adrian Fenty, offered to help. Three days after the catastrophe, the Mayor's staff with help from Homeland Security set up a Command Center at the Embassy. We were equipped with twenty computers and as many monitors, plus staff. On January 19, a week after the earthquake, Mayor Fenty came to the Embassy to observe the work of the Center and to give a joint press conference with me where he pledged the city's support in Haiti's time of need.

The Command Center was operational on a 24-hour basis. While in Washington, we had a virtual view of Haiti, especially of the Port-au-Prince area. From the basement of the Embassy, our operators were linking families together in Haiti and coordinating aid in the Washington metropolitan area. Also, the Embassy coordinated with the State Department to facilitate the travel of several Haitian officials who were stranded abroad.

The Greater Washington Haiti Relief Committee changed its name to The Greater Washington Relief Fund and went into action. Two years earlier, after Hurricanes Ike and Hannah had devastated Gonaïves, in north-central Haiti, I had urged the various Haitian humanitarian groups in the Washington metropolitan area to form a permanent organization to be ready in times of crisis. The earthquake of 2010 was their first major crisis and they performed admirably.

With no official instructions or directives from my superiors in Port-au-Prince, I could have done what a Haitian diplomat told me was the grounds of his successful career. "You know, my friend," he told me, "whoever presents his head gets it chopped." On that basis, he had been in the Haitian diplomatic corps for nearly four decades.

Oblivious of what others said or thought, during the first days following the earthquake, I plunged into full representation of Haiti at all levels. Meanwhile, I kept hoping that the higher-ups in Port-au-Prince would eventually speak up or contact me. When, on January 14, two days after the earthquake, Haiti's President René Préval spoke publicly, it was to display his despondency. "My palace collapsed," he cried. "I am also homeless! I don't know where I am going to sleep tonight!" Dressed shabbily, the words from President Préval's mouth left most Haitians at home and abroad adrift and disgusted.

Despite any negative feeling I may have had concerning the performance of the president during the crisis, I defended him. Appearing on several television programs, I challenged people to put themselves in his shoes. "Imagine that Washington would have been crushed as badly as Port-au-Prince is," I said. "Imagine the White House destroyed. The Pentagon, Police departments, the CIA and FBI headquarters! Imagine the banks, hospitals, restaurants, schools. Imagine that there are no means of communication, because all the telephone companies have been silenced. So are the radio and television networks. For, almost everything is concentrated in Port-au-Prince, the capital, which is destroyed."

"Do you think your president would have appeared immediately on the air to speak to the Nation?" I asked.

While I spoke like that publicly, internally I kept saying to myself, *But Signal FM was still operating and all our top officials were alive. Why did none of them show up?* Haitian officials seem to be guided by the same principle that my diplomat-friend shared with me and felt it best not to question authority. If the President of the Republic has not spoken, no one, not even the prime minister, dares to say anything. Any action on their part would appear as usurpation of power. Some said, "The President was under shock." If so, he should have delegated power to someone less shocked. He should have put aside his dislike of Signal FM which had been critical of him and his team. The country needed to hear him.

Mario Viaud, the proprietor of Signal FM, told me that he was ready to make the station available to the government, but no one had contacted him. Therefore, he remained the private voice that kept listeners informed, especially in the diaspora. Other stations, more restrictively, because of their lack of Internet connection, were also operating locally like Mélodie FM and Radio Maximum. No official visited them to rally the people.

Meanwhile, from Washington, I responded to any direct or indirect attack on Haiti. Reverend Pat Robertson, the conservative evangelical icon from Virginia, gave me the best opportunity to shed light on Haiti.

In an interview with Rachel Maddow on MSNBC, Rev. Robertson said that the earthquake that hit Haiti was God's punishment for the pact that the Haitian leaders had signed with the Devil to obtain their independence. He was no doubt referring to the "Ceremony of Cayman Woods," in northern Haiti, not far from Cap-Haïtien, Haiti's second largest city. On August 14, 1791, a slave named Boukman, of Jamaican ancestry, presided over a big nocturnal religious ceremony that is considered the debut of the slave insurrection against the French slave holders. It was their usual Saturday night Voodoo ceremony and one would suspect that it would be well attended. At one point in the ceremony, a huge pig was slain and its blood passed around for all to taste. The sharing of the blood represented a pact to work against their oppressors.

I was in the Washington studio of NBC when Rev. Robertson made his offensive remarks. I declined to answer Ms. Maddow's questions about the earthquake until I addressed the statement of the conservative minister. "Some people don't know the history of their country. Otherwise, they would have known that the so-called pact with the Devil signed by the Haitians had allowed the United States of America to become the country it is today. For, it was our defeat of Napoléon Bonaparte's army that forced the

French to sell the Louisiana Territory in 1803." Indeed, with the stroke of a pen, the new American nation more than doubled its territory overnight.

"It was also that pact with the Devil that allowed Simon Bolivar to depart from Haiti in 1816 with boats, arms, ammunition, and men to go liberate *Gran Colombia*. Obviously, Haiti is the only country which has yet to benefit from the alleged pact with the Devil."

My comments on CNBC brought me an avalanche of mail, all laudatory and supportive. I don't know what kind of response CNBC got, but I would venture to say that it must have been overwhelming. Somehow, this short history lesson had an impact that put Haiti in a new light for many. For months afterward, I was approached in restaurants, on flights and elsewhere by complete strangers to thank me for speaking out on their behalf.

The Congressional Black Caucus (CBC), the bloc of African American legislators in the US Congress, came to my support immediately. Soon after my intervention on CNBC, a CBC delegation, led by its chairperson, Congresswoman Barbara Lee (Democrat of California), came to the Embassy to give a press conference in support of Haiti and of what I was doing. Moreover, I was invited to Congress to address the Black Caucus. One Congressman stood up and, no doubt, echoing the sentiment of almost all, spoke emotionally, "Brother, you spoke for us when you responded to Pat Robertson the way you did."

———

Churches, synagogues, and schools invited me to speak about Haiti. I addressed several congregations around Washington, including in Maryland and Virginia. I traveled to states like California, Florida, Texas, Missouri, Pennsylvania, New York, New Jersey, Connecticut, and Massachusetts, to tell the history of Haiti and how it is intertwined with that of the United States and of the Western Hemisphere.

I addressed students of all levels—from elementary schools like the prestigious Georgetown Day School in Washington to universities such as George Washington University, Yale, Princeton, University of Virginia and others. I was often asked about Haiti's alleged influence in changing the course of history in America and in the Western Hemisphere. With a dose of incredulity, students often asked about how a country as poor as Haiti could have helped America.

Haitians fought for America's freedom, even before Haiti gained its own independence. The participation of soldiers from Haiti under the command of French officers, like Comte d'Estaing in the Battle of Savannah, Georgia, goes back to 1779. Many of those soldiers were also at the Battle of Yorktown under General Lafayette. Finally, in 2007, the City of Savannah unveiled a monument in the center of town to the memory of the *"Chasseurs Volontaires de St. Domingue,"* the elite fighters who covered the retreat of the American forces. Those fighters were precursors of Haitians.

However, the Louisiana Purchase remains the most important indirect contribution of the Haitian revolutionaries to the United States. Faced with the loss of their wealthiest colony, the French dispatched about 40,000 troops to the colony in 1802. Their mission was to squash the slave revolt and continue on to the "Northern Territories," or Louisiana, which was comprised of land west of the Mississippi River to the Rockies, and from the Gulf of Mexico to the Canadian border. The French plan was foiled when the Haitian combatants signed a pact of unity at Arcahaie on May 18, 1803. Former Black slaves had teamed up with freed mulattoes to fight the French.

When the French learned about the "Congress of Arcahaie," they knew they could no longer resist such a united force. Retroactively, they signed, on April 30, 1803, the document finalizing the sale of the Louisiana Territory. There is no doubt that the French did not want the Haitians to get credit for setting up an empire in the New

World. On November 18, 1803, six months after the May 18 unity pact, the French were vanquished at the Battle of Vertières, near Cap Haïtien.

Haitian involvement in the development of the United States is paramount to this country's history. It is not generally known that Jean-Baptiste Pointe du Sable, credited with having the first trading post with the Potawatomi Indians on the Chicago River, was a native of Haiti. He is considered the founder of Chicago. The US Post Office issued a Black Heritage 22-cent postage stamp in his honor on February 20, 1987.

Pierre Toussaint was a slave attached to the household of the Jean Bérard family which escaped from Haiti in 1787, ahead of the revolution, to establish themselves in New York. When Bérard died and his family was in dire financial straits, Pierre Toussaint provided for the widow to help maintain her status in society until she died. A hairdresser for ladies of high society, Pierre Toussaint became a wealthy man who attended to the needy. He built a school and an orphanage for poor Blacks, and is known to have discreetly provided financially for some French expatriates in need. A devout Catholic, it is written that he attended mass daily at the St. Peter's Roman Catholic Church in New York. He contributed handsomely for the advancement of his church which, in turn, has honored him in death. The church where he worshipped in downtown New York City is located on Pierre Toussaint Square, at Barclay and Church Streets, near the World Trade Center. In 1990, the bones of Pierre Toussaint were transferred from the old Negro cemetery in downtown Manhattan to a vault under St. Patrick's Cathedral on Fifth Avenue, the only layman to share that dwelling with departed bishops and cardinals.

Mother Mary Elizabeth Lange, the nun who arrived in the United States around 1817, is credited to have founded the first school for Black girls in Baltimore. Her work allowed the emergence of an educated class of Black women in Baltimore.

Haiti has produced giants in various domains and they have impacted America and the world in immeasurable ways. The tragic earthquake allowed me to talk about Haiti in a new light. Undoubtedly, Haiti would not be the "poorest country in the Western Hemisphere" today, had it not challenged slavery and the economic order in force over five centuries. Haiti did not obtain its independence in the '50s and '60s when many countries in the so-called Third World were shedding their colonial yoke and were being wooed by East and West looking for potential allies in the ideological war that shook the world.

The earthquake allowed me to appreciate human solidarity and kindness in adversity in America. Reportedly half of US households contributed something for Haitian relief. Children in schools collected their dollars and cents that were delivered to the Embassy. Great was my surprise when my secretary announced that a group of homeless folks from Washington had come to see me. They had a special donation to make for the victims of the earthquake.

I received them in my office. The delegation of about a dozen homeless men and women had brought their dollars which were counted in front of me. It amounted to less than $100. Marie-Claude Malebranche, the secretary, recorded their donation along with the checks for thousands of dollars, yea millions, contributed via the Embassy of Haiti for the victims of the devastating earthquake. By the time I resigned on August 1st, 2010, I had collected more than $4 million that was deposited in a special account at the branch of Citibank in Washington where the Embassy kept its accounts. All the money was transferred to an emergency account at the Ministry of Finance.

Sometime in February, I received a $3 million check from the Ambassador of Ghana in Washington. That transaction caused a commotion when our bank advised that it was in local currency.

President Préval, who was aware of the substantial check, told me that it would amount to only $100,000 to $200,000. I told the President that I would not accept anything but $3 million in US currency, because that's what the Ghanaian ambassador had told me it was. Along with a delegation, the ambassador had his photo taken with me in my office at the Embassy, while I was accepting the check.

On receiving the report about the Ghanaian check from Citibank, I contacted the Ghanaian ambassador to explain the anomaly. He said he would follow through with his ministry. Days later the ambassador called me to apologize. He explained that the accountant had made a mistake and wrote the check from a local currency account instead of the dollar account used for international operations. He assured me that this would be rectified.

In late April, I received a new $3 million check. I waited for it to clear before letting President Préval know that the sum of $3 million in US currency was in the earthquake emergency account. For, one of the first questions the President had asked when we met in New York at the International Donors' Conference on March 31, 2010, was: "Ambassador, where is the $3 million from Ghana?"

If President Préval appreciated what I had done for Haiti after the earthquake, there was no indication of that. Instead, I sensed resentment on his part. The Haitian *teledyòl*, or grapevine, was rife with comments about the insult felt by "The Palace" about my usurpation of power after the earthquake. "He was acting as president," they said, of my jumping into the void of leadership on the part of my superiors. Perhaps the Palace folks were reacting to comments by some viewers of television programs who had asked whether I was Haiti's president. After all, the president and all his ministers were absent in the first two days following the catastrophe that left the country somewhat rudderless. As I already explained, I had to assume responsibility for Haiti at a time when it appeared forlorn.

On February 12, one month after the earthquake, I accompanied a Congressional delegation on a one-day trip to Haiti to assess the situation. The bipartisan and bicameral delegation, headed by Speaker Nancy Pelosi, included several senior legislators, including Congressmen Charles Rangel, John Conyers, and Senator Frank Lautenberg. When the delegation met with President Préval and his staff, he snubbed me. On presenting the officials seated at the table with him, the President never mentioned me. When Speaker Pelosi's turn came to speak, she rectified the slip—or snub—by acknowledging me, the ambassador who had accompanied the delegation and who had worked diligently since the earthquake. That's when all those seated at the long table with President Préval turned to see me sitting in the back row behind the President's team.

The action of President Préval was deliberate, as will be shown a few months later when he came to New York for the Donors' Conference at the United Nations on March 31, 2010. Sheila Caze, the secretary of the president, told me there was no ticket for me to join the presidential delegation in the official section reserved for the Haitian delegation. Their boorishness did not hinder me from obtaining the credentials to sit in the official section. They must have wondered how I had managed to outmaneuver them. Imagine, the president's ambassador to Washington being humiliated so shamefully.

The hostility of the president toward me was more obvious on July 12 during the ceremony commemorating the six-month anniversary of the earthquake. When acknowledging and decorating those who had contributed in special ways during Haiti's most tragic hours, President Préval did not mention me. At one point in his speech that day, he cited some of the names of contributors who had given even one dollar; these were the homeless who had come to the Haitian Embassy in Washington. He bestowed honors on Anderson Cooper of CNN, deservedly so for his thorough coverage during several days after the earthquake.

Anderson Cooper had, unsuccessfully, tried to have me criticize the Haitian authorities. While in the Haitian capital, Cooper was thwarted in his attempt to reach Haitian officials to address the issue of corpses that were unceremoniously dumped in mass graves in Titanyen, with legs poking through the dirt. I furnished him names and telephone numbers of officials in Port-au-Prince that he could contact. Cooper told me that the Minister of Information would not comment, alleging that she had just returned from abroad. So, I told him, "If she cannot comment, how can I comment on something that is happening thousands of miles away, while the officials on the ground cannot say anything?" Anderson Cooper would add in his reportage that "even the ambassador in Washington refused to speak to me."

At the July 12 ceremony, President Préval also honored several deserving Haitians for their role in the earthquake. Among them was former Army General and twice Foreign Minister Hérard Abraham for his management of petroleum distribution after the earthquake. But not I. He did not mention that I was responsible for signing and making arrangements for delivery of the 225,000 barrels of the Venezuelan petroleum products via the border of Haiti with the Dominican Republic.

Not only was I not honored along with the others, the president refused to receive me, although I had requested a meeting with him weeks earlier. He appeared very surprised when he saw me seated on second row from the front at the Palace grounds where the ceremony was held. The superb politician that he is, he greeted me amiably. However, his wife, who accompanied him, was glacial. As if to say, "What are you doing here?"

I was not officially invited to the event, although the Palace was aware of my presence in Port-au-Prince. I had visited the Ministry of Foreign Affairs soon after my arrival a few days earlier. I had met Foreign Minister Marie Michèle Rey, and inquired whether my request to see the president had had a response. It was negative. At that point, I told her the reason for my request. I wanted to discuss with the president my intention to resign my post and announce my candidacy to the presidency. I felt it was the respectful—and loyal—thing to do: to sit down with my boss first before I go public with my intention. I spent more than a week in Port-au-Prince and was never received by President Préval.

On returning to Washington, I wrote a letter to the president in which I told him how much I regretted that I had to announce my resignation to him so formally. Unfortunately, he was unable, I wrote, to receive me during my stay in Port-au-Prince. The resignation, I stated, would be effective August 1st, 2010. Later I found out about the president's motive for distancing himself from me. He had already decided that Jude Célestin would be his candidate for the presidency. Thus, he would not do anything that could be misinterpreted as a boost for me in public opinion, though he had little credit left.

Chapter 2

Fraudulent and Arbitrary Elections

My decision to run for President of Haiti was not taken in haste. Ever since January 12, 2010, when the earthquake devastated one-fifth of Haiti's landmass, including the capital of Port-au-Prince and surrounding communities, I felt the need for new leadership in the country. It was obvious that the current leaders had failed the people.

My wife, Lola, who often railed at my participating in Haitian internal politics, supported my idea to seek Haiti's highest office. She was apparently swayed by a string of people who came to our home to insist that I run for president. An influential group of Haitians in Salisbury, Maryland, also known as the "Salisbury Group," was quite forceful in its advocacy. Some of them said they had discovered in me the leader that Haiti needs. They were particularly struck by watching me explain on television the role of Haiti in the flowering of freedom in the Western Hemisphere. They applauded at how I had defended Haiti's global reputation in its most desperate and tragic hours, and were energized by my vision of a decentralized Haiti.

Many of those who came to see me were enamored of a statement that became like a leitmotiv in my interventions: *We must build and develop the Republic of Haiti instead of the Republic of Port-au-Prince.* Many visitors told me that we need that kind of change. A Committee to Elect Raymond Joseph was set up by some important figures in the Haitian community. And they promised to work with me to make it happen.

Lola was but one, albeit the most important one as far as I am concerned, to come forth with the idea of my candidacy to the presidency. The voice of a young man that I admire and for whom I have great respect was as important in helping me make my decision. Vladimir Jeune, 25 years old, had been living with us at the Ambassador's residence in Chevy Chase, Maryland, since the fall of 2008. He would be graduating from Georgetown University Law School in June of that year. He was like a son to us, a very amiable and wise young man, who fully integrated into our household. One evening after I came home from a televised presentation, Vladimir walked up to me and said, "Ambassador, this is your time, you should run for president this year. I will work for you. I know young people will be excited by your candidacy. We need someone with your vision."

I looked him straight in the eyes and said, "But Vladimir, isn't your father a candidate for the presidency?" He shot back: "No, no. Things have changed. Even my mother does not agree with his running." He paused, and added: "Ambassador, you should do it. You will be surprised about the support you will find. You have become our voice and I do speak for the youth."

That day, reflecting on what Lola and Vladimir had told me, I thought that the Bible may be wrong, at least once. Does it not say that *"A prophet is not without honor except in his own country and in his own house?"* (Matthew 13:57). Here, my household is fully behind me. And people from various sectors are calling on me to lead. Perhaps I should not refuse.

For more than four decades I had been involved in Haitian politics from my base in New York. Yet I had never been infected with the *candidaturite* bug once denounced by the famous priest Jean-Bertrand Aristide. By the way, Aristide would finally succumb to the bug in September 1990.

I concluded that it would not be hypocritical on my part if I were to change my mind at this late juncture in life and declare my candidacy for the presidency of Haiti. I was deeply convinced that I was not on an ego trip. I felt strongly that I must do something in response to the irresponsibility and the apathy displayed by the leadership that was managing Haiti after the earthquake.

Although I was physically fit, I still had some doubt about plunging into internal Haitian politics at the age of 79. I even wondered about supporting another candidate. Through the years, I had the knack of creating coalitions. Perhaps I should do that again to push a viable candidate. Besides, my "nephew" Wyclef Jean had confided in some people that he would declare his candidacy for president. Since he was under forty years old, he would relate better to the electorate, of which more than half was below the age of thirty-five. Moreover, the pop star had been involved in charitable work in Haiti with his Yelé Foundation. Indeed, Wyclef would have been unbeatable.

However, from unimpeachable sources, I had learned that he would be ruled off the ballot on the issue of residency. I could not discuss that with Clef, because it would appear self-serving. I was also a candidate. Some close relatives, including Clef's mother, told me they would discourage him and ask him to support me. Thus, I kept my candidacy alive, especially since I knew I could not be ruled off on the residency issue or on any other issue for that matter. How wrong I was. I had failed to take into consideration the duplicity of Haitian officials, especially the president.

I made a concerted effort to obtain advice from a broad cross section of the Haitian electorate before I made my final decision.

In light of what Vladimir had told me about his father, I decided to approach Pastor Chavannes Jeune, an influential Protestant minister who at one time was president of the MEBSH (*Mission Evangélique Baptiste Sud d'Haïti*), the same association of Baptist churches in southern Haiti of which my late father was the second president. On March 31, at the International Donors' Conference on Haiti at the United Nations in New York, I had an opportunity to meet Pastor Jeune privately. He was the first person, other than members of my immediate family, with whom I discussed my intentions to run for president.

I hedged in what I told Pastor Jeune. I said that I am under strong pressure from various quarters to run for president this year. I knew that he may also be a candidate, so I wanted to know what we could work out. I did not want to split the Protestant vote, especially since we both came from that sector. Moreover, I have been an ally of his family since the days when his late father and uncle were superintendents of churches in the MEBSH under the leadership of my father. In my youth I often visited the seaside fishermen's community of Morency from which his family hailed. My best friend Pélège Pierre had married a belle from Morency, which is only five miles from Cayes. So, confiding in Pastor Jeune was like speaking to a member of my extended family.

I was relieved at his response. "Listen brother," he said, "if you finally decide to run, you will not have me facing you, but backing you." He paused, and added, "But you know how these things work. Often it is not you or I who are the problem. It is the people behind us." I thought I understood his hedging.

Events will prove that he had prepared me for what would eventually happen. He entered the race anyway and was approved by the Electoral Commission which placed him seventh in a field of nineteen approved presidential candidates. He was allotted 1.80 percent of the general vote in the November 28, 2010, first round of balloting, far from the 5 percent he had scored in the presidential race of 2006.

I had put out feelers to the Protestant community in Haiti and received positive response to my candidacy. Some delegations came to Washington to convince me that I should run, because they said the Protestant community needed a fresh face and someone who is not tainted. I never asked what was meant by "someone not tainted," but it was obvious to me that the Protestant community was not satisfied with past Protestant candidates, such as Pastor Jeune and Pastor Luc Mésadieu. The Protestants, who had shun politics in the '40s and '50s, have become quite active since the late '80s after the collapse of the Duvalier dictatorship. Considered more homogeneous as a group, Protestant voters can swing an election. In Haiti religion plays a big role in politics, just as conservative evangelicals do in the United States. The Protestants were late coming into the political game but now they represent a pivotal group.

I was particularly honored when former followers of Pastor Elysée Joseph came to see me to tell me that with his passing, I should pick up the mantle. Pastor Joseph, they told me, had spoken warmly about me, telling them that I was like a mentor to younger Protestant leaders like him. Therefore, they felt it natural that whatever support he had should be channeled my way.

In August 2009, before the earthquake, Pastor Elysée Joseph had visited me with a delegation at the Villa Creole hotel in Pétionville during my vacation there. The presence in his delegation of Dieudonné Fardin, the founder of *Le Petit Samedi Soir* magazine, impressed me. Pastor Joseph stated that God had called him to be the candidate to usher an era of change in Haiti; that he wanted my support in his venture. He spoke about the ties that bound us, going back to his late father, Pastor Volney Joseph, who was a superintendent of churches under the leadership of my father. Although we had the last popular family name Joseph, we were not blood relatives, but our friendship certainly was not of yesterday.

I saw sincerity in the face of Pastor Joseph as he explained that he had not come lightly to the weighty decision of challenging the entrenched powers in Haiti. I had listened with much attention. Then, I told him that other Christian brothers had also told me they had heard the Lord's call to assume leadership in Haiti at the highest level. Since Protestants were being wooed by many candidates, I proposed that Protestant leaders show solidarity among themselves. Instead of fielding several candidates of similar religious persuasions, I advised that they pull their resources together. They should organize a nominating convention which would be like a primary election in the United States. All those who received the call of God should be invited for a discussion, leading to one single candidate to represent the Protestant sector.

Pastor Joseph looked at me intently and said, "You know how much you are held in high esteem. I would suggest that you call for that conference. I will be the first to support that. Certainly, the majority of Protestant leaders will respond to a call coming from you. It is a very good idea. Will you do it?"

"I would have liked to do it," I said, "but I am an ambassador, on active duty. I cannot take that kind of initiative." (An ambassador must resign before assuming leadership in partisan politics.)

I continued, "However, if the conference is convened and I am invited, I will definitely attend and help in reaching a consensus."

The wheels were in motion to organize the conference when about four months later, the devastating earthquake hit, causing thousands of deaths, including that of Pastor Elysée Joseph. God had called him home. Imagine the eerie feeling that came over me when some associates of the dead pastor approached me to say that their late leader spoke glowingly about me and that I should step forward to fill the void he had left.

Unquestionably, the death of the pastor had cleared the way for others who also sought Haiti's presidency. The campaign manager of another Protestant candidate came to see me to announce that a crippling disease had landed Pastor Mésadieu in a Boston hospital, knocking him out of the race. "God is working in mysterious ways," he added. Without saying so, this brother was apparently warning me to drop out of the race. Finally, he was very direct. "They won't let you get on the ballot," he said. "They could even evoke the residency issue to stop you, because you became ambassador in October 2005. That means your ambassadorship did not fully cover five years when you resigned on August 1st, 2010. You should join our campaign."

I had become a resident of Haiti since April 2004 when I assumed the post of Chargé d'Affaires, with my work address being the Embassy of Haiti in Washington. Moreover, I occupied the ambassador's residence. As chief of mission, I had full diplomatic immunity since April 2004. Nonetheless, in their frantic search for a reason to disqualify me, the political decision makers had even contemplated using the residency issue against me, as was done in the case of Wyclef Jean. They would have looked ridiculous had they taken that path. Finally, residency was never used to disqualify me from the presidential race. At the last minute, on the evening of August 20, 2010, the Provisional Electoral Council evoked *décharge,* or the lack of Good Governance Certificate, to bar me from running.

Having resigned on August 1st, 2010, I had requested an expedited audit of the Embassy in Washington by the Ministry of Foreign Affairs. That was done. The Ministry of Foreign Affairs had delivered me a "Certificate of Good Governance," attesting that no financial irregularities were registered under my administration, which covered six years. Based on that certificate, *La Cour Supérieure des Comptes et du Contentieux Administratif* (CSCCA), the equivalent to the General Accounting Office in the United States, also provided me a Certificate of Good Governance.

But the Electoral Council, under the dictates of President Préval, decided not to accept my documentation. The last minute decision of the Electoral officials was blatantly arbitrary, because some former and current ministers, including two former prime ministers, were exonerated from presenting their Certificate of Good Governance.

The real reason for disqualifying me was the president's belief that I could benefit from the support of my "nephew" Wyclef Jean. Though ousted from the race, he still had a large following, especially among the young people. President Préval believed that a secret pact existed between Clef and me, and that he would steer his fans my way. With Clef's support and that of various Protestant organizations, I was a potential threat to the president's chosen candidate.

Privately, the president had said that any candidate who could potentially garner 15 percent of the vote in the first round of balloting should be eliminated by any means. On that basis, Mayor Lydie Parent of Pétionville was also barred from running for the presidency. The Electoral Council alleged that as a sitting mayor, she had not obtained *décharge*. Yet, Wilson Jeudy, the sitting mayor of Delmas, was kept on the ballot without *décharge*. Wyclef was considered a sure winner and I a "15 percent" candidate. Certainly, we must be eliminated by any means.

When supposedly independent institutions become submissive to orders from on high, there is no way for justice to prevail. The court challenge that I undertook, even all the way to *La Cour de Cassation,* Haiti's equivalent of the Supreme Court in the United States, was repeatedly delayed until the case became moot. I was never discouraged in following the process to its ultimate conclusion. Not by naïveté or overconfidence, thinking that I would have won the case in the end. Rather, I was intent on proving to all that justice and democracy did not exist in Haiti; that the Executive branch, more often than not, dictates the decisions of the other so-called independent institutions. On September 9, 2010, the *Christian Science Monitor* published my position in an article on the matter. One sentence summed up the whole article: "This year, the elections in Haiti have begun arbitrarily, they will also end arbitrarily."

By all accounts, the legislative and presidential elections of November 28, 2010 were fraught with fraud. The decried Préval administration, with the complicity of the corrupt Electoral Council, attempted to steal the elections at all levels. Long before the vote was tallied, Senator Joseph Lambert, the then coordinator for the *Inite* (Unity) party of President Préval, had announced publicly that Jude Célestin, the party's candidate, had won with 52 percent.

Despite the millions spent on the campaign by *Inite* for its candidate, Célestin's candidacy had failed to catch fire. Nonetheless, in the first round of the elections, the Electoral Council placed him second with 22.48 percent of the total vote of 1,074,056. Pop star Michel Martelly came in third with 21.84 percent. The apparent victor of the November 28 first round was Mirlande Manigat, the professor of Constitutional law. Supposedly, she had garnered 31.37 percent of the vote. It was unbelievable that well-known notary public Henri Céant only scored 8.18 percent, placing him fourth. Trailing were former Prime Minister Jacques Edouard Alexis and industrial/businessman Charles Henri Baker, respectively in fifth and sixth positions with 3.07 percent and 2.38 percent of the vote.

The Electoral Council had taken its sweet time to juggle the numbers. When, on December 7, nine days after the vote, it officially released the results, rioting broke out in various parts of the country. Port-au-Prince and Les Cayes felt the brunt of the enraged voters who shouted that they had not voted for Célestin. They went on a rampage, destroying several government offices and the Port-au-Prince headquarters of *Inite*, the government's party. It took the heavy pressure of the international community, including that of Secretary of State Hillary Clinton and the Organization of American States (OAS) to force a recount of the vote. An OAS commission confirmed that Célestin was in third position, thus disqualified to face Professor Manigat in the runoff. That benefitted pop star Martelly.

The original results were manufactured by the Electoral Council to ensure the eventual victory of Jude Célestin, President Préval's candidate. The percentage of 31.37 percent given Professor Manigat would not have changed that much. That was evident when she faced Martelly in the March 20, 2011, runoff. Her score only edged up to 31.74 percent against Martelly's 67.57 percent. If President Préval had succeeded in his stratagem, Jude Célestin also would have trounced Mrs. Manigat. Her presence in the race was only to lend it credibility. Thus, the Préval electoral coup d'état would have been a done deal.

But Martelly spoiled it for them. After Wyclef Jean's disqualification, not to anger those who believed the government was biased against musicians, the Electoral Council kept Martelly in the race. Moreover, the foul-mouthed singer was not considered a serious candidate. He was not among the "fifteen percenters." I am told that the president of the Electoral Council, Gayot Dorcinvil, wept when the results of the November 28 vote came in. He bemoaned his decision of not having ruled Martelly out at the same time with Wyclef Jean.

Most Haitian politicians are not guided by principles. It is interesting to see their contortions when they reverse their positions publicly to benefit from certain advantages. By noon on November 28, long before the polls were closed, a dozen presidential candidates, including Manigat and Martelly, had called a press conference at the Karibe Hotel in Pétionville to denounce the electoral fraud. They railed at the government and the Electoral Council and vowed not to accept the results. Both Manigat and Martelly had endorsed the call to annul the vote. The next day, however, the two reversed their position and said they would wait for the final results. Confidentially, they had been contacted by OAS, UN and American officials who advised them that the eventual results would favor them.

The results that placed Martelly in second position were not unanimously accepted. According to a report by the Washington-based Center for Economic and Policy Research (CEPR), the conclusion reached by the OAS concerning the elections resulted from a political decision. The OAS and MINUSTAH, as the United Nations Mission in Haiti is called, feared continued violence if Martelly were to be denied victory. Another dissenting voice was that of Ricardo Seitenfus, a Brazilian professor of international relations who was a special OAS representative in Haiti since 2008. For denouncing the heavy hand of the international community, he was forced out of Haiti, with pay, two months before his contract term ended in March 2011.

Seitenfus has since written *"Haiti: Dilemas e Fracassos Internacionais"* ("International Crossroads and Failures in Haiti"), a critical book in Portuguese about his experience. For him, the whole process was a failure manufactured by the international community, including the United States, the OAS, and MINUSTAH.

It is criminal for those entrusted with positions of responsibility to violate so blatantly the will of the people. Under lawful governments some officials would be blamed and punished for the violence that their actions cause. In Haiti, however, impunity is considered the rule. The leaders know that their punishment would merely result in losing their post in government, but not the thousands or millions of dollars they've unlawfully gained. Unless the country breaks from this laissez-faire attitude at the top, there won't be any salvation for Haiti.

While the international community apparently addressed the fraud perpetrated in the elections at the presidential level, nothing was done to redress the fraud in the legislative races. The electoral fraud of 2010 has resulted in the most corrupt Legislature. For example, the analysis of the vote in Haiti's Northeastern Department (one of Haiti's ten Departments, as the mini states are called) by the elections observer team of the Washington-based Democracy Project (an NGO based in Washington, was an official observer of the elections in the Northeast) showed a pattern of fraud. The numbers released by the central tabulation office of the Electoral Council generally consecrated the victory of the government candidates. However, those numbers differed substantially from the ones that were posted at various voting precincts.

The breakdown for the legislative vote in six precincts in Ouanaminthe, in Haiti's Northeastern Department, is telling. Joazard

Claude, the legislative candidate of the government's party *Inite* for *Député* (Congressman) came first at all the polling places when the Electoral Council in Port-au-Prince officially released the figures on December 7. But the numbers posted by central tabulation were in flagrant conflict with those photographed on November 28, 2010, at the doors of the polling places by Democracy Project. Joazard Claude's 18 votes at the polling place *Ecole Nationale Mixte* in Ouanaminthe became 118 at central tabulation. Thus he was catapulted to first position from third; behind him came Noel Luckner of the party *Alternativ* who had 77 votes, and Emilien Patrick of the party *Ansanm Nou Fò* who had scored 24.

The fraud was obvious even in the numbers posted by central tabulation. When dealing with the breakdown of the vote, central tabulation provides the same information as that photographed at the doors at the precinct level. In all the polling places, Joazard Claude was actually in third position, but through the fraud engineered at central tabulation he was placed first and declared the official winner. In the four polling places at the *Ecole Nationale Mixte* in Ouanaminthe, central tabulation systematically added 100 votes to the actual vote Claude had received. Thus 15 became 115; 30 turned into 130 and 10 into 110. The generosity of central tabulation knew no bounds. In two polling places at *Collège Georges Muller* in Ouanaminthe, Joazard Claude's total was boosted by 200, thus 19 became 219 and 20 turned into 220.

This was repeated in precinct after precinct, and not only in the Northeast. The conclusion, therefore, was that the 2010 legislative elections were a vast fraud and should have been challenged in the same manner that the presidential vote was.

In an Opinion article that appeared January 12, 2011, in the *Wall Street Journal*, I denounced the electoral fraud at all levels and called for new legislative and presidential elections. However, privately, some American and OAS officials claimed that they had already spent $29 million on the elections. They could not afford to waste all that money. There would be a review of the figures for the presidential candidates, but the results of the legislative elections would stand, except for those in the Ouanaminthe district where Democracy Project had clearly documented the fraud.

There was no way to oppose or derail the plan of the international community to foist half-baked elections on Haitians. I strongly thought about ignoring the second round which pitted Professor Manigat against Mr. Martelly. In the end, I decided to be involved in the camp that I believed represented change. Moreover, I was contacted by my "nephew" Wyclef Jean with a compelling message. "Uncle," he said, "the campaign is being presented as a battle between 'Morality and Immorality.' All the pastors are said to be in the camp of Mrs. Manigat. I know you can change that perception. Let us back Micky together!" Wyclef had already thrown his support to Michel Martelly when he had joined his fellow singer on November 28 as they paraded together in Pétionville while denouncing the electoral fraud.

Wyclef and I decided to support Martelly because we saw through President Préval's game. There was evidence that the president had chosen his candidates for the runoff. He wanted Mrs. Manigat to lend credibility to the exercise, as I have already stated. But Jude Célestin would be the winner. Since we were both denied to run by order of President Préval and he had ordered the CEP to kick us out of the race, we were about to turn the tables against him, a sort of political tit for tat.

This was the first time that Wyclef and I were going to do something political in concert. With the help of my cousin and senior adviser Dumel Joseph, we mobilized some pastors in Florida and contacted several others in Haiti. We called a press conference at the Plaza Hotel in Port-au-Prince for March 8, 2011, twelve days before the vote scheduled for March 20. Pastor Jean-Claude Pierre, from Fort Lauderdale, Florida, opened the session with prayer. Candidate Martelly was joined on the dais by Wyclef.

Reporters and cameramen jammed the second floor conference room at the Plaza for the most important news of the day. When Pastor Pierre spoke, he was addressing the whole country and the diaspora via Internet. He gave candidate Martelly a full endorsement as a family man and a compassionate leader. He praised the bad boy on the music scene who has turned his back on his previous life to embrace the call to serve. Now two former popular presidential candidates, including singer Wyclef, were officially endorsing Martelly. It's big news and was treated as such.

<hr />

Michel Martelly was visibly moved by the words of Reverend Pierre and was lost for words to thank the pastor for such a laudatory endorsement. Seeing me seated on front row, and aware that I had engineered the event, Martelly called on me to introduce the next speaker. "The ambassador is better qualified than anyone to present him," he said. He pointed at Wyclef.

In my short introduction, I said, "We came to offer a choice to the country. But both of us—my nephew and I— were disqualified. They were afraid we would win. President Préval feared a fair election. But what is happening today is the fulfillment of a passage of the Scriptures, Matthew 21:42: *'The stone which the builders rejected has become the chief cornerstone.'* Wyclef, it is all yours." All the cameras switched to Wyclef, who gave a full endorsement to his friend Michel and asked his supporters to come out in force to support his presidential bid.

The next day, pastors throughout the country were calling to declare their support for Michel Martelly. Two days after our press conference, the influential Pastor Chavannes Jeune threw his support to Martelly. In less than a week, the "Morality versus Immorality" damaging message of the Manigat camp had been blunted.

Candidate Martelly was experiencing the power of the Scriptures. On a pre-election visit to Tampa, Florida, in late February 2011, I pointed to him a biblical verse that befitted his situation:

"When I was a child, I spoke as a child, understood as a child, I thought as a child; but when I became a man, I put away childish things." (I Corinthians 13:11) I was not officially campaigning with him. But this was a first meeting at which he invited me to see him in Port-au-Prince. He had told me, "Ambassador, this is exactly me!" He asked me to write the verse on a card for him. He stuck it in his pocket.

With the 2011 elections behind us, I began thinking seriously about the book I began to sketch before the earthquake. I had often been asked how was the group of which I was secretary general able to organize an opposition to the Duvalier dictatorship. How were we able to infiltrate everywhere—into the ministries, the Armed Forces, the Police, even into Papa Doc's own Palace? That mystery continues to intrigue many who wonder whether I may not revert to the same techniques of the '60s to denounce the excesses, even the crimes, of current or future officials.

Prior to the electoral campaign of 2010, President Préval had listened to the advice of one of his advisers who told him to apologize to me about the treatment I was given when he snubbed me during my visit to Port-au-Prince in July. After speaking with me on the telephone for more than ten minutes, the president invited me to his residence for a chat. Among other things, he told me he was planning to invite the other presidential candidates also. What do I think of that initiative? A positive undertaking, I told the president.

President Préval was also intrigued by Wyclef Jean and me declaring our candidacy for president. "You must have a common strategy," he said.

"No, we are having parallel campaigns," I responded, "but politics will not cause division in our family."

The president's most intriguing and surprising comment was, "Ambassador, you are not coming here with another *Vonvon*, are you?"

Was he speaking in jest? Or, was he hinting that I probably will find myself in opposition soon, just as I had been for most of my life?

"No, Your Excellency," I responded, "in this age of the Internet and with all the technological breakthroughs registered, the techniques of *Radio Vonvon* are no longer necessary. In fact, *Vonvon* is very much passé. Moreover, Mr. President, the word has been liberated in Haiti. It will be very difficult for this country to get to a situation where a new *Vonvon* would be necessary."

On leaving President Préval that day, I felt quite uneasy as I reflected on his last words to me. I felt that the president feared both Wyclef and me. I realized also that after all that has happened since the 1960s when I had organized the clandestine *Radio Vonvon* against François Duvalier's dictatorship, that period still remained a mystery. Obviously, many Haitian politicians in Haiti and elsewhere in the diaspora, some in the highest spheres, still think that I am a dangerous person who must be watched closely.

Chapter 3

The Wyclef Jean Connection

There is some confusion about my family relationship to Wyclef Jean, the pop star who should be given much credit for boosting the pride of a generation of Haitians and Haitian Americans. In his late 20s, he was not known as my "nephew" when he started an overnight movement in America in 1997. The new generation may not know it, but it was Wyclef who instilled pride in many young compatriots with one spontaneous gesture.

In 1997, when Wyclef draped himself in the flag of Haiti at the Grammy awards, he unleashed the pent-up nationalism of young Haitians throughout America. Most of them, especially students in elementary and high school, were ashamed of their roots. Made to feel inferior by all sorts of debasing monikers, including "yo, boat people," young Haitians used to lie about their origins. In the eighties, there was an armada of sailboats from Haiti as desperate Haitians tried to reach the shores of the United States. So, those new immigrants were called "boat people" compared to earlier middle class Haitians who fled the Duvalier dictatorship and were known as "boeing people." Young people rathered be islanders from Jamaica, Trinidad, Guadeloupe, Martinique, anything but Haitian.

In a flash, that changed one evening with the coming out of Wyclef on a national stage in New York adorned in Haitian pride. The next day, Haitians took to the streets in Brooklyn and Queens, which had large Haitian agglomerations, with Haitian flags unfurled. It was not different in the Oranges in New Jersey and elsewhere in other American and Canadian cities. All of a sudden, there were not enough Haitian flags to go around. Overnight, a Haitian flag industry exploded in America and elsewhere. Feeling proud of their origin, young Haitians wanted the whole world to know who they were. It's as if they were coming out of the closet.

The Haitian flag became attractive attire worn as a headband, belt, bandanna or whatever. In all sorts of shapes, it was hanging from the visors of cars. In states where only one plate is required on a vehicle, the Haitian flag was displayed instead of regular plates. Unquestionably, Haitians wanted to be known as such. Those who were hiding their identity waved at each other on the streets. *Sak pase* (What's up?) became a trademark expression, as Haitians and their foreign friends shouted at each other in form of greeting. It was an instant cultural revolution whose repercussions were felt by other ethnic groups who also began to display the flags of their countries. For once, the Haitians were being mimicked in America.

A less spectacular event would reveal Wyclef's relationship to me. One evening in April 2005, about a year since I took over at the Embassy of Haiti in Washington, I received a telephone call from Clef who told me, "Uncle, I'm coming to Washington. You have to be there tomorrow night." He told me about his being honored at an event that the Pan American Development Foundation (PADF) was organizing for Yéle's partnership in the "Clean Streets" program in Haiti. He would like me to be his guest of honor. "Certainly, I will be there," I said.

The following evening, when I arrived at the Fairmont Hotel, I knew immediately that things wouldn't be the same afterward. Three chairs were set up at the table in front, with the mistress of ceremony, Ms. Amy Coughenour Betancourt, seated in the center. Wyclef was seated at one side and I at the other. When the time came for Wyclef to speak, he turned toward me and said, "It's an honor to have with us tonight the Ambassador of Haiti to the United States, my uncle Raymond Joseph!" Somewhat in unison, all heads turned to look at me, as if to say, "You are his uncle?" That was the first time he had mentioned our relationship.

After the event, I was approached by several people with whom I had been interacting since I arrived in Washington the previous year. They kept saying, "Ambassador, you never told us you were Wyclef's uncle!"

"What reason did I have to tell you that I was his uncle?" I responded.

From that day on, for many, I was not so much Haiti's ambassador to the United States, but Wyclef's uncle.

The next day I received several phone calls, including from former colleagues at the *Wall Street Journal*, who wanted to know if what they had read in the press was true. "Are you really Wyclef's uncle?" What could I say but yes? The cat was out of the bag. Since then, the press has often referred to me as Wyclef's uncle. I hadn't disclosed this information because I didn't want to jeopardize his career. My politics would have closed some doors for him. For example, my nemesis, President Aristide, was a fan of the Fugees. Had he known Wyclef's relationship to me, he definitely would have blocked the concert of the group in Haiti.

Prior to that public announcement, I had disclosed the family connection in a very unusual manner. Soon after I arrived at the Haitian Embassy in 2004, a banal incident forced me to let some of my employees into the secret. While on an inspection tour of the building on Massachusetts Avenue, I got to the fifth floor, home of the passport unit. I noticed a pile of passports in a big carton box. I picked up one which was on top of the heap. When I opened it, the picture of Wyclef Jean popped up. I asked the manager of the unit what was being done with those passports. "They are being returned to the consulates where they came from," he said, "because there is conflicting information regarding their holders."

"What conflicting information do you have for this one," I said, as I showed him Wyclef's passport.

"Oh, for him, it's a matter of birthplace," he said. "Some documents mention St. Marc as his birthplace; others say Croix-des-Bouquets."

"Croix-des-Bouquets is the right place," I said, with a smile on my face.

"How do you know, Chargé?" (When I arrived in April 2004, I was Chargé d'Affaires, head of mission. I would become a full ambassador in October 2005.)

"I know," I said, "because he is my young cousin. His mother and I are first cousins. We are from Croix-des-Bouquets." That's when I knew that Wyclef was not an American citizen. All along I had thought that he had been naturalized as were his parents and younger brother Sam. His other siblings were born in America. Reflecting on it, I said to myself, *Oh, he's the only one of the bunch who has done as Leo (my brother) and I.*

After more than forty years in America, we had not chosen to become American citizens because we did not want people to say we had no right in addressing Haitian issues. We were opinion leaders through our weekly organ, the *Haiti-Observateur*. I concluded that our young "nephew," without knowing about our decision, was probably guided by the same principle.

I had new respect for Wyclef. Not that I object about others who make the choice of adopting a different citizenship. All the members of my immediate family and of Leo's are American citizens, something we have encouraged. For naturalized Haitians, exercising their voting rights can effect change in their adopted land to benefit their country of origin. At the same time, we felt that as long as the Haitian Constitution barred dual citizenship, we should keep to our nationality to have a say in Haitian national affairs.

Officials of my own government were skeptical about the family link between Clef and me. In time, that will be put to rest. When I got Wyclef to give me a big push in the passage of the HOPE Act in Congress, I dispelled all doubts. The HOPE bill would allow Haitian products, especially textiles, to enter the US market without tariffs. I was lobbying Congress and needed all the help I could get. In November 2006, Haiti's Finance Minister, Daniel Dorsainvil, came to town to meet some officials, including US legislators, about the HOPE Act which some people believed was in jeopardy. Dorsainvil told me he wished someone could get to Wyclef Jean. "With his influence, he could give us a big boost," he said. "That can be arranged," I responded. But I did not tell him about my relationship to the influential singer.

That same day I called Clef and told him about several meetings we had scheduled on Capitol Hill the next day. I also mentioned that the finance minister was in town, especially to lobby for HOPE. I wondered whether he could come down to give us a push.

"At what time, Uncle?" he asked.

"At 11 a.m."

"Wow," he exclaimed. "I have a gig in New York tonight which probably will last till 4 a.m." He paused a little and said, "I think we can make it down before 11. I can sleep in the limo." Then, it was an affirmative "Yes, Uncle, I'll be there."

I called the minister to tell him that Wyclef will be with us on Capitol Hill in the morning. "Really," he exclaimed. "Ambassador, you have much influence." I said nothing.

At about 8:30 the next morning, I received a telephone call from Jerry—that's Jerry "Wonda" Duplessis, Clef's cousin and bass player who's often referred to as Clef's sidekick. Jerry said, "Uncle Ray, we are on Route 50. How do we get to your place?" Route 50 in Washington is off I-495, the beltway surrounding the capital. That meant they were about thirty minutes from the residence at Kenwood, in Chevy Chase. I indicated a shortcut they could take.

By 9 a.m., the black stretched limo pulled into the driveway. They had about one hour to shower, and change. "Don't worry, Uncle, we're like soldiers," Clef said. "At least I am. I hope Jerry will hurry up too." I directed them to two bathrooms and told them that breakfast was waiting. They were soon ready. They hurried through a delicious breakfast that my wife had prepared. By 10:15 we were out of the residence and heading to Capitol Hill. By 10:55 we pulled up on Independence Avenue, in front of the building where the Ways and Means Committee has its office. As we emerged from the limo, Minister Dorsainvil, who was already waiting with Leslie Délatour, exclaimed, "Wow, Ambassador, you have really delivered."

When we arrived at the office of Congressman Charles Rangel, I began to introduce the visitors. Before I could say much, the Congressman, pointing at Wyclef, said, "Mr. Ambassador, that one needs no introduction." He gave Clef a warm accolade and invited us to his conference room. Succinctly, Clef interceded for his country. "Haiti needs a hand up, not a hand down, he said." Charlie Rangel responded, "You're preaching to the choir, brother!"

It was a fruitful day on Capitol Hill, but not before a mini concert that night offered by Clef and Jerry at the request of Senator Mike DeWine (Republican of Ohio). When we had met him that day in his office, he said, "Musicians don't travel without their instruments, isn't that so?" Clef said, "We can find the instruments." As soon as we left the Hill, Clef called his contacts in Washington and got them to deliver the instruments in time for the evening show. Clef was ready with a ditty he had hurriedly arranged for HOPE.

That evening became news the next morning. *"Capital Police showed up Wednesday night at the Hartt Senate Office Building, where Wyclef Jean was loudly rocking the house,"* one read in the Reliable Source column of the *Washington Post*. *"The hip-hop star teamed up with outgoing Senator Mike DeWine (R. Ohio) to lobby for a trade bill with Haiti (Jean's uncle is the Haitian ambassador), then launched into an impromptu 40-minute set. When an officer approached Jean, staffers feared the ex-Fugee was in touble—but the cop just wanted an autograph for his daughter."*

Senator DeWine, who had lost his seat in the legislative elections two weeks earlier, was helpful in maneuvering around last minute hurdles thrown on the path of HOPE by two Southern Senators: Elizabeth Dole of North Carolina and Lindsey Graham of South Carolina.

In March 2007, I invited Wyclef back to Washington to help me when I was lobbying Congress for a liberalized HOPE Act. Although the bill passed by the Republican Congress in December 2006 allowed Haitian textiles products to enter the US market without tariffs, there were many restrictions on the origin of the fabrics used. Also, the benefits were limited in time. In about three years, some benefits would have been lost, unless renewed.

The recently inaugurated Democratic Congress was taking up the bill and Clef came to the rescue. This time he was addressing the Western Hemisphere Subcommittee of the House Foreign Relations Committee chaired by Congressman Eliot Engle (NY Democrat). Getting the endorsement of this subcommittee was crucial in obtaining a liberalized HOPE Act. And we had a sympathetic ear in Chairman Engle. Clef delivered a message in rap mode.

We had spent a whole afternoon rehearsing at my residence with Clef, Jerry, and Hugh Locke, the director of Clef's Yéle organization at the time. Hugh masterfully adapted my prose to rap style which Clef perfected. I had written the basics about the bill. But the rapper transformed it to make it his. Long after, Clef would tell me, "That was great, transposing philosophical thought into rap." His conclusion was more philosophical than anything that I had written. In his appeal to the legislators, he said, "To live for yourself is to live selfishly. But to live for others is to live eternally." The applause was deafening. We eventually got an enhanced HOPE bill for Haiti. But that's another story.

Considering Clef's contribution in changing positively the image of Haitians, and considering all the help he had given me, I lobbied my superiors for an honorary title for the singer. In January 2007, President Préval named him roving ambassador of Haiti. It took months after that and several telephone calls on my part to finally get him his diplomatic passport. On his birthday, October 17 of that year, he was partying at SOBs in downtown Manhattan. To his great surprise, I delivered him the document, which had arrived the day before from Port-au-Prince, thanks to an employee of Yéle who had traveled especially with it for the occasion.

As much as Clef and his siblings and even Hugh Locke showed me respect by always referring to me as "Uncle Ray," there came a time when "Uncle" had to take a back seat. When I heard about Wyclef mulling over a run for Haiti's presidency, I confess that I thought it was a joke. Although he was a big-hearted philanthropist dedicated to his country's welfare, Wyclef, I felt, was not ready yet to become Haiti's president. I couldn't tell him so because it would have sounded self-serving, especially since I was thinking about running for president also.

I felt that Wyclef lacked the training and experience to be president. Moreover, he provided the Haitian officials material to disqualify him. Although he had a business in Haiti, the Telemax television station, he always entered the address of his residence in New Jersey on the immigration form when he traveled to Haiti. The Ministry of Interior collects all this information which can be used at the discretion of the officials for whatever purpose they choose. In Clef's case they used the information to disqualify him from running for the presidency.

In my case, I knew residency couldn't be evoked. They manufactured their own arbitrary reason to disqualify me, as I have already explained. Despite the strains caused by the 2010 campaign, Clef and I managed to come together in support of Michel Martelly. In that sense, what I have always said stands: "Politics shall not divide this family."

I want to clarify the confusion about Wyclef being my nephew. In Haiti, younger cousins call their older cousins uncles. Wyclef's mother Yolanda, who most people know as Solange, is my first cousin, as I already said. Wyclef's maternal grandmother, Idalie, was a younger sister of my mother Julienne. There were two other sisters, Pauline and Gracilia, and two brothers: Tombold and Ménélas. My elder sister Laurette was Wyclef's godmother. So, Wyclef is my second cousin.

The strong family bonds that existed in Haiti were maintained after we migrated to the United States. In 1972, when my cousin Solange came from Haiti to join her husband in Brooklyn, she invited me to visit them. I was introduced to Gesner Jean, the Nazarene preacher with whom I developed real rapport. Pastor Gesner, as he was called by all, had known of my existence as a "brother-in-law" who had been to Bible School in America. But little did he know that I was the translator of the Creole New Testament with Psalms that he had been using while in Haiti. When he found that out, this cemented our bond.

Since that translation work in 1960, I had become a dangerous relative about whom little was said. It's understandable, because I had long embraced another cause which had put me on a collision course with the Duvalier dictatorship. I was even condemned to death in absentia for my anti-regime activities, the most spectacular of those being *Radio Vonvon*, the broadcast from New York. Meanwhile, some of my cousins, brothers of Solange, were part of Duvalier's gestapo-like police. Now in the United States, Solange and her husband felt at ease to seek my company, although we did not broadcast our relationship.

I knew when the two young sons of the Jeans, Wyclef and Samuel, were brought to the United States. I don't know what and when their parents told them about their "uncles" Leo and Raymond. But when I first met the youngsters they began calling me uncle and have never stopped. While they were growing up, I had little contact with them. But Solange and Gesner maintained telephone conversation with me and my brother. Solange would often call to ask advice regarding the boys, especially Wyclef, in their strained relationship with their strict preacher-father.

The family situation deteriorated as Wyclef became increasingly involved in music that his father considered trash. Although Clef had first learned to play in church where he was involved in the choir, he was also very talented in playing what Pastor Gesner called *mizik lemonn, vye bagay nèt* (worldly music, trashy stuff). So, one Friday afternoon, I got a call from Solange. She told me she could no longer keep peace in the house; that Leo and I should pay the family a visit after church the following Sunday around 3 p.m. By that time, the Jeans had moved from Brooklyn to East Orange, NJ. Leo lived in Queens and I was in Manhattan's Upper West Side.

Leo picked me up around 2 p.m. We got to East Orange on time. As usual, Solange had prepared a sumptuous meal. The kids were not around when we arrived. She had planned things well, so no indiscreet ears would be listening to our conversation. Being fully briefed by her about the situation, I was ready with my arguments.

After the meal, we moved into the more relaxing living room. I told Pastor Gesner to get his Bible, because he would need it. I had brought mine. "Let's open to Romans 12:3-8." I read aloud. The passage was about the "gifts" that God bestows on his servants for the benefit of all. And no one should think himself better because of his gifts.

Pastor Gesner had a pensive look, probably wondering where the conversation would lead us. Then, I asked a question: "Pastor, do you remember what gifts your father was dealt?"

"Where are you coming from, Ray?" he asked.

"I am coming from nowhere, Pastor. But I am quite sure that you remember that your father's gifts were not the same as yours. Neither are my gifts the same as those of my father. Remember, my father was a pastor like you. Most people thought I would have followed in his footsteps. I even graduated from the Pastor's course. But today I am an editor. Whenever I write an editorial, I feel that I am preaching to the world, albeit not in the same way as my father used to do. You get me, Pas?"

I didn't say anything about his father, because it was unnecessary. You see, Gesner Jean's father was a *houngan,* a Voodoo priest, something that the pastor had totally rejected and which caused a major break between him and his father.

Pastor Gesner was still pensive. But I think he may have understood by then where the conversation was leading us. I broke the silence by saying, "Listen, my brother, please let the kids play their music. God has given them gifts that are different from those he gave you and me. Don't inhibit them in what they are trying to express. I have listened to their music, Pas, and it's not trash. In their own way, they are exalting God but in a mode that's very different from what you are used to hearing. Believe me, Pas, it's not trash! If you listen closely to what they're saying in their music, I am sure you will agree with me. Trust me."

Pastor Gesner Jean drew a deep breath and said, "Okay. If you say so, I believe you." Being among the oldest of the extended maternal Bonny family, I was often contacted by some of my cousins in need of advice. Somehow, they trusted me and often followed my advice. Pastor Gesner, no doubt influenced by Solange, had developed a certain respect for me. My being a Bible scholar had impressed him. So, he did not take lightly what I said. I can't say how relieved I felt when he said "*D'accord!*" (Okay.)

My work was only half done, because I had to deal with the kids also. When they came home that Sunday we had finished our adult conversation. I told the boys that I was taking them out. We were going to McDonald's, their favorite restaurant. They were so happy they could not wait. They jumped into Leo's car and we went to Main Street in East Orange where there was a McDonald's. We told them they could order anything.

We had a conversation with them which went something like this: "Listen, you guys, we don't want you to play your music in the house. Neither on the church instruments! Your uncle Reynold (that's Jerry's father, Reynold Duplessis) is fixing up his basement for you to play there. That's where you will be practicing. Is that okay?"

"Yeah, yeah, that's okay! We understand," Wyclef said.

The rest is history. In that basement, which was named Booga Basement, Wyclef joined with Pras Michel and Lauryn Hill to launch the Fugees, short for refugees. From that basement, the group went to conquer the music world. I was not involved in their inner doings—and for good reason. But I rejoiced in the fact that Pastor Jean had paid attention to what I had to say. By giving his blessing, though grudgingly, to the kids, he had contributed to their success. He wouldn't regret it.

In 1997, when the Fugees hit Platinum and Wyclef had become an instant millionaire, he did something for his parents. Before he was married and had a house for himself, he bought mom and dad a big house on Highland Street, in South Orange. Those familiar with the Oranges in New Jersey know well that South Orange, partially on a hill, is like *Morne Calvaire,* an exclusive section on a mountain in Pétionville, the upscale suburb of Port-au-Prince, Haiti's capital. There was a world of difference between their new dig and their modest house in East Orange. It was as if the family was being rewarded for what they had endured in the Brooklyn projects that Wyclef describes in his book *Purpose, An Immigrant Story.*

For the inauguration of what I called "The Chateau Jean," Leo and I were invited. On arriving, I spotted Pastor Gesner down in what passed for the basement. It was tastefully decorated and adorned with expensive furniture. Pastor Gesner was enjoying the evening, as he played domino with his Christian brothers who were also there for the great occasion. I cleared my throat loudly, as Haitians usually do when wanting attention. "Pastor Gesner, I see that you are well established here," I joked.

He gave me a bear's hug and we winked at each other. Without saying anything, we were silently acknowledging the conversation we had in his living room about five years earlier when I had convinced him that Wyclef's music had nothing to do with Satan. Here, that music had made it possible for the family to have this lavish reception in a mansion of their own. It was indeed a marvelous evening.

A few months later, Leo asked me if I had taken a ride in the late model Lincoln Continental that Wyclef had bought his father. No, I had not. Leo went on to say that he was floored by what he heard coming from a cassette that Pastor Gesner had on.

"Isn't that *konpa* I'm hearing there, Pas?"

"That's *konpa kretyen*" (*Christian konpa*), Pastor Gesner retorted. *Konpa* is the most popular beat of Haitian dance music. These days, *Christian konpa* is part and parcel of Gospel music in almost all Haitian churches, including in the staid Catholic Church which has also embraced popular culture, drum et al.

I was pleasantly surprised when I saw Pastor Gesner Jean at what must have been his first pop concert. In an elegant white suit, with his cane draped over his arm and his no less elegantly dressed wife at his side, the pastor climbed up to the balcony at Carnegie Hall in New York to take his seat. That was in 2001 when Wyclef had broken another musical barrier. He had taken what he called his "All Star Jam" to Carnegie Hall which was usually reserved for classical music and jazz.

For me, the stars of the evening were not Stevie Wonder, Eric Clapton, Marc Anthony, Mary J. Blige, Macy Gray and the others. Not even Wyclef himself. When, in the middle of the show, Clef stopped everything and noted that his father was in the house, the audience went wild. When the spotlight was trained on him, Pastor Gesner Jean and his wife stood up. Beaming, they graciously acknowledged the honor that was bestowed on them.

I was not at Carnegie Hall that evening. I purposely took a distance, at least publicly, from the Jean family. I knew that

Jean-Bertrand Aristide had become a fan of the Fugees and was discussing with Clef about a concert in Haiti. It was no secret that the *Haiti-Observateur*, the weekly that we published in Brooklyn, was in opposition to Aristide, who had publicly denounced the paper years earlier. In no way were we going to jeopardize Clef's relationship with Aristide. Nonetheless, my cousin Solange always kept me abreast of everything, even when she acted as a maid to take Aristide's calls to Clef. "He's not here," she would say humbly. "I will tell him. Thank you." Aristide did not know that he was speaking to Clef's mother, a wily diplomat if there ever was one.

Another political leader with whom I had been at odds for years did not know about my relationship with the famous Jean family. From his exile in France, Jean-Claude Duvalier was in touch with the Duplessis, including my cousin Solange. At times he would dispatch his partner Véronique Roy on mission to New York. When Véronique came to town, she often lodged at Solange's home in New Jersey and was chauffeured by some of my young cousins. Through Frantz Bataille, who became a columnist at the *Haiti-Observateur*, I met Véronique a few times in New York. All the time, she was not aware that Solange was my first cousin, someone with whom I was in constant communication.

In such circumstances, I always think about the wisdom expressed in certain Creole proverbs. *"Pèsonn pa konnen kijan dlo fè pou rantre nan kokoye!"* ("No one knows by what process the water gets into the coconut!")

Chapter 4

Setting Up a Dictatorship

From its inception, Haiti has not known democracy. During the nineteen-year American occupation that ended in 1934, a semblance of democracy was set up with presidents elected by the Legislature. In 1950, the first popular election brought to power Paul Eugène Magloire, a general who had participated in the coup d'état which brought down President Dumarsais Estimé. When I left Haiti in 1954, I didn't feel the heavy hand of government. There was a flowering of free speech. But with the presidential election of 1957, which brought François "Papa Doc" Duvalier to power, Haiti took a path that would lead it to a cruel dictatorship.

When I returned to the country in 1959 after five years of studies in the United States, I found myself in a frighteningly different country. The feeling would creep upon me imperceptibly, even though I had no reason to fear anything. I was in no way involved in politics.

I felt a duty to go back to my hometown Cayes, in southwest Haiti, especially to the West Indies Mission, now Worldteam, to lend a hand at *Radio Lumière,* the first Evangelical Protestant station in southern Haiti, which was inaugurated February 20 of that year. Pastor David N. Hartt, a visionary man, finally had accomplished his mission. For years he had dreamed about having a radio station to spread the gospel countrywide from the mission's base in the outskirts of Cayes.

Years later I will learn in a book, *Drumbeats that Changed the World* by Joseph F. Conley, that I was responsible for the name *Radio Lumière* (Radio Light). It was taken from the name of the first Sunday school publication in Creole that I started in 1950—*Reyon Limyè* ("Rays of Light"). Since then the name of the mission compound has changed to *Cité Lumière* and other *Lumière* institutions, including television, hospital, and university, have sprung up. (*Radio Lumière,* now based at Côte Plage in Port-au-Prince, is a network with several stations throughout Haiti.)

I knew that *Radio Lumière* was looking for good programming. I offered to host a series entitled *Bouki* and *Malis,* based on the two mythical personalities of Haitian folklore that, I believe, generally helped to mold Haitian character. I wanted to put *Bouki*, the fool, on equal footing with *Malis*, reputed to be "Mr. Smart." From time to time, *Bouki* would beat *Malis* at his game.

Soon I had to stop my program, through self-censorship. Some friends told me that I should be very careful about the conversations of *Bouki* and *Malis.* They noted that the country was changing politically and that some of my scenes of *Bouki* and *Malis* could be misinterpreted as criticism of the authorities who, too often, pull the wool over the eyes of the people, not unlike what *Malis* does to *Bouki* all the time.

Also, a sensitive situation was developing around the mission compound concerning my financial standing. I was volunteering my services because I had a handsome contract with the American Bible Society. So, the Raymond who had left the mission with a meager salary of seventy-five gourdes per month in 1954 had a salary superior to that of the North American missionaries. (At that time the gourde, the Haitian currency, exchanged at five to one US dollar.) Besides, I was paying my help much more than the twenty-five gourdes per month paid to servants. I was causing havoc at the mission in more ways than one. My stay in Cayes lasted only three months. I moved my family, including the two servants, to the capital area where I no longer felt under the constraint of mission life.

Now in the new milieu of Greater Port-au-Prince, I became more aware of the changes that were taking place in the country. Certainly, those changes were more pervasive in the capital than what I had felt in Cayes where people were more laid back. Other than eminent acquaintances in Protestant religious circles, I had some friends and contacts in the ranks of university and seminary students. For the most part, the pastors were supporters of François Duvalier's government that had assumed power in 1957 in a cloudy election backed by the Haitian Army. Generally, the students, unlike their parents, provided a more sinister picture of what was happening in the country. Eventually, they proved to have been more accurate than their parents in their evaluation of a dangerous and frightening evolving political situation.

I was disturbed about what I considered the lack of political vision of Haitian Protestant leaders who felt comfortable with Duvalier. They had embraced Papa Doc mainly on the basis of his opposition to the powerful Catholic Church. Although I understood the reason for their attitude, I felt that the evolving grip of Duvalier on the country would be deleterious for all.

The Protestant leaders were reacting to the persecution they had endured in the 1940s during the *Rejete* (Reject) movement that was sponsored by the Catholic Church and supported by the Haitian government. Ostensibly, "Reject" was an anti-superstition campaign that targeted Voodoo whose practice was to be violently eliminated from Haiti. Some Catholic priests, leading chanting congregants, barged into *hunfors,* as the Voodoo sanctuaries are called, and destroyed sacred objects. They cut down trees, like the giant *Mapou* where the *loas,* or Voodoo gods, allegedly live. In the process, some evangelical Protestants were victimized, especially in South Haiti. Some of their churches in the countryside were invaded and left in shambles. The Catholic Church was alarmed by major gains that the Protestants were making in Haiti's countryside. A popular *Rejete* campaign song stated it clearly, *"Ni pwotestan ni lwa, nou pa kapab nan sa."* ("Neither Protestants nor *loas* [the Voodoo gods or spirits], we can't accept.")

Duvalier had adroitly and successfully tapped into deep anti-Catholic feelings within the Protestant community and in the larger Voodoo culture to build his reputation among those groups. Even my father, who was apolitical, as were the majority of Protestant ministers in those days, spoke glowingly about freedom of religion that had gotten a boost with the presidency of Duvalier. The Protestants applauded when the new president locked horns with the Vatican in his determination to create an indigenous clergy.

The penchant of the Protestants for Duvalier was expressed in a letter that an admirer and supporter of mine had addressed to me. It's obvious that Pastor Luc Nérée had found himself in an uncomfortable situation of divided loyalty. The influential minister of the "Baptist Church of the Cities" in Delmas (Port-au-Prince) was like an older brother to me. On April 18, 1966, while on a visit in the United States, he wrote me from Milwaukee, Wisconsin, expressing support for my struggle against the dictatorship. On the other hand, he spoke glowingly of the new political reality in favor of Protestants in Haiti.

Writing in French, he stated, "I firmly believe that victory will be ours. However I have an important question to discuss. It has to do with the status of Protestants who currently enjoy full freedom to preach the Gospel. It is a fact that the Romanists [Catholics] are very uneasy on account of the progress scored by the Gospel in Haiti. I wonder if one should not ponder calmly the question of Protestantism in Haiti before the participation of the Roman Church imposes

certain conditions on a future government that will restrain evangelical activities."

Reverend Nérée was especially nervous because rumors were rife
that the movement that I spearheaded had teamed up with certain
Catholic priests who were in opposition to the Duvalier regime. The
priests of the Holy Ghost order were expelled from Haiti in part on
this false assumption. So was the leader of the Jesuits.

While the Protestant leaders counted their blessings, I was getting
another reading of the new Haitian government from the students,
many of whom were young Protestants who did not live through
the horrors of *Rejete* in the 1940s, as did their parents. In a matter
of two decades, a chasm had been created between offspring and
parents on an issue of national importance.

The students were especially preoccupied with an amorphous
civilian organization called *Les Cagoulards,* from *cagoule* (French
for a kerchief disguise that serves as a mask). These were Duvalierist stalwarts who had begun to operate under civilian commanders
without any connection to the Army. The parents had paid little
attention to the new group. "A government must defend itself" was
a familiar phrase in the mouths of the parents. As a candidate, Duvalier had leaned on the Army to assume power, but he profoundly
mistrusted the military. From the outset, he set out to make the
Army a subservient tool, devoid of power to stage a coup. Thus, he
organized a parallel force to the Army that would eventually defang
the military.

I had my first encounter with a civilian patrol of *Cagoulards*
one evening in 1960 on Bourdon, the main artery linking Port-au-
Prince and Pétionville, the suburb five miles east of the capital. I
was transporting two University students to a hiding place. Masked
men at a barricade waved my little British Austin car to the side of
the road. Immediately I stopped, put the car in neutral and pulled
the safety brake. I told the guys in the back not to make a move. I
jumped out, somewhat annoyed, and in an authoritative voice, said

in earthy Creole, "Damn it! What's going on! Since when do dogs eat dogs? . . . Tell me, please!"

The apparent leader of the group responded sheepishly, "Forgive me, Master. We are just obeying orders. We did not know who you were. I am sorry, Sir." And he waved me by, after giving me a military-style salute. Which I duly returned!

My daring instincts in acting like an official had saved me that evening. And the young students in my car also, who probably would have been arrested, had their names been on the list of rebellious University students who were being tracked down. Certainly, the inexperience of the *Cagoulards* in the early days of their formation was our salvation.

These *Cagoulards* eventually dropped their makeshift masks for black glasses and assumed the official title of *Volontaires de la Sécurité Nationale* (VSN), the blue-denim-clad militia with red kerchiefs around their necks. Deridingly called *Tontons-Macoute* (TTM)—bogeymen—they became the ubiquitous enforcers of Duvalierist power. Their status was undeniable, especially since Papa Doc ordered that they occupy their own posts, usually built in close proximity to Army posts.

Eventually, the TTM dwarfed the Army in numbers and superiority of arms. The military mainly excelled in parades. Also Papa Doc often dispatched the soldiers to track down and fight rebels in the border areas or in distant mountain redoubts. However, for social and political control, as well as for repression, the dictator depended on the TTM, or VSN, as you wish. The literature on Haiti is replete with atrocities attributed to the *Tontons-Macoute*.

Although I was neither involved nor interested in politics, my home in the capital had become like a magnet for some University students who felt at ease venting their frustration at what was happening to them—and the country. The government was recruiting students to be auxiliaries to the *Tontons-Macoute* in their schools. Some resented being turned into spies against their fellow students.

Duvalier feared that the students could eventually rise up against his rule, not unlike what they had done against previous presidents who, once in power, used all sorts of stratagems to hold to power illegally. This has been the scourge of the country. As for Duvalier, who had decided even before being "elected" that he would be president-for-life, he began by co-opting the students from the outset.

Among the students who were leading the charge for Duvalier, I will point to two medical students—Roger Lafontant and Fritz "Toto" Cinéas—as well as to Luckner Cambronne, an enterprising young businessman. They recruited many students to Duvalier's cause. Their method of operation was bribery and intimidation. But not all the students succumbed to the temptation of easy money or advantage in school. Many left the country to escape death.

Lafontant was the muscle man that many students feared and denounced. Eventually, he became a diplomat, representing the Duvalier regime abroad. He was a mentor to Jean-Claude "Baby Doc" Duvalier. Lafontant, MD, came back to Haiti in 1990 and declared his candidacy for the presidency. Ruled off the ballot, he attempted a coup d'état on January 6, 1991, to derail the February 7 inauguration of President Jean-Bertrand Aristide, who had won overwhelmingly on December 16, 1990. Lafontant was assassinated in his jail cell at the National Penitentiary in Port-au-Prince on the evening of September 29, 1991, while the Army coup d'état against President Aristide was in progress.

As for Cinéas, MD, he was the most moderate. He became a career diplomat, representing Haiti in several capitals, including Washington. Currently, he is Haiti's ambassador to the Dominican Republic. Over the years we developed a friendship and have mutual respect for each other.

Luckner Cambronne rose to become the financier of the regime who was involved in all sorts of deals. In his most shady deals, he had a company selling corpses of indigents to foreign universities for research. He also made a high profit from selling blood plasma extracted from the poor on the international market. A real vampire! When he was ousted from Haiti in 1972, he asked to meet me and revealed that I was an enigma for his deceased boss "Papa Doc," who died without ever discovering my sources in Haiti.

President Duvalier wanted total control. Besides the *Tontons-Macoute* (bogeymen), he also organized a feminine terror group called *Fillettes Lalo* (body snatchers) that terrorized women accused of being anti-Duvalier.

It is estimated that about 30,000 people were murdered under the dictatorship of Papa Doc Duvalier. Early on, I was shocked by the horror stories, even death, attributed to the newly elected government. The case of Yvonne Hakim Rimpel remains the cruelest perpetrated in the early days of the dictatorship. The feminist activist had supported Louis Déjoie, Duvalier's opponent in the 1957 election. A writer, she had criticized the role played by the Army under candidate Duvalier. On January 5, 1958, Duvalier's emerging gestapo-police kidnapped her at her home in Pétionville. The next day she was found on a street, unconscious and naked, covered in blood from a severe beating. She is believed to have been raped. After two months in a hospital she recovered, but Lady Hakim Rimpel remained silent until her death in June 1986.

I was particularly unhinged by the desecration of a dead man's body by Duvalier's thugs. Clément Jumelle, a former minister of finance in the government of Paul Eugène Magloire, had been a candidate for the presidency. He went underground as soon as Papa Doc was declared the winner of the "election" in 1957. He was in hiding for eighteen months before he sought asylum at the Cuban Embassy in April 1959. Four days after he checked in at the Embassy, he died from kidney failure. He was unable to follow treatment in his unknown hideout.

On April 12, 1959, the hearse taking his body to burial in his native hometown of St. Marc was halted by the *Tontons-Macoute* who violently dispersed the mourners. His body was seized and taken to the Palace. The empty coffin was interred in St. Marc. It was said, and generally believed, that Papa Doc had met in a secret place with his dead rival Jumelle. The tyrant made people think that his Voodoo power enabled him to interrogate even a dead man to get useful information.

To me, the kidnapping of the corpse was the height of disrespect. Even the dead were not safe from the brigandage that was being set up as government. I had resolved at that point that one day I would avenge even the dead. Unknown to me at the time that we got connected, Georges Rigaud and Hubert Legros Sr., two individuals about whom I will discuss in the next chapter, eventually became the pillars of *Radio Vonvon* in Haiti and were close associates of Clément Jumelle.

I confess that I felt more powerless when I became aware that Papa Doc's control of the people went beyond naked repression. Through his use of Voodoo lore, he had gained a psychological advantage over the great majority of the society. Papa Doc made people believe that he had the power to transform himself into spirits or animals to carry out certain missions. It is hard to get that deep into people's minds. The attitude of the people changed whenever you spoke about Duvalier. Their eyes shifted right and left to see whether their conversation was being listened to. It was a pervasive mental attitude. And I decided that with accurate information against the dictator, I could get people to believe that he no longer had that power. It was a mental game. To shake his hold appeared an insurmountable task. But I was determined to find a way. That meant I had to learn more about Voodoo.

Chapter 5

For Whom the Dogs Spy

When Papa Doc assumed power in 1957, he incorporated Voodoo lore into his system of governance. Dressed in black most of the time, and often wearing a black humbug hat, he exuded the air of *Baron Samedi*, the "Master of Cemeteries." Indeed a powerful and malevolent Voodoo spirit! In a land where animals and inanimate objects are thought to have soul, Papa Doc adroitly exploited the people's beliefs to keep his stranglehold on power.

A medical doctor, Duvalier was a member of the *School of the Griots*, a fiercely nationalist group that embraced Voodoo. Having also studied anthropology, the doctor was an astute mystic. He had also built the reputation of a healer during the anti-yaw campaign of the 1940s when he worked with "Point IV," the precursor to United States Agency for International Development (USAID).

As a Public Health official, he made efficient use of penicillin to help eradicate yaw, a nasty skin disease akin to leprosy that was prevalent in Haiti's countryside. That's how he earned the moniker of "Papa Doc." Above all, his ability to transform himself into some kind of animal provided Papa Doc the most powerful tool of control.

While practicing medicine, Papa Doc had greater ambitions—to become president with the help of the Haitian Armed Forces. On one occasion, he gave his followers ample evidence of his Voodoo power. Duvalier was a major opposition leader to the regime of Paul Magloire, nicknamed *Kanson Fè* (Man of Steel) for his stranglehold on power through the Army. One night the police of President Magloire had dispatched a unit to arrest the activist who was located at Ruelle Cameau in Port-au-Prince.

Having been warned in advance by his high level mole at the Police that a detachment would be leaving at a specific time to arrest him, Papa Doc mounted a scenario to impress his followers. Minutes before the Police arrived, he told them he sensed danger. He ordered them to scatter and hide and to watch through peepholes or door cracks to see how he would handle the situation.

Papa Doc took off his black jacket, turned it inside out and put it on again. Then he sat on a straight-back chair backward, his legs astride. He put on his black humbug hat and rested his forehead on the back of the chair, totally motionless, like a scarecrow.

When the Police arrived at the location, the commanding officer, who had been briefed by his superior on what to do, ordered the house surrounded. He went inside alone to make the arrest. He passed by Duvalier and purported to see nothing. He paced back and forth, noted that a meeting had been in progress, because there was physical evidence of it. Several glasses and cups were still half full. However, there was no one in sight, except for the figure on the chair which, mysteriously, escaped his gaze.

Ten minutes into the operation, it was called off. Papa Doc, still motionless on the chair, coughed loudly, a signal that it was safe for all to come out of hiding. They rushed out and surrounded him as he slowly got up from the chair. Without saying a word, he took off his jacket and refitted it properly. He looked around somberly at his awe-stricken followers and flashed a broad smile. He told them that they had just experienced what *dedouble* was all about.

Dedouble, in Haitian mystical terms, is a transformation of self that allows one to do feats beyond the ability of a common mortal. It was his *dedouble* status that allowed Duvalier to either momentarily blind the police officer or for Duvalier to totally disappear.

When the commanding officer returned to Police headquarters that night, he was visibly shaken. He reported that on entering the house at Ruelle Cameau, he came under a spell and his vision became blurred. Although he knew that some people had been there, he could not see anyone. He only saw cups and glasses, some half full. The longer he stayed in the house, the more he felt a paralyzing force that overwhelmed him. He hurried to get out before something worse could have happened to him.

During the first eight years of his regime, Papa Doc faced much opposition. Beginning in 1959 through 1964, he had to deal with eight armed exile groups that sought to oust him. With a good intelligence network throughout the country, the dictator succeeded in defeating his challengers. But he intimated that he was helped by occult powers.

He gave a show when he tracked down one of his former aides who had turned against him. On April 26, 1963, Clément Barbot had failed in his attempt to kidnap 13-year-old Simone and her 12-year-old brother Jean-Claude, Papa Doc's youngest offspring. The dictator used that pretext to carry out a bloodbath in Port-au-Prince.

When he was told that Barbot was responsible for the failed attempt, he set out methodically to find Barbot's hiding place. Meanwhile, he had ordered that all black dogs around Port-au-Prince be shot, because Barbot had turned into a dog to escape capture, he was told. After two months of search, Papa Doc's intelligence service located Barbot in a cane field in La Plaine, about eight miles from the capital. One evening, accompanied by three or four of his bodyguards, Papa Doc took a secret reconnaissance trip to the area. Around midnight, he went through some ceremonial artifices by the cane field. The next day he sent a detachment of soldiers and *Tontons-Macoute* to the cane field with specific information on where to look for Barbot. The cane field was set afire and Barbot rushed out and was captured without a shot being fired. That action impressed many about Papa Doc's occult powers.

The fear of Duvalier was more widespread than I ever thought. In late November 1960, only three years after Papa Doc had ascended to the presidency, I had an experience that profoundly changed the course of my life. It was about 5:30 p.m. when a new acquaintance and I were lounging by the swimming pool, as he discussed the evolving political situation with me. I had moved to a house in Frères, a still undeveloped section of Pétionville at the time. It was a securely fenced property of about three acres of land with tropical fruits galore in a tranquil neighborhood, less than a mile from the then Military Academy.

The sun was going down fast, as it happens in the tropics. And darkness would soon intrude. Suddenly, Jean Lecroyant—not his real name—put his index finger over his tightly closed lips and looked at me intently. He quickly veered his eyes to the left to indicate that we had a visitor. There, a black dog was sniffing around for food. In Haiti's countryside and even in town, some animals, especially dogs, freely roam around in search of food. As the sun finally disappeared in the distant horizon, we both watched the dog leave. As it crossed the threshold of the property, Lecroyant, in hushed tones, asked: "Do you understand these things?"

"Yes, I do."

Lecroyant was surprised at my response. He said he had no idea that I understood these subtleties of Haitian life. He knew my father was a Protestant minister.

In the same breath, he admonished: "You see, you have to be very careful these days about what you say and where you say it. You should be extra careful when animals are around, because you don't know who sent them. You can't even trust some trees, like the

Mapou, because that's where the spirits dwell." He paused and kept nodding his head to emphasize his point.

Although raised in Haiti, I knew little about Voodoo, because I grew up in a Protestant household where the word was never mentioned. But having decided to study social anthropology after my theological studies, I became interested in the cultural aspects of Voodoo. Lecroyant, who knew of my upbringing, thought he was about to teach me something new. What disturbed me is that Lecroyant would believe that stuff. So, I decided to deal with him at his level.

He said: "Of course, you know, that black dog was from Duvalier who sent it to spy on us!" Since Lecroyant was involved in politics, he might have had the task of softening me for Duvalier by letting me know the power of the man. On the other hand, as a friend, he may have wanted me to be careful about the dangerous world in which we lived. I couldn't tell his motive, but he appeared to be sincere.

Lecroyant had returned home from Spain where he had been studying for four years. He had married a Spanish woman whom he had brought to Haiti with him. We were in the same league, so to speak. I, too, had been studying in the United States—for five years. My wife then was a white American whom I had brought home with me. Feeling some rapport with me, Lecroyant was uninhibited when in my company. That evening I got an instructive lecture on Haiti's evolving politics.

Lecroyant told me that Papa Doc had infiltrated the *hunfors,* or voodoo shrines. The *hungans,* or voodoo priests, were in Papa Doc's pay and comprised a vast spy network. The *hungans* are thought to have occult powers enabling them to accomplish uncommon feats, even to turn people into zombies. Since many Haitians trust *hungans* with their problems, Papa Doc had built himself a reliable information network.

Up to that point I was not in the least interested in politics or Voodoo. I had left Haiti in 1954 to study biblical languages at the

Moody Bible Institute in Chicago with the goal of translating the Bible into Creole. My translation of the New Testament with the Psalms was the first. Published under the auspices of the New York-based American Bible Society, it appeared in October 1960, one month before the black dog incident.

Immersed as I was in Christian religion, and deeply involved in Bible translation, I had paid little attention to Voodoo. But the reaction of Lecroyant to the appearance of the black dog totally unsettled me. When he left that evening, I had a headache. I took two aspirins and sat in the living room thinking. I said nothing to my wife Beth (Elizabeth), who had just become pregnant with our second child. She went to bed early, as I continued to mull over in my head about what I could do to loosen Papa Doc's hold on the psyche of Haitians.

In addition to my biblical studies, I had earned a BA in social anthropology from Wheaton College, in Wheaton, Illinois. Among the things I retained from my studies was to never minimize the beliefs of people, silly though they may seem. It's normal that to enter in the good graces of those you want to accept your point of view that you show deference to their own philosophy. So, I acted as if I also believed in Voodoo. But I knew better.

I reasoned that if Lecroyant, educated abroad and appearing sophisticated as he was, could believe in the black dog as he did, Papa Doc had full control of the land. Certainly the masses were more pliant than Lecroyant. I was overwhelmed at the thought that one man could have so much power by using the lore and customs of the land. Worse yet, that he used that power not to bring meaningful change to the country, but to perpetuate his power.

It was impossible for me to convince Haitians that dogs, cats, lizards, tarantulas or any other animal can't spy. I couldn't succeed by minimizing the idea of supernatural forces working in mysterious ways. I would have been dismissed as naïve, because many had experienced Papa Doc's power. He had gained notoriety as a Voodoo manipulator long before he became president.

I got confirmation of Papa Doc's supernatural power from an impeccable source. One Friday evening in April 1986, while at a party in Cayes-Jacmel in Haiti's southeast region, I was introduced to a gentleman who took me aside for a short conversation. His eyes opened widely, as if he wanted to peer inside me. With an air of amazement, he asked, "Are you the Raymond Joseph of *Radio Vonvon?*"

"Yes," I responded.

"I want to see you alone. We have things to discuss. Would you come by my house tomorrow where we can be alone?"

I nodded in agreement after he had given me the information on his address. Throughout the evening, I could sense the joy that the gentleman felt. He was beaming every time our eyes crossed. It was as if he could not wait for the next day.

On Saturday morning, at 11:00 sharp, alone at the wheel of a rented car, I pulled up in front of the residence, in Jacmel, of the military commander of the Southeastern Department. The late Colonel Gambetta Hyppolite, in khaki shorts and a white T-shirt, wearing sandals, welcomed me warmly. He yelled out to the servant: "Prepare us coffee quickly, we have an important visitor with us!" It was obvious that the Colonel felt at ease with me, important though he may be. I would soon discover the ties that bind us.

"Sit down, sit down," he said, excitedly. "I have so many questions to ask, I don't know where to begin. I cannot believe I am in front of you, Raymond Joseph. For many years I dreamed about you and have asked if I would ever have a chance to meet you, the master of *Radio Vonvon*. Please, tell me how did you do it?"

I paused a few seconds. Looking him intently in the eyes, I said, "I don't know whether I can tell you how I did it, because I don't know when I may have to start another *Vonvon.*"

He cut me off. "But you should know that I was also a *Vonvonist,*" he exclaimed.

"I did not have you on the list," I replied.

"Oh no, there were many of us who knew where to go deliver the information without giving our names for any list. It was too dangerous. So, you see, I was one of yours without you even knowing it!" He continued: "By the way, as a young army officer, I was sent on missions to find the *Vonvon*. I was sent to Port-de-Paix, to look for it in a cave."

"Did you find it?"

"Of course not. Neither did I find it at Fort Liberté, nor at Fort Jacques where I was also dispatched. . . . We knew where it was. . . . At Osso Blanco and at the Coast Guard." (Osso Blanco was a high class butcher shop that spotted a large antenna near the Champ de Mars across from the National Palace. The Coast Guard was headquartered in Bizoton, south of Port-au-Prince center city.)

The colonel looked at me, as if to get my approval of what he had just revealed.

I did not respond to that. But I told him, "I will tell you a story which may help you understand something about *Radio Vonvon*." Then I began to recount the experience of the black dog by the pool in Frères. He was following me with unusual intensity. When I reached to the part where Lecroyant told me that the dog was a spy dispatched by Duvalier to listen to our conversation, the colonel bolted from his chair.

Staring me in the eyes, he exclaimed: "Mr. Joseph, no! . . . The dog was no spy that the old man had dispatched. The dog was Duvalier himself. Let me tell you, Sir, I was there when Duvalier used to *dedouble* himself into dog, cat and whatnot. I have experienced it, Sir. That's why in Haiti, people know that you are *pwofonde* (profound), because the old man died without ever finding out how you were able to infiltrate everywhere. . . ." In other words, he meant I am profoundly endowed with mystical power.

I just looked at the colonel, but said nothing about his revelation of what was generally thought of me in Duvalierist circles. He kept looking at me waiting for I don't know what. Certainly, I was not about to reveal anything to him.

To complete the conversation, the colonel said, "Sir, you can count on me for anything. You are an unusual person. It's well known."

If I am unusual, it happened early in life when I lost my fears. Growing up in Haiti's countryside, at an early age one learns about *lougawou,* the werewolves who rule the night and who may kidnap children—and even grownups—to take them to the netherworld. Usually those stories are told at night, especially when there is a bright full moon. The extended family would sit in a large circle in the yard, and in turn this one or that one would tell a riddle. They would start by saying out loud, *Krik!* And all would respond *Krak!* At times a storyteller would depart from the norm and start with a scary story. One such story haunted me for a long time. It went like this:

It was past midnight and this young fellow happened to be out quite late. He did not know how late it was, because he did not have a watch. Going by a cemetery, he was struck by the sight of several figures dressed elegantly in black and white. Some had long canes draped over their arms. The young man, somewhat disoriented by the spectacle, asked one of the men, "Sir, what time is it?" In a booming voice, the man said, "Young man, it is that time of night for the living to rest and for the dead to take their stroll!"

The young man dashed away to escape what could have been a kidnapping to the netherworld, the land of the dead. The moral of the story was left to us to figure out. Undoubtedly, it was meant to scare us, young ones, and to deter us from thoughts of running away from home. It worked, because that story sealed my fear of darkness.

When I was about 12 years old, I lost my fears. A neighbor had died in Simon, upstream from the pristine water source called *La Perle* (The Pearl) that flowed in the valley near our house. This was the first wake and funeral that I can remember attending. Very inquisitive, I was intrigued by the beautiful elongated black face of the lady lying in a laced white dress in the coffin. After the religious ceremony which was held in the yard of the family, the party left for the burial ground. I never saw where she was buried.

In those days when morgues did not exist in the countryside, custom called for the corpse to be buried within twenty-four hours. In most parts of Haiti's countryside, this is still the practice. That same night, the beautiful black lady in her white dress, just as I saw her in the coffin, appeared to me in the most unusual way. I went to the outhouse down some thirty feet from the main house. A few feet behind the outhouse was a steep cliff at the bottom of which flowed The Pearl. Usually, when I was doing my business, I would close my eyes. When I opened them that night, I swear that I saw the lady standing at the only door by which to leave the outhouse. My heart began to pound within my chest. I did not know what to do. I closed my eyes again and still sitting, I said in a loud voice: "Have you come for me? If you have come for me, take me and go with me. But if you have not come for me, I am asking you to leave and let me go!" When I opened my eyes, she was gone.

That night I changed my usual habit of dashing into the main house after relieving myself. I was in no rush this time. I strolled in the small cornfield I had planted, admired the stars for the first time and became enamored of the night which was fresh and quiet. After about ten minutes enjoying the outdoors alone, I remembered about my parents, little brother and sister. I did not want them to think that something untoward had happened to me. So, I leisurely walked into the house. I said nothing about my experience. But from that day on, I had lost my fears—all sorts of fears. I felt that there was not a thing that I could not do. This experience would serve me well throughout my life.

Around that same time, I began to awaken spiritually. I was a fervent churchgoer and reader of the Bible. I did not go to church just for the social setting that the occasion provided. I was curious about the deep meanings of the Bible and of life itself. In reading the Epistles of Paul, I came unto a verse to which I felt a connection. It is in the epistle to the Philippians 4:13 – *"I can do all things through Christ who strengthens me."*

Having conquered my fear of the night and all sorts of fears, this verse was like a tonic. I knew nothing about Superman back then. But in retrospect, I saw myself as Superman who defied the dead. For, in Haitian culture, the dead are among the most powerful on earth. I felt that nothing could stop me from doing what I set my mind to do, especially good things.

Chapter 6

Fighting Fire with Fire: The Legend of Radio Vonvon

About nine months after the black dog experience by the pool, in July 1961 I left Haiti with my wife and our two children in the nick of time. The Secretary of State at the Ministry of Interior, Michel Aubourg, had tipped me about impending danger. Somehow it became known that my house had been a safe haven for dissident students who were planning strikes against the regime. Although I was not involved in their organizations, I was targeted for being an accessory to their crime by providing a hiding place for some who were being sought for arrest. All demonstrations and opposition activities to the regime were banned. Even folks who were not involved in politics became victims of the Duvalierists who used their power to settle scores of any sort. Arbitrariness ruled.

I had met Aubourg in Chicago in the summer of 1955 while he studied at Northwestern University in Evanston, a suburb of the Windy City. I was then enrolled in the Pastor's course at the Moody Bible Institute in Chicago. He and I had developed a friendship around the English language. Although a brilliant anthropologist from Haiti's School of Ethnology, Aubourg did not yet master

English well enough to write his thesis. I told him to write in French and I would adapt it in English. This sealed our friendship, although I resisted his political views.

Aubourg was fully convinced that Papa Doc, who had spent a year at the University of Michigan studying public health, would be Haiti's next president. Since he was a member of the doctor's inner circle, he wanted me to be part of Haiti's upcoming revolution, that of the black middle class, he said. I declined.

Now six years later, we are back in Haiti and Aubourg holds a powerful position in the government. In a private conversation, he told me, "Raymond, you always wanted to continue with graduate work, right?" He paused. "Well, now it's the time to do it." He wanted me to run. "Go see your friend Ford and he will prepare your passport and clear you for departure as soon as possible."

My friend Guillaume Ford was the interim director at the Office of Immigration and Emigration, next door to the Ministry of Interior, where Michel Aubourg had his office. Moreover, Immigration was—and still is—a unit under the oversight of the Interior Ministry. I had two friends at the pinnacle of power in terms of immigration control. This was critical, because the budding Duvalier dictatorship had set up a system to block potential enemies from leaving the country.

A business of *non monte, non desann* had flourished. Literally, one's name supposedly had to "*monte*"—"sent up" (to the Palace)—and it had to "*desann*"—"come down" (from the Palace)—before one could leave the country. This was applicable especially in political cases, but soon it developed into a vast system of corruption. Fortunately, I was spared this waiting game.

I flew out of Haiti with my family on a Friday in late July. Later I would learn that the following Monday, early in the morning, a detachment of *Tontons-Macoute* descended at the house where I lived. But I was already in Puerto Rico, bound for the mainland. Michel Aubourg must have known what was about to happen when he urged me to leave immediately. He may even have been the one to give the *Tontons* the information that I was preparing to leave the country and that they should move speedily to block me—after the fact.

Apparently, Aubourg did not totally ascribe to Duvalierist doctrine. For, one of the maxims of that doctrine, borrowed by Papa Doc from Machiavelli's *The Prince,* was: *En politique la reconnaissance est une lâcheté.* (In politics, gratefulness is weakness.) No doubt, Aubourg remembered what I did for him while he was at Northwestern. A humanist, he is credited with having saved many lives. Apparently, the regime found out about his acts of mercy. He died, allegedly of poisoning.

Once I arrived in the United States, I began to think about how to counteract the dictator back home. It was not an easy task. As previously mentioned, when Papa Doc assumed power in 1957, he incorporated Voodoo into his system of governance. He made people think that his mystical power knew no limit. To successfully challenge the dictator, his mystical influence had to be minimized.

We discovered the workings of his system. Other than his mystical intelligence network rooted in the *hunfors* and backed by the roaming animals, Papa Doc also relied on the Army's intelligence unit. Besides its plain clothes operatives commonly called *detektif* (detectives), the Army depended on the rural constabulary called *Police Rurale* to gather information. The presence of the constabulary was pervasive through its civilian auxiliaries, the *soukèt lawouze,*— literally the "dew shakers" who usually beat the bush early in the morning in search of information. The *Tontons-Macoute* militia provided extra cover as far as intelligence was concerned, but their main attribute was repression.

To counteract the dictator's vast network, we set up the *Bureau Central* in Port-au-Prince to infiltrate the intelligence networks of the dictator. In the *hunfors* the Bureau relied on the *hunsis,* as the servants of the *hungans* are called. They are the lowliest in the hierarchical ranking of the *peristil,* another creole term for a Voodoo shrine. Thus, while Papa Doc was getting his information from the *hungans,* the *Vonvon* operatives relied on some *hunsis* to keep tabs on the doings at the *peristil.*

In Army ranks, it was easy to find the disgruntled at all levels, especially since the military had been unofficially demoted with the advent of the *Tontons-Macoute.* We were not asking anyone to take up arms. Our sole interest was accurate information that we used in our broadcasts to Haiti. Broadcasting such information all the way from New York had a mystical effect. People felt that Duvalier no longer had total control of events. Another powerful force was at work.

Building a network of informers was a delicate and dangerous task. We did not pay anybody, because we couldn't have matched the dictator if we had ventured into the monetary system of corruption. He could always outbid us in such a situation. However, the organizers of the *Bureau Central* were very resourceful and they managed to find true patriots among the disgruntled around the dictator willing to provide information. At times we did some favors for these secret agents, such as a visit to the United States for a sick relative, some help to defray the cost of a funeral or extra cash for the schooling of the kids. We were family.

One such patriot was Bossuet "Bobo" Delva, a *detektif* (undercover) who was working at the *Recherches Criminelles,* the "Criminal Research" branch of the Police in Port-au-Prince, based across the plaza from the National Palace. At four feet five inches tall, with very dark skin and low-keyed in personality, wiry Bobo would not have been thought of as a major player in the intelligence network. He became our main mole at the Police. Since he was the most trusted investigator for sensitive cases, the organizers of the *Vonvon* became connected at the highest level of the dictator's spying network. We were ready to undertake psychological warfare against Papa Doc.

I was extremely busy juggling graduate school, lecturing, and providing for a growing family. Still, in Chicago where I was at the University, I found time for weekly meetings with prominent Haitians who were disturbed and concerned about the political situation in our homeland. One, Ernest Lafontant, eventually joined the ranks of the regime and became Duvalier's consul in Chicago. There was Dr. Janin Raoul whose son Kwame Raoul became a State senator in his own right after he was picked by State Senator Barack Obama in 2000 to fill the remainder of his term in the Illinois Senate. However it was the trio—the late Dr. Jean François Conte, the late Raymond Chassagne and I—that would, with internal support, eventually shake the foundation of Duvalierist power.

Dr. Conte was a successful surgeon who lived on Woodland Avenue in Hyde Park, not far from the Chicago residence of the Obamas. He had a prosperous clinic on the south side of Chicago. Initially he bankrolled our movement. Raymond Chassagne was a former officer in the Haitian Army whose brother Roland Chassagne, also an Army officer, had been murdered by the *Tontons-Macoute* in the massacre of April 26, 1963. Raymond was the philosopher and political strategist of the group.

I was the youngest of the trio, but I had developed contacts beyond our ingrown community. I had an idea that my two colleagues fully embraced, after I had explained to them the experience of the famous black dog at Frères, Pétionville. We must have a radio program to challenge Duvalier and his goons, I insisted. That is the only way for the opposition to eventually flourish.

I convinced my foreign contacts also about the need to have a democratic voice to counteract the Haitian dictator and others who espoused communism. Two broadcasts—from Havana and Moscow—were touting the benefits of communism. And after Fidel Castro's defeat of Fulgencio Batista in Cuba, I saw the possibility of a communist victory in Haiti. I felt that Duvalier, just like the right-wing dictator Batista, was indirectly sowing the seed for a communist takeover in Haiti. Although I had been pro-Castro in college, I became disenchanted when he started his *Al Paredón*—to the wall—campaign, the summary executions of real and imagined enemies lined up against the wall.

I had met Fred Schwarz, a medical doctor from Australia who was campaigning against communism. He had abandoned a prosperous practice in Adelaide to come to the United States to warn America about the evils of communism. His book *You Can Trust the Communists (to be Communists)* became a bestseller. Dr. Schwarz, who was based in Long Beach, California, put me in contact with his friend, a former movie star named Ronald Reagan. He had not yet become Governor of California. Those contacts would be helpful to me when the decision was made to start our broadcast.

As the dictator unleashed his murdering machine on a defenseless population, anger boiled within me. The tragic event of April 26, 1963, was a turning point in my resolve to do something instead of nursing a constant hurt. As previously mentioned, there was an attempt that morning to kidnap Jean-Claude Duvalier and his sister Simone. As the youngsters got off their chauffeured car in front of College Bird, the reputable Methodist institution on Rue de l'Enterrement in the capital, shots rang out. One bodyguard and their chauffeur fell dead. Jean-Claude and Simone rushed into the school and out of danger.

Duvalier went into a rage. Without any investigation, he ordered a pogrom. Nearly 100 citizens were murdered on that day, including 80-year-old retiree Auguste Léandre. Lieutenant François Benoit and his wife Jacqueline, née Edeline, suffered the most. Gunned down were the officer's father, mother, four servants and a dog. The couple's nine-month-old son was taken alive from the house, never to reappear. At least eight relatives of Jacqueline Edeline were murdered on that day, including her mother, father, brothers, sisters and in-laws. Benoit Armand, a lawyer, was murdered because of his surname. Why such cruelty against one family? The dictator had surmised that only Lieutenant Benoit could have pulled the coup with such precision. The young officer and his colleague Lieutenant Monod Philippe were international stars who had won top medals in shooting competitions in Panama. Lt. Benoit, whose roots are in southern Haiti, was considered a partisan of Louis Déjoie, the candidate who lost to Duvalier in 1957. However, Lt. Philippe was a known Duvalierist. On that basis alone, the madman carried out his murderous operation. Most of the victims that day were mulattoes and considered partisans of Louis Déjoie. The action of Duvalier that day added impetus to our determination to go on the offensive.

Dr. Conte, Raymond Chassagne, and I spent about three years raising funds among friends and relatives. We also worked on elaborate plans on how to prepare Haitians back home for a general uprising against the dictator. Two tragic events, one in Dallas, Texas, and the other in Port-au-Prince, became the final catalysts to our action. On November 22, 1963, President John Fitzgerald Kennedy was assassinated in Dallas. It was a bizarre scenario in which his assassin, Lee Harvey Oswald, was himself gunned down two days later by Jack Ruby, a night club operator. Convicted on March 14, 1964, of Oswald's murder, Ruby appealed the conviction and death sentence. He died of lung cancer on January 3, 1967, before the appeal was heard.

Many conspiracy theories swirled around the assassination of President Kennedy. But not much importance was given to Papa Doc's boast that he was responsible for the undoing of the popular American president who did not hide his dislike for him. Opponents of Duvalier, including me, were scandalized by the insensitivity of Papa Doc. On learning about President Kennedy's assassination, Duvalier had a champagne drinking party at the National Palace that evening. He claimed that he killed Kennedy exactly on the 22nd of the month, his magic number.

For the record, Duvalier was "elected" on September 22, 1957, sworn into office October 22, gave himself a second mandate April

22, 1961, declared himself President-for-life on April 22, 1964, and supposedly died April 22, 1971. In Duvalierist circles, Papa Doc's boast about Kennedy's assassination reinforced his invincibility. But as opponents to his rule, we became more determined to rid Haiti of the murderous dictator.

Another tragic event nearly a year later was the last straw that broke the camel's back. On November 12, 1964, Papa Doc organized a circus for the execution of two rebels, the remnant of thirteen who had left their university studies in the United States to undertake guerrilla action against the dictator in Haiti. All but the two, Marcel Numa and Louis Drouin, were killed in action. Papa Doc ordered a special holiday. He asked that school children in uniform be brought to the cemetery of Port-au-Prince to watch the execution. Radio Nationale and Channel 5, the only television station in Haiti, covered the event.

The images remain fresh in my mind. Each victim, standing erect, was tightly tied to a post. A taller figure, with dark skin, dressed in long dark pants and a white shirt, contrasted with his shorter fair-skin colleague. The darker man was Marcel Numa and the mulatto Louis Drouin, both from Jérémie, the southwestern city nicknamed "The City of Poets." Amid the hoopla of a festive day, something tragic was about to happen. The execution squad raised their carbines in unison as the group leader barked the orders. All of a sudden there was quietness all around and one could hear the last distinct order: Fire! Afterward, a young Army officer, Frank Romain, strode over quickly and administered the coup-de-grâce. Papa Doc pushed his cruelty further. The body of the rebel Yvan Laraque, tied to a chair, was displayed for a few days at a major intersection on the northern outskirts of the capital. Guards with masks kept the dogs away.

Nearly 1,800 miles away in Chicago, I was ashamed and seething with anger. My American classmates were buzzing about what Duvalier had done. Every time I heard about the cruelty, it felt like salt being rubbed on a fresh wound. Then, Duvalier ordered a massacre in Jérémie. The relatives and friends of the thirteen rebels were killed without mercy. Undoubtedly, the dictator thought that he had finally deterred all opposition to his rule. By having the children watch the horrific execution, the dictator was conditioning their young minds to accept his new culture of official violence while instilling fear in them at a tender age. Diabolical, indeed!

We had an emergency meeting. The three of us who formed what some of our friends called "The Three Musketeers" or *L'Equipe Solide* (The Solid Team) agreed that this was indeed the last straw. Time had come to do something. Raymond Chassagne was in touch with his brother in New York, Albert Chassagne, a dentist. Raymond would ask Albert to arrange for a meeting in New York with top political and military brass in exile. Dr. Conte, the treasurer, said we were ready financially. About $50,000 was already earmarked to begin our operation. I would contact my various acquaintances throughout the United States for more financial backing.

In contacting political leaders, we told Albert Chassagne to be as inclusive as possible. We asked that he contact Daniel Fignolé, who had been President of Haiti for 19 days before the election of Duvalier in 1957. He was toppled by a coup d'état in June of that year and had been in exile in New York ever since. He wanted all opposition to coalesce around him. He claimed that he was still President of Haiti and insisted that we acknowledge his title and rank before he would join any discussion. We moved ahead without him.

I told my two colleagues that since we were coming from Chicago in America's Midwest, we would be considered hick town cousins by the bigwigs of New York and Washington. We must find a way to impress the Easterners. I suggested that our meetings be held at the Waldorf Astoria Hotel, one of the most prestigious addresses on New York's Park Avenue and a pied-à-terre of presidents and other luminaries. My colleagues agreed.

For a weekend, beginning Friday night, we took a suite of three rooms, with a large room in the center for general discussions, and adjoining rooms on each side for private caucuses. The invitees were impressed, just as we had figured. The first evening was more like a social gathering of get-to-know each other. Saturday morning, beginning at 9:00 and continuing until 8:00 p.m., we had fruitful discussions. Continental breakfast, lunch, and coffee breaks were served at the suite at our expense. On Sunday morning at 10:00 when we reconvened, it was to officially approve a two-page statement which was like an operation guideline.

At the outset of the discussions, the majority of the participants wanted to plan another "invasion" of Haiti. We successfully outmaneuvered those who wanted another invasion. We noted that they had been at their eighth so-called invasion in as many years of the Duvalier regime. Each military operation, we argued, apparently strengthened Papa Doc's grip on the country. We had a different plan. First, we would win over the minds of the people before transitioning to more active opposition. Moreover, we disposed of $50,000 to launch the radio broadcasts. That was not an insignificant sum at the time.

The partisans of an invasion argued that $50,000 was good seed money to attract more. And we would be in a stronger position than other groups to undertake a successful invasion. When some said that "words cannot topple a dictatorship," we held to our position. To win over the minds of the people was the most important first step. To do that, we had to speak to them, and radio was the only suitable medium for that task.

Paul Magloire, the ex-president and former general of the Armed Forces, was the first among the group to espouse our logic. Indeed, it makes sense, he said, to prepare the people first for an eventual change. The proponents of military action dropped their objections, although they held to their original position that radio cannot overthrow a government. But we did not say that overthrowing the government was our top priority. Foremost in our strategy was the psychological preparation for an eventual change.

It took another five months of preparation to launch *La Voix de l'Union Haïtienne Internationale* (The Voice of the International Haitian Union). Through my American contacts we discovered "Radio New York Worldwide" (WRUL), originally housed above the Paris Theatre on Fifth Avenue at 58th Street in Manhattan. The shortwave station, owned by the Mormon Church, hosted the broadcast of the anti-Castro Cuban exiles. On Monday, July 23, 1965, our first broadcast hit the waves at six o'clock, with the theme song: *Maria Leve! Maria, ou pa tande premye son lanmès sonnen?* (Maria, Wake up! Maria, haven't you heard the first bell for mass?)

Instead of flowery French, we chose Creole as our medium of communication. This was revolutionary in itself at a time when broadcasting was done mainly in French, then the only official language of Haiti. We did not totally ban French from the programming, because we still harbored in our midst those who believed that the only way to express intellectual thought was in French. In time, even the purists came to accept that the most effective messengers were the Creole speakers, especially *Frère Lepoule* (Brother Chicken), a first-ranked comedian. (We also had published a booklet in French, entitled *Programme de la Coalition Haïtienne* [Program of the Haitian Coalition] which was our agenda for governing Haiti.)

The broadcast gained traction when Brother Chicken came on board—for seven to ten minutes of the half-hour show. The two original speakers, who were not identified by name or nickname, were Raymond Chassagne and me—"the two Raymonds"—as our intimate friends referred to us. Later, we added a third Raymond—Raymond Montreuil.

Brother Chicken played the part of a Voodoo priest. He always started his session with his *asson* or divining instrument, which is a bell with a distinctive sound. There was no way to mistake the sound of the *asson*, especially for Voodoo practitioners. Moreover, Brother Chicken was the only one who refused to speak regular Creole.

In his well-rehearsed broken French, he sounded like a top-notch comedian. He became the darling of the listeners.

We began the radio program as a "cultural voice" from abroad without any hint of our political agenda. At one point some Duvalierists even said that Papa Doc was behind the broadcast, a way to show his international reach and connections. We did not object. In fact we rejoiced in the apparent confusion, because it was helping to popularize the broadcast among those we considered our main targets. There was no reason to antagonize the dictator and his minions at the outset. To have them as indirect allies was a coup that brought us instant recognition.

It did not take long before we got called on the carpet. The board of directors of CHFD, the *Coalition Haïtienne des Forces Démocratiques* (Haitian Coalition of Democratic Forces), the umbrella organization responsible for policy for the radio broadcast, called a rare Saturday morning meeting. The main topic of discussion was Brother Chicken. Who was he? Where did he come from? Are we not giving a bad reputation to the broadcast by introducing Voodoo into the mix and by having such an uncouth personality on the air?

Some board members had received unflattering reports from Port-au-Prince about the broadcast. Some listeners, no doubt among the intelligentsia, asserted that the program was being trivialized by a so-called witchdoctor who was talking trash in a language that was neither French nor Creole. The board wanted to hear what it was all about. I produced a tape recording of our broadcast. On a portable Wollensak tape recorder, the staid board members were enjoying Brother Chicken who was doing his thing. Amused though they were, the overwhelming majority voted to cut Brother Chicken out.

I was heartbroken when I had to break the news to Brother Chicken. I told him he had to take a rest until the situation was sorted out. I emphasized, however, that he should not despair, because in the end I was confident that we—that is, he and I—would win.

Two weeks had elapsed without a crow from Brother Chicken. Then, we received a letter from the *Bureau Central* in Port-au-Prince wanting to know what had happened to Brother Chicken. Didn't we know that he is the most popular character on the show? And the guys in Port-au-Prince insisted that we must do whatever must be done to get Brother Chicken back on the air—immediately!

Three weeks after the last board meeting, I called a meeting of my own. I made two photocopies of the letter from Port-au-Prince. I passed a copy to those sitting on one side of the long table and the other copy to those on the other side, and held onto the original. Although I put on a serious demeanor for the occasion, I was chuckling inside. I managed to keep my composure as I waited for them to finish their reading. This time it was Luc Fouché, the erudite former ambassador to Washington, who spoke first. "We have no choice but to bring Brother Chicken back," he said, adding that "the Central office is adamant on this point. And let me say here that those guys on the ground know better than we what is needed. Let us not forget that we are just echoing them."

Unanimously, all embraced Brother Chicken, who felt invigorated when he resumed broadcasting after a month of silence. He literally crowed and flapped his wings in a sign of victory before he began to talk in his usual manner. To hear him, one would believe he was a real rooster, albeit a rooster endowed with the gift of language. A first-class showman, Brother Chicken had mimicked perfectly a crowing rooster that was flapping its wings.

He said he had gone on vacation and was sorry to have deprived his fans of good fun for a whole month. Next time, he will cut his vacation into segments, not to be away for long. Through biting humor, Brother Chicken was demystifying Papa Doc. Indeed, that was the main objective of the broadcast. Referring to a fable of Jean de Lafontaine, the French master storyteller, Brother Chicken found a new name for Duvalier. He took some liberty with Lafontaine's original story about a tomcat called *Rodulard Duce* who was so mean that he killed all the rats in the neighborhood. Whether he was hungry or not, *Rodulard* would kill the rats, at times leaving their corpses to rot under the sun.

One day the Dean of "Ratdom" called a conference of all living rats to discuss what to do with *Rodulard Duce*. A young thinking rat said he had a solution. A small bell should be tied around *Rodulard's* neck. Thus, whenever he is coming around, all rats will be alerted and could quickly disappear into their holes.

The Dean smiled and congratulated the young thinker for his brilliant idea. He said this was a stroke of genius on the part of such a young fellow. Whereupon, the Dean asked for volunteers to do the job of slipping the bell around the tomcat's neck. A great silence fell upon the assembly. One by one, the rats slipped out the back hole, leaving the Dean at the podium by himself. Even the young thinker who first came up with the idea had disappeared. Fixing his spectacles, the Dean let out a big sigh and murmured to himself: "Just a bunch of cowards! What can be expected from an assembly of rats!" Dejected, he left the scene.

The gist of the story is that *Rodulard* became *Wodila* in Creole, because the true Creole speaker cannot pronounce the French "r" and "u", which automatically become "w" and "i" (*ee* as in Lee). From that day on, every time Papa Doc did something obnoxious, Brother Chicken would embellish on it and talk about *Wodila* doing this, *Wodila* doing that. A name had been coined for Duvalier without mentioning him directly. He had to own up to the name.

Nonetheless, people were not fooled. They understood exactly what was being said. And Papa Doc could not do a thing about it. We began receiving reports from the *Bureau Central* and letters from listeners with the name *Wodila* replacing that of Duvalier. Brother Chicken's renditions were the closest we had come to political discourse in the early months of the broadcast. All of a sudden, there was no longer any doubt about our political leanings. This could not be a Duvalierist voice from abroad.

When Papa Doc began feeling vulnerable to the radio broadcast from New York, he became enraged. We were informing the people about the evils of the regime and we could not be silenced. Certainly, that couldn't have happened on Haitian soil. After a listening session around eleven o'clock one morning, the dictator was so agitated that he almost broke his wrist as he slammed his fist on his desk and blurted out: *Destroy that Vonvon! Kill it!* The next morning, we changed the name of the six o'clock broadcast from *La Voix de l'Union Haïtienne Internationale* to *Radio Vonvon*—The Bug bugging the old man.

"Yes, Sir," Brother Chicken said in the broadcast, "From now on it is *Radio Vonvon*! Thank you, Sir, for the name!" (A *vonvon* is a black insect slightly larger than a bee which sounds like a dragonfly as it buzzes by.) The broadcast had become a nuisance for Duvalier.

In line with our original policy of a cultural show, we eschewed politics in the beginning. We had planned to become political by increments, as we built up our audience. After the first two months, it was obvious that we had deep penetration in Haiti. A new technological breakthrough had given us a big boost. *Radio Vonvon* came on the scene at a time when transistor radios were gaining wide popularity. Massive distributions of the battery-powered transistor radios had been undertaken throughout Haiti. The *Bureau Central* had used schools, churches, and neighborhood clubs to carry out distribution through wholesome competition. The transistor radio revolutionized radio listening in the far reaches of the country. Almost overnight, *Radio Vonvon* was dubbed "The Six O'Clock Mass" that few wanted to miss.

It was also a novel voice with a message distinct from two other broadcasts from abroad: the Creole broadcast of Radio Havana, initially headed by René Dépestre, and Radio Moscow's program which René Théodore directed. Those two broadcasts were heavily ideological while we came along more like comic relief. Moreover, our Saturday show targeted the youth, with the latest French and

American popular hits dominating the programming. Johnny Halliday, Petula Clark, Elvis Pressley, Soeur Sourire, and the Beatles were among our most popular artists.

We also used Haitian singers whose songs included ambiguous messages that could be interpreted as poking fun at the authorities. One such song by an unknown artist became a recurring theme in our broadcast: *Sese te di konsa, mwen granmounn nan tout kò mwen!* (*Sese* [a funny nickname] said, I am endowed with power all over my body!) The listeners understood that we could only be referring to Papa Doc who considered himself the embodiment of all power. He enjoyed his many self-bestowed titles, such as "The Immaterial Being," "The Effective Chief of the Forces of Air, Land and Sea" and "The Haitian Flag, One and Indivisible" to which we deridingly added, "Yeah, the Floating Flag." We poked fun at him by adding the demeaning *Sese* nickname to his lofty collection of titles.

The needling of Brother Chicken got the best of Papa Doc, who finally exploded with his "Kill that Bug" order. He also protested to the US State Department about a broadcast from New York which was destabilizing his government. He could not specify those responsible for the challenge to his rule, because the names of the organizers were kept secret. He was thrown off track when an article in an obscure publication mentioned Ray Jozèf as the leader of the group. Duvalier and his experts said this was a *nom de plume*. The writer of the article had only written my last name in Creole, and the nickname Ray had not yet taken hold. I was always known as Raymond, or by the nickname Mong for friends and close relatives. This allowed me a full year of anonymity to organize without my real identity being detected. What we were able to accomplish in that year was phenomenal. We managed to set up a network of informants that covered the most sensitive State agencies in Haiti.

We went fully political after a front page story in the *New York Times,* September 2, 1965—"Duvalier Bids U.S. Bars a Broadcast: Daily Program Beamed by Private Station Protested." The State

Department had asked through Radio New York Worldwide for some recordings of our broadcast. After seeing an English translation of what was being said in Creole, the State Department responded to the Haitian government that the broadcast does not break Federal laws or broadcasting regulations. The organizers are only exercising their right of democratic dissent. Nothing can be done to silence them.

The name of former President Paul Magloire surfaced as the financier of the broadcast. He gained some notoriety for being among the group's sponsors. The response of the State Department became like a seal of approval. From then on, we were no longer inhibited from naming Duvalier or his cohorts whenever there was an occasion to do so. However, the listeners had become so enamored of the name *Wodila* that it stuck as a regular nickname for Papa Doc.

Brother Chicken did not like the name Duvalier. He deformed it into *Divage* (with a hard "g") which is a play on an expression meaning blah-blah-blah, or speaking nonsense. Brother Chicken once undressed the old man to make him look stupid. Speaking in broken French, he said, "Hello, *Divage*, I see that you're looking for the bug (hidden microphones) in the curtains, in the refrigerator, somewhere and everywhere. Well, I'll give you some advice. Take your pants off, your shirt, the undies also, I mean your undershirt, underpants, and your socks, to be plain naked as your mother made you. Take off your heavy glasses and get inside a tub full of water. Then you'll speak without the bug catching you." He paused a few seconds, then added, "Oh, no! That won't work, because of your gold teeth."

Indeed, based on Brother Chicken's messages, Papa Doc was certain there were bugs planted in his residence at the Palace. Bugs as in electronic devices! But our devices were human beings speaking on telephone lines that had been tapped.

When he threw a tantrum one morning about a breakfast that he didn't like, people commented about it in front of a *Vonvon* informer, and so Papa Doc heard Brother Chicken recount the event from New York. We had really infiltrated the regime for good.

"Look, man," Brother Chicken said, "you are Mister President, right? Not any insignificant little two-bit President, you know. You are President-for-life. If you don't like the eggs the way they were prepared, just return the stuff and have them do it over. You don't need to throw a tantrum like a kid. Come on, stop that stuff."

As proof mounted that Papa Doc was losing it over *Radio Vonvon's* inroads, we discovered new ways to intensify his madness. When he had an altercation with Simone, his wife, who was throwing fits of jealousy about Papa Doc's affair with his secretary, he slapped her violently. That same night Simone telephoned General Gracia Jacques to complain about her husband. Gracia was Papa Doc's most trusted bodyguard. Two days later, Brother Chicken was embellishing the fight over *Radio Vonvon.* The *Bureau Central,* which was on the same telephone circuit as that of Gracia Jacques, had managed to tap Papa Doc's bodyguard's line.

But the best test of Brother Chicken's power was his visit to Haiti, announced on the air on a Tuesday. In his flavorful broken French and Creole mix, he invited his friends and devotees to meet him at *Kalfou Difò* (Carrefour Dufort) on a Saturday at 1:00 p.m. He disappeared from the broadcast.

Carrefour Dufort, southwest of Port-au-Prince, on the National Road No. 2, is a major junction teeming with people who come from long distances to do commerce. Moreover, being a *Carrefour*— a crossroads—it fits in voodoo lore as a place where great things happen. For, the spirits and werewolves meet in the dead of night, usually around midnight, at crossroads, before going on their missions. Thus, Carrefour Dufort, on a Saturday, met the requirements for a major audience with the man-spirit who had eluded the dictator and his henchmen.

Overnight Friday, there were discreet civilian patrols in the vicinity of Carrefour Dufort. All the roads leading to the Carrefour were under watch. By 10:00 a.m. that Saturday, a detachment of the Armed Forces under the command of Colonel Edner Nelson arrived at Carrefour Dufort to be deployed at strategic points. Observers had been dispatched to the area by our *Bureau Central* since Thursday. Not to draw attention on them, most of our observers were from the locality.

That Saturday, Carrefour Dufort was unusually busy. People had flocked there to get a glimpse of their radio idol, the man who taunted Duvalier in their behalf and who seemed untouchable. The faint-hearted stayed at a distance to see what would happen. Others never left their homes for fear of being arrested by the *Tontons-Macoute* who were understandably edgy.

As the one o'clock hour approached, the tension was palpable. Then an eerie silence fell on the marketplace exactly at 1:00 p.m. When a young corporal turned his head fast, his cap fell off. He quickly picked it up. Eyes were shifting, right and left. The spies of all stripes were fidgety. The soldiers were ready for all eventualities. Then, nothing happened. At least nothing that was detectable to the naked eye. There was a big sigh of relief on the part of the dictator's men and no small disappointment from the partisans of Brother Chicken. However, it did not take long for feelings on both sides to change.

The Tuesday following the Carrefour Dufort event, Brother Chicken was back in the studio in New York. What a session it was! He was extremely angry. He violently shook his special bell, the *asson*. He fulminated about the intrusion of *Divage* who thinks he's in control while controlling very little. He said it's not the troops of *Divage* or his stupid spies, the two-legged, the four-legged or the crawling type, that would stop him from making the rounds and accomplishing his announced mission. "Once I set up an appointment," he said in his usual manner of speaking, "I keep it no matter what. You get that old man? You cannot mess up my program. Anyway, did I set up any appointment with you and your troops?"

Then, Brother Chicken got down to specifics. Addressing the commander in charge of the troops that were dispatched to

Carrefour Dufort, he said: "Colonel Nelson, next time I set up appointment with my people and you show up, I'll break your neck!" Colonel Nelson, who was a strong believer in mysticism, must have had close to a heart attack.

Brother Chicken went on a tirade in which he displayed his mystical powers. He said that he had come for the meeting when he saw the troops that Duvalier had dispatched to welcome him. He was not about to play the fool and allow them to catch him. To show that he was really there, he singled out Corporal Joe who was part of the troops and told him, "At one o'clock in the afternoon, when your cap fell off your head, did you not feel a funny noise in the tunnel of your ears? Well, that was me, All Powerful! I turned into a wind and landed anyway under everyone's glare." He chuckled and flapped his wings to underscore their helplessness when dealing with him.

He ordered Corporal Joe to go tell his superiors what he had felt when his cap fell off his head. "I know your eyes aren't trained to see me," he said, "but I know you felt me for sure, because you were trembling. You'll never see me unless you get the power that I only can bestow. You'll live a long life if you follow my orders." The episode at Carrefour Dufort had a profound effect on the lives of many. For weeks after that event, I kept getting letters from people who said they saw Brother Chicken in their neighborhood. They could not explain the appearance of a big, red rooster that showed up from nowhere and disappeared before they could photograph him. They were sure it was not any regular, run of the mill type of a rooster. One person vowed that he saw the rooster transforming into a big black pig that disappeared into the sea after roaming through several neighborhoods of Port-au-Prince and Pétionville. People were convinced that it was Brother Chicken doing his thing, just as he had announced on the radio before he went off the air.

It took more than a year for the Duvalier regime to find out my identity. Once that happened the soft approach was used. There is a saying that "Everyone has a price." In Haiti, where the majority of people struggle to escape poverty, easy money has a great pull. In that light, Papa Doc and his advisers decided that through corruption he could easily silence the voice that was challenging him.

There was much discussion about the effectiveness of André Théard, Papa Doc's ambassador in Washington at the time. Apparently, he was unable to deal with the most vexing problem for the dictator since the summer of 1965: *Radio Vonvon*. He had failed in getting the Johnson administration to silence the broadcast from New York. Arthur Bonhomme said he knew Raymond Joseph very well and proposed that he be entrusted the task of making contact with me. On that basis, he was named Ambassador to Washington to replace Ambassador Théard.

I knew this to be true because, again, most of our secret agents were in attendance at most important conversations.

Bonhomme took office in January 1967. Soon thereafter, he contacted me. A Protestant like me, Bonhomme had set up the Haitian Bible Society, and was quite familiar with my work. He was approaching me as a brother in Christ. I received a telephone call from Washington and he invited me to a meeting—not at the Embassy, of course. We agreed to meet at the famous Mayflower Hotel on Connecticut Avenue in Northwest Washington. Although it was to be a one-on-one meeting, I did not fully trust my brother in Christ. I arranged to have a shadow at a reasonable distance to observe what would happen.

Ambassador Bonhomme complimented me about my dedication to bring freedom to our land. He said perhaps the Lord had placed him in the position he now held to be of service to the cause. He noted that such things happened in the Old Testament when God placed his servants in pivotal positions at specific times. He mentioned Joseph who was sold by his brothers and rose to be Prime

Minister in the land of Egypt. Finally, he was instrumental in saving his whole family at a time of great famine. He also talked about Esther, the stunningly beautiful Jewish virgin, who won the heart of Ahasuerus (Xerxes), the powerful king of Persia and Media, and became queen in the land where the Jews were in captivity. Eventually, at a critical time, she saved the Jews from extermination.

Ambassador Bonhomme had spoken the language that he knew would soften me up for his next proposition. It must be very expensive to operate a broadcast from New York, he said. He was now in a position, he said, to help me. Certainly, he could find funds to alleviate the burden for me. Listening to the ambassador, one would have thought that he had espoused my views of the regime he was serving and that he was ready to do his part for regime change in Haiti.

At one point in the conversation, he said he could help the fellows of our *Bureau Central* by providing impeccable sources of information and funds also. But I would have to put him in contact with them in Haiti. Stringing him along, I asked "how much money are you talking about?" He had available to him as much as $250,000. At that time the exchange rate with the Haitian gourde was five to one dollar. In a subtle way, Ambassador Bonhomme and his associates thought that no one would refuse such an offer to become a Haitian-style millionaire. In exchange, however, I would have sold him the guys of the *Bureau Central* under the guise that he would be collaborating with them.

After hearing him carefully, it was my turn to play the Bible scholar role, just as he had done. "Mr. Ambassador," I said, "you no doubt know about the forty days of temptation of Jesus Christ by Satan in the desert. For sure, you remember the final act when Satan took him to the highest peak and showed him all the wealth of the city and said, 'All this I will give to you, if you bow down and worship me.' Certainly, you remember Judas Iscariot also who betrayed the Master for thirty pieces of silver. That led Christ directly to the cross, right?"

Then I stood up and said, "Until today I considered you a brother in Christ, although I don't agree with your serving such a despicable regime. As of today, I see Satan in front of me, and from this day forward I will treat you as Satan. The $250,000 sum falls in the same category of Satan's offer to Christ and the thirty pieces of silver that Judas had received to betray his Lord. Keep the money for yourself." And I left without a handshake.

From that day, I became a thorn in the flesh of the ambassador. Whenever he was invited to a public forum, I showed up to taunt him with embarrassing questions. Once I traveled all the way to Topeka, Kansas—from New York—when he was invited to speak there. Ambassador Arthur Bonhomme had failed at the mission entrusted him.

When I took over as Chargé d'Affaires of the Haitian Embassy in 1990, Ambassador Bonhomme, who was then living in Washington, came to pay me a visit at the Embassy. After our conversation, before he left, he told me, "Brother, forgive me for what happened back in 1967." I gave him a handshake and said, "All is forgiven."

I do not know what Ambassador Bonhomme may have told his sons before his death in June 1992. When I came back to Washington in 2004 to take over the Haitian Embassy a second time, one who befriended me and with whom I had good rapport was Pastor Charles Henri Bonhomme, the son of Arthur Bonhomme. (Charles Henri died in 2012.)

———

Ridiculed and belittled by Brother Chicken, and fully aware that his whole system of government had been infiltrated, Papa Doc decided to mount a professional and very sophisticated operation to discover the brains behind "The Six O'Clock Mass." He summoned Serge Beaulieu to the Palace and entrusted him the secret mission of discovering the sources of *Radio Vonvon* in and out of Haiti.

Beaulieu had been successful in infiltrating opposition groups in New York over the years. His last major exploit was the infiltration of *Jeune Haïti,* the "Young Haiti" movement which was dismantled in 1964 when the thirteen rebels were killed in Haiti, with the two executed publicly. Some of the leaders of *Jeune Haïti* were studying in major American universities, such as Princeton, Yale, and Columbia. The Kennedy administration had been financing the schooling of some promising young Haitians who were being groomed as potential leaders in a Haiti liberated from the dictatorship of François Duvalier.

When President Kennedy was assassinated, the "future leaders" of Haiti felt they had lost a hero and saw their dream of a liberated Haiti coming to naught. The Kennedy administration had cut foreign aid to the dictatorship to protest against the various human rights violations perpetrated by Duvalier. They did not trust President Lyndon Johnson to continue with the University scholarships that President Kennedy's administration had approved.

During the summer of 1964, the young warriors of the *Jeune Haïti* movement slipped out of New York heading to Haiti. They had hoped to reenact in the mountains of southwest Haiti what Fidel Castro had successfully done in the Sierra Maestra in Cuba. As the "thirteen" left New York, Serge Beaulieu also slipped out of the Big Apple. He took a flight to Haiti where, on landing at the Port-au-Prince airport, an official vehicle whisked him off and drove him directly to the Palace where his boss was waiting.

Beaulieu was the bearer of several documents, including the green cards of the would-be "guerrilleros." Beaulieu had gained access to the apartment that *Jeune Haïti* had used as headquarters on Lexington Avenue in Upper Manhattan. He stole the identity papers of the "thirteen." As they were landing on the southwest peninsula of Haiti, their photos were splashed on the front page of *Le Nouvelliste,* one of the two major dailies in Port-au-Prince at the time. (On May 1st, 2014, *Le Nouvelliste,* the only remaining daily in Haiti, celebrated its 116th anniversary.)

As I mentioned previously, for the next three months, the rebels were hunted down and killed. The last two rebels were publicly executed.

Serge Beaulieu, the dictator's master spy, set out methodically in his quest to add another feather to his cap. Based in New York, he needed a counterpart in Port-au-Prince. He turned to a young man in his 30s, Bossuet Delva, nicknamed Bobo, the investigator at the Police department which was called *Recherches Criminelles* ("Criminal Research"). Beaulieu knew Bobo well, because the two had worked together at *Recherches Criminelles* before Beaulieu was assigned to New York, then the base of the majority of political exiles. Unbeknownst to Beaulieu, Bobo had already been recruited by our *Bureau Central*, which had discovered in him a true patriot profoundly troubled by the increasingly repressive dictatorship.

Instead of providing Beaulieu accurate information about the *Bureau Central*, Bobo had become our main mole at the Police. Since Beaulieu relied on him for damaging information on our Bureau, Bobo had firsthand knowledge of all the operations under way to track us down. In the process, we obtained accurate information on Serge Beaulieu himself. He lived on Hicks Street in Brooklyn Heights, an upscale neighborhood of Brooklyn just across from Manhattan. His wife at the time was a Swiss citizen who kept her maiden name and had an unlisted telephone number in her name. That kind of arrangement provided Beaulieu an excellent cover to carry out his dirty business. Moreover, he was registered as an official correspondent at the United Nations for *Radio Caraïbes* in Port-au-Prince.

Serge Beaulieu was entrusted with an impossible mission. He was operating against *zombies*, or rather "dead men on furlough." The two organizers of the *Bureau Central* had supposedly been executed by Duvalier's *Tontons-Macoute* years earlier. Thus, no one could have suspected them of being part of an organization fully alive.

Hubert Legros Sr. and Georges D. Rigaud were brilliant lawyers in their early 40s. They had been closely associated with Clément

Jumelle, the presidential candidate who formerly was Finance Minister in Paul Magloire's administration and whose body was stolen from a hearse by Duvalier's thugs. Strong opponents of the budding Duvalier dictatorship, Legros and Rigaud had been targeted for execution by Papa Doc. On the day that the order was given to pick them up, the two lawyers were notified before the executioners arrived at their office. They escaped by a back door minutes before the brutes arrived at the front door.

Those dispatched to carry out the execution feared Duvalier's reaction if he knew that they had failed in their mission. Thus, the list of the executed with the names of Legros and Rigaud at the top was presented to the dictator with an **X** drawn over it. This meant "mission accomplished." Papa Doc was satisfied that his bitter enemies had departed to "The Land of the Hatless," as Haitians refer to the dead.

However, in their alleged death, Legros and Rigaud accomplished much more than during their life in the open. Lodged in a villa in Bourdon, high above the capital, the two lawyers built a network that reached into practically all Haitian governmental institutions and departments, including into Duvalier's palace.

Rigaud, a fair-skinned mulatto, had assumed the identity of a foreign relative of the Belgian family that owned the villa. And the darker skinned Legros acted as a gardener and keeper of the grounds. Since the *Tontons-Macoute* did not venture into those upscale neighborhoods, the two "dead" men had the perfect cover to operate. And operate they did, often venturing out at night dressed as women. Their effectiveness was unparalleled. Close members of their families were aware of their whereabouts, but they played their part by wearing mourning clothes for a year.

A la guerre comme à la guerre, states a French proverb. (All's fair in war.) The fellows of the *Bureau Central* used certain situations to recruit informants, sometimes against their will. The trusted male confidant of Papa Doc, Gérard Daumec, was caught in a

compromising position with the president's female secretary, Francesca "France" St. Victor. Using that information, the fellows at the
Bureau Central recruited both of them as informants. Through *Bwa
Piwo* (The Stilt Guy), a trusted emissary who went by that non de
plume, the *Bureau Central* informed Daumec that his affair with the
lady would soon be aired on *Radio Vonvon*.

Gérard Daumec became frantic. He asked for a favor, and in
return offered to cooperate. By no means, he said, should the information be made public by *Radio Vonvon*. If that were to happen, it
would certainly be his death sentence and that of the lady also. He
said he was ready to pay whatever was asked so the New York guys
wouldn't air the affair.

Daumec expected *Bwa Piwo* to ask for a substantial sum. But
we were not interested in his cash. Our patriots were not motivated
by money. We knew that if we had let corruption intrude into our
operation, we would lose out. There was no way we could have kept
pace with the dictator who was flush with cash to buy cooperation.

Daumec was in shock when he heard what was being asked of
him. Not a penny, he was told. The *Bureau Central* only asked for
him to be an informant of *Radio Vonvon*. He drew a deep breath
and said he agreed. Then *Bwa Piwo* told him that he would have to
enlist the lady also. She had to know what he was doing to save her
from Papa Doc's rage. She, too, had to join the club. There was a
long minute of silence. And *Bwa Piwo* added that there should not
be any misunderstanding to what he was agreeing. He won't be able
to fib once he joins the club, because just as we found out about his
affair, we will also know when he is lying. Then *Bwa Piwo* told him
to go talk to the lady and get back as soon as possible with a positive
answer. Daumec pleaded with him not to go public with the story
until he came back.

Two days later, according to Rigaud, Daumec contacted *Bwa
Piwo* and asked for a face-to-face meeting. The lady, he said, agreed
to the deal. They are both in the club. He was given a number for

himself and one for the lady. All major informants, or club members as they were called, were assigned a number which was aired on the radio, whenever needed, to acknowledge that their information had reached the intended destination. Since we could not divulge the names of informants, we had to devise a method to let them know that their information or request had reached us.

Francesca "France" St. Victor, née Foucard, was Papa Doc's trusted secretary—and then more. A fair-skinned woman endowed with natural beauty, she was the most envied female at the Palace. The Duvalier women hated her. This was especially true of Papa Doc's wife, Simone Ovide ("Mama Doc"), and Marie Denise, the first daughter, nicknamed Dédé. Their feelings toward France were understandable, because it was widely rumored that France also performed other duties for Papa Doc. He somehow confirmed this when, speaking publicly one day, he turned and looked at France with a broad smile on his face and said: *"Quand je veux danser j'appelle ma femme de chambre et nous esquissons des pas, n'est-ce pas, France?"* ("When I want to dance I call on my bedroom lady and we pirouette around. Isn't that so, France?")

There was complete silence in the audience as people looked at each other. Simone, who was also present, just froze. But no one dared say anything to Papa Doc. For days *Radio Vonvon* embellished on this off-the-cuff indiscretion of the President who had found sweetness somewhere other than in his conjugal bed.

France St. Victor engineered the marriage of her younger brother Luc Albert Foucard to Papa Doc's second daughter Nicole. While this greatly pleased Papa Doc, Mrs. Duvalier and first daughter Marie-Denise were livid. That caused a rift in the family, because the dictator's wife and her strong-willed eldest daughter greatly resented the light-skinned Mme. St. Victor. Although Duvalier espoused *noiriste* (Black power) philosophy, he couldn't resist the charm of the *femme fatale*—to the greatest displeasure of his own wife and daughter.

The family rift played out openly. Marie-Denise married Colonel Max Dominique, whom Papa Doc didn't much trust. However, Dominique became a protégé of Mrs. Duvalier, who encouraged him to keep his group of officers ready in case something happened to the old man. Duvalier, a diabetic, never enjoyed good health, and Mrs. Duvalier saw in her son-in-law Dominique a shield for uncertain days.

An air of conspiracy reigned at the Palace with the camp of Mrs. Duvalier accusing Mrs. St. Victor of treason for revealing State secrets. Meanwhile, the St. Victor camp asserted that Max Dominique, an ally of the First Lady, was planning a coup with his fellow Army officers. From New York, *Radio Vonvon* kept fanning the fire of discord. Caught in the middle, Papa Doc took sides in a most spectacular way.

The feeling of betrayal pushed Papa Doc to the brink. The execution, on June 8, 1967, of nineteen Army officers, including seven of the Palace Guard, was intended to eradicate whatever sources the *Vonvon* had at the Palace.

Most of the victims were friends of Colonel Dominique or members of his group of Northerners. That underscored the insecurity that Papa Doc felt even in his most immediate circle. There was a lively altercation between father and daughter when Papa Doc wanted to add the name of Max Dominique to the list of those to be executed. It is said that Marie-Denise told her father, "Then add my name to the list also."

Thus was Max Dominique spared, but he was forced by Papa Doc to participate in the execution of his men at the infamous *Fort Dimanche* prison, adjoining the La Saline slum, next to Cité Soleil. The executioners were placed in front of each victim. There was a second tier of armed men, all *Tontons-Macoute*, placed behind the executioners. And Papa Doc barked the command to fire. Afterward, the sadistic doctor called out the names of each executed officer, and answered himself "Absent!" All this was broadcast on Haiti's State radio and television.

Following this gory spectacle, a decision was made at *Vonvon* headquarters in New York not to broadcast information emanating from the Palace. The intended effect was to insinuate that we had lost our sources. Indeed, word spread quickly that Papa Doc had finally done away with the vipers in his bosom. Moreover, Marie-Denise and her young sister Simone together with Colonel Max Dominique were exiled to a plush diplomatic post in Spain.

Three weeks passed without news from the Palace. We waited a month to allow the *teledyòl,* the Haitian grapevine, to widely spread the information of Papa Doc's victory over *Radio Vonvon.* When the Palace began to rejoice about its great feat, we suddenly resumed giving Palace information, often with more accuracy than before.

A great disappointment was felt by the dictator and his henchmen—to the great satisfaction of *Vonvon* listeners who became the more convinced of our invincibility. We encouraged a rumor that spread faster than Papa Doc's alleged victory. People believed that the executed officers had joined the netherworld of spirits, even more powerful than the *zombies* of the *Bureau Central,* in their work for the radio. Thus, in death they had become more powerful and more dangerous.

Taunting Papa Doc, Brother Chicken referred to reports that he had received recently from the field telling him about night appearances around Port-au-Prince of some of the men who had been executed. He told Papa Doc that he acted foolishly when he gunned down the officers, because they had become *zombies* who can penetrate everywhere without being discovered. He advised Papa Doc that if he wanted he could regain their control by also becoming a *zombie.* "But, Sir," Brother Chicken snickered, "to reach the state of *zombification,* you must first taste death." Flapping his wings, he crowed victoriously.

Chapter 7

To Eradicate the Voice

Papa Doc was not to be so easily defeated. He decided to borrow a leaf from Dominican dictator Rafael Leonidas Trujillo y Molina. To silence a fierce critic, Trujillo had ordered the kidnapping of Columbia University Professor Jesús de Galindez in 1956. According to public records, Professor de Galindez was last seen entering a subway station in New York. He had given an evening lecture at Columbia on March 12, 1956, on Latin American government. Months later it was concluded that the professor was kidnapped and flown to Santo Domingo to be tortured before he was murdered. It was said that his body was fed to the sharks in the Santo Domingo Bay, off the Dominican capital.

That daring act of Trujillo had caused the deterioration of his relationship with the United States and sealed the eventual assassination of the powerful Dominican dictator. That was State terrorism carried out inside the United States by a so-called ally. Papa Doc was so upset by his powerlessness in dealing with faceless challengers, that he apparently did not weigh the ramifications and think through the consequences of any terrorist act that he was about to perpetrate on US soil.

Serge Beaulieu was summoned from New York by Papa Doc and given a top secret assignment. He had to kidnap me and bring me to Haiti alive—or dead, if must be. Once commissioned, Beaulieu returned to New York. On the same Pan American flight that Beaulieu arrived, there was our live courier from the *Bureau Central* with the detail of his mission. The day following Beaulieu's arrival, we broadcast a terse communiqué over *Radio Vonvon*: "By the Pan American World Airways flight, last night Mr. Serge Beaulieu arrived in New York on a special mission."

The broadcast could not be heard in New York. It was beamed on shortwave to Haiti and other points in the Caribbean. Of course, Beaulieu himself had not heard the broadcast and knew nothing about the bad news concerning his mission until his boss told him. Papa Doc was very upset after he had listened to the morning's taped broadcast of *Radio Vonvon*. Religiously, he had listened to the show every morning, in the company of a few trusted lieutenants. The old man realized that Beaulieu's mission was compromised. Immediately after hearing the latest on *Radio Vonvon*, the dictator telephoned Beaulieu in New York and told him to be careful and to desist for the moment. The mission is compromised.

On his second night in New York, Beaulieu also was unpleasantly surprised. He received a telephone call from me.

"Hello, I would like to speak to Serge Beaulieu."

"This is he," he replied in his gruff voice.

"I am Raymond Joseph from *Radio Vonvon*."

"I don't know *Radio Vonvon*, I know *Radio Lumière*," he said. Rather than acknowledge *Radio Vonvon*, Beaulieu insinuated that he knew me from the Creole show that I hosted in late 1959. The show about the mythical Haitian personalities *Bouki* and *Malis* aired on *Radio Lumière* in Cayes.

"No, I am not talking about *Radio Lumière*," I retorted. "That's ancient history. I am speaking about *Radio Vonvon* which broadcasts every morning at six o'clock. We usually interview recent arrivals from Haiti, and we would love to interview you."

"I give no interviews," he snapped, somewhat annoyed.

"That's too bad! I thought you would be a good subject. But I understand. That's okay."

I was about to hang up, when he rushed to say, "But I would like to meet you."

"Okay, that can be arranged."

"When?"

"Tomorrow, if you will."

"At the United Nations? You'll come to the United Nations? We could talk at the Delegates Lounge."

"No, I won't come to the UN. That's your territory."

At this point, even if he was not going to kill me, he could arrange to have me identified by people who would be working with him to eventually kidnap me. They could have been sitting in the Delegates Lounge. I was not paranoid, just cautious. I had studied counterintelligence and knew not to accept any seemingly harmless invitation.

"Where, then?" Beaulieu asked.

"At a street corner. And we'll decide where to go."

"At Dag Hammarskjöld Plaza, on 47th Street and First Avenue, at 9:00 a.m.?"

"Okay, at nine o'clock sharp."

Then Beaulieu began to describe what he would be wearing. "A light tan trench coat," he said. *No doubt, like those worn by secret agents or FBI operatives in the movies,* I thought.

"Mr. Beaulieu, you don't need to give me any description of yourself, I know you very well," I said.

I heard complete silence at the other end. I said, "Goodbye. See you tomorrow."

The next morning, at around 8:15, I told the fellows in my office what I was about to do. Their collective response was disbelief. "Isn't he the one who is supposed to kidnap you?" asked one. "Don't you think you are too daring?"

"With the last two shows we gave him," I said, "the broadcast yesterday morning of his special secret mission and the telephone call last night to his private, unlisted number in Brooklyn Heights—it is he who should fear me. Really, have no fear for me, because I have the momentum. I know how to handle these situations." And I left the office, then at the Park Sheraton Hotel, now Park Central.

I quickly disappeared in a subway entrance on 7th Avenue and 55th Street, boarded the R train, got off two stops later at 42nd Street, transferred to the Grand Central Shuttle, and got out at Lexington Avenue at 44th Street. Exactly at 9:00, I arrived at the designated place, at the same time with our agent-in-trench-coat. We shook hands, and immediately he said, "We are so close to the UN, why don't we go to the Delegates Lounge? We can really talk freely there."

"No, I am not going to the UN. Don't insist. I already told you it is your territory."

"Okay," he said, "let us sit here then!" He motioned to one of the benches in the park.

"Nothing doing," I said, "I don't like publicity. You never know who may see us together. I don't want to jeopardize your job. Why don't we go to a restaurant?"

"Which one?" he asked.

"Anyone, there are a few around here."

"Let's go to that one," he said, pointing to a restaurant which overlooked the plaza on Second Avenue and 47th Street. So we did. On entering the restaurant, he quickly took a seat from which he could look at the street. I would soon find out the reason why. I sat at the end of the table with my back to a wall.

We ordered coffee and croissants. While I sipped my coffee, he smoked one Havana cigar after another. Smoking had not yet been banned in restaurants and closed places. I don't smoke, but it did not bother me then. (A few years later, I developed an allergy to cigarette smoke.) I did not mention his "special mission," but relentlessly I tied him to his despicable role of a spy for Duvalier. He protested my characterization of him and claimed innocence.

At about fifteen minutes into our conversation, he drew my attention to the street, just at the place where we would have sat, had I accepted his offer to speak on the bench. A man was walking by slowly. Beaulieu said, "There, that's the correspondent of Tass (the Soviet news agency). Wouldn't you like to meet him?"

"No," I said emphatically. "I am here to talk with you. I don't need anyone to see you with me, as I already told you." During the Cold War, Tass, the Soviet news agency also served as a cover for agents of the KGB, the soviet spy agency. I was not a friend of the communists. What business do I have meeting a Tass correspondent!

That was to be a smart move on Beaulieu's part. Apparently he had thoroughly rehearsed his meeting with me. The Tass agent did not show up just by coincidence. Beaulieu had sensed that he wouldn't succeed in luring me to the Delegates Lounge. He thought, however, that I might fall for the idea of meeting at a public place where no one would be listening to our conversation. Had I accepted his bait to meet the Tass correspondent, he may have devised a back-up plan.

We were at the height of the Cold War. Imagine that I would be standing in conversation with a Soviet agent while someone posted with a camera at a high floor zooming in on us. And Beaulieu would have had the evidence he needed to prove that I was a communist informant, if not an agent. He could have used that picture to black-mail me. Of course, Beaulieu, himself, would have been airbrushed out of the picture.

On the other hand this could have been a golden opportunity to help the "correspondent/KGB agent" identify an enemy to eventually eliminate. It was no secret that I was a dedicated anti-communist who had lectured extensively in the United States on the evils of communism. A close-up view of me by the Soviet agent would have been a great coup. In either case, it would have been a sweet victory for Serge Beaulieu.

I sensed a certain frustration in his voice after I refused his offer to meet the so-called Tass correspondent. His face had hardened. Apparently he had run out of options. At one point, I said, "It is rather interesting that *Radio Caraïbes*, which cannot pay $50 a month to a speaker in Port-au-Prince, has found $1,000 a month, plus expenses, for a correspondent at the United Nations." In other words, he was not fooling me about his connections and his real mission in New York. I wanted him to know that.

I drew a big breath and told him, "Listen, when you were back home, working for the *Criminal Research Department* (of the Police), you knew some of what was going around Port-au-Prince. Now, removed from the scene, a lot of what goes on in the homeland escapes you. If you need any information about things back home, not only in Port-au-Prince, give me a ring at any time and I will see how I can help." I handed him my public business card and added, "Yes, you may call." I got up, paid the bill and left.

That same afternoon, about fifteen minutes before our team was to leave for the recording studio at 485 Madison Avenue, Serge Beaulieu called. His voice could not hide his rage. "Listen," he said imperiously, "I am an expert at these things too."

"What things?" I asked.

"Intelligence, as they say in the business."

"Oh, yes, I know. You were not sent to study in Israel and Canada for nothing. I know all about that—and more." At our meeting in the morning I never hinted about his background; that I knew where he had been trained. Yet, the *Bureau Central* had briefed me thoroughly about Serge Beaulieu. He became angrier. "I am an expert at other things also," he shouted in the phone.

"Such as?"

"Machine guns," he sputtered.

"Oh yeah," I said. "Look how nice and reserved you were this morning when we were face to face. Now behind the security of your telephone, you are threatening me. Listen, man, I am not an expert at machine guns, or at any gun for that matter. But let me tell you, when I need the experts in machine guns, cannons, bazookas, grenades, even silencers, I know where to find them. When you have better things to say, give me a call." I slammed the phone down with such force that his eardrums must have felt it for days.

Earlier, when I had returned to my office everyone wanted to know about how it went. I only said, "He is dangerous. From now on, we are going to watch all his moves."

The threatening phone call confirmed for me that we could not treat Beaulieu lightly. I lost no time in alerting our *Bureau Central* in Port-au-Prince about my "meeting with the Devil" and how I had undressed him, so to speak. "Now what I need from you," I told the fellows at the *Bureau Central*, "is to keep close tabs on him whenever he comes to town—from the time he lands at the airport to the time he leaves the capital. Don't worry about us here. We have him under control."

About a month after our New York encounter, Serge Beaulieu was in Port-au-Prince at the famous Hotel Oloffson, the setting for Graham Greene's novel *The Comedians*. It was the usual sort of Saturday evening affair, and the dandy Petit Pierre, described in Greene's novel, was showing off. A band was playing, and Petit Pierre, a.k.a. Aubelin Jolicoeur, walked up to a female German journalist who was visiting Haiti and asked her to dance. She politely declined. Petit Pierre then turned to her companion, another German, and repeated his demand. She also refused. Whereupon, Petit Pierre gave her a *souflèt marasa*—(a twin slap as it is said in Creole when slapping a person on both sides of the face). In a huff, he walked away briskly. The women were stunned.

Serge Beaulieu, who happened to have been there and saw what had occurred, came to the rescue. He called out to Aubelin Jolicoeur and ordered him to apologize to the lady.

Jolicoeur asserted that he had slapped her for a good reason. She deserved what she got for having declined to dance with him. "Me Aubelin Jolicoeur," he shouted. He was about to turn away when Beaulieu blocked his path. Jolicoeur was a frail waif compared to the strapping Beaulieu. So, Aubelin froze.

Whereupon, Beaulieu buttoned his jacket and drew himself up straight as an iron bar and blurted out, "In the name of the President-for-life of the Republic, I order you to apologize to the lady—immediately!"

In a second, Aubelin Jolicoeur was transformed. He became as meek as a lamb. He knelt down in front of the German lady and begged for forgiveness. He departed the scene soon thereafter. And Serge Beaulieu, his gallant self, ordered drinks for the ladies. He asked them not to judge Haiti by the boorishness of the good-for-nothing pedant.

Aubelin Jolicoeur, as a columnist for the daily *Le Nouvelliste*, was also a spy who pried tidbits from the few visitors who still ventured to visit Haiti in those turbulent days. His real job was to discover the mission of certain visitors, because the Duvalier regime thought that they could not be only simple tourists. Haiti had lost its mystical allure for foreigners, as Papa Doc strengthened his stranglehold on the country. Thus, the few tourists who still came were considered suspicious elements. Jolicoeur's job was to ferret out as many foreign agents as possible by offering to write about their visit to "Haiti, the Pearl of the Antilles," as he was so fond of saying.

Two days after the incident at the Hotel Oloffson, *Radio Vonvon* was broadcasting it from New York. We kept the listeners on a leash throughout, with snippets of what was to come, until a few minutes before the end. Then we told the story about Aubelin Jolicoeur's boorishness and of Serge Beaulieu's gallantry.

Two weeks after that broadcast, Papa Doc ordered that Serge Beaulieu be named the official press attaché at the Haiti Mission to the United Nations. He had been smoked out, or rather was brought in from the cold. He could no longer be an effective spy, the infiltrator par excellence of exile groups. Till his death, reportedly by lung cancer, in New Jersey, on December 12, 2004, he never forgave me for derailing his lucrative underground career.

=======

By late 1967, the change in the Haitian people had been substantial. From our headquarters in New York, we had tested our strength by secretly ordering simple tasks to our forces on the ground. We ordered that they place certain mystical objects at various *carrefours,* or four corner forks in the road, throughout the country. Invariably, these operations took place at night around midnight, or in the wee hours of the morning. Usually *kwi,* the peasant eating bowl made from half of a gourd, would contain roasted peanuts and corn, as well as some candies, food that the spirits traditionally enjoy.

Papa Doc's allies became nervous and enraged when they woke up in the morning to find the objects everywhere. Yet, they did not know how they got there. Obviously, Papa Doc, their boss, was no longer "Master of the Crossroads" and did not rule nighttime events, as he was thought of having power to do. A more powerful force was at work in Haiti, especially with our clandestine CH (*Coalition Haïtienne*) or Haitian Coalition clubs sprouting all over. The time was ripe for a military strike against the dictator.

The task of training the freedom fighters was entrusted to Roland Magloire, a former lieutenant of the Haitian Armed Forces who had joined the Coalition in New York. We would not do any training on US soil. Neither would we finance our bellicose activities from America. The treasurer of the group, Edouard "Routo" Roy, was a practicing physician in Montreal, Canada. The Bahamas, formerly a British Crown colony, became our recruiting ground.

Whereas financing the radio was originally painstaking, funds for military action came readily. For example, at a face-to-face meeting in Nassau, Bahamas, Oswald J. Brandt, a well-known industrialist in Port-au-Prince, handed me seven bank checks of $5,000 each, with no names in the line for the beneficiary. Weeks later, Routo would tell me, "Raymond, you passed the honesty test, as far as Oswald is concerned. You know he asked me how many checks you had given me. When I told him seven, he exclaimed, 'Well, well, we still have some honest Haitians.'" The money flowed. In one week, we had raised $250,000, most of it from wealthy Haitians. In 1967 that was a fortune.

The late Luc Fouché, former Cabinet Minister and Ambassador of Haiti to the United States, used to call me *Ti Jòzèf*—Joey. During our fund-raising campaign for military operations, he told a few friends, "*Ti Jòzèf* is a masterful cajoler. For him to get Paul to fork over $20,000, he must be a miracle man, because Paul never parts with his money. He only gives advice and his name. Indeed, we are really going places."

He was referring to Paul Magloire, the former President of Haiti who had been living in exile in New York since 1957 after he had fled to Jamaica in December 1956. President Magloire was an avid supporter of the *Vonvon*, but he never disbursed a penny for the "psychological operation." Nonetheless, he was always delighted to have me come on weekends to his residence, at 175 Devonshire Road at Jamaica Estates, to play some of the broadcasts of the week. Mrs. Magloire (Yole) was a fanatic of the *Vonvon* and made sure that the "listening show" would be a social occasion to which friends and relatives were invited.

The popularity of *Radio Vonvon* was greatly affected when a group of dissidents from the Coalition undertook military action in Haiti. The debacle of May 20, 1968, caused despair in the underground which was methodically organizing the downfall of the regime. On that date, about a dozen men landed in Cap-Haitien, while their colleagues dropped three crude bombs on Duvalier's Palace in Port-au-Prince. The bombs caused no damage to the Palace. The B25 used in the strafing was left at the Cap-Haitien airport, a trophy for Papa Doc.

Meanwhile, the leader of the would-be liberators, Raymond Montreuil, flew back in a Cessna to his base in the Bahamas, together with three colleagues. They left ten poorly trained invaders to face the hordes of Duvalier in northern Haiti. Although the invaders killed Prosper Mora, the military commander of Cap-Haitien, and his aide-de-camp, they were all killed, except for two, captured alive: Ernst Renois and Maurice Magloire.

This was a major blow. At the time Roland Magloire, overall commander of Coalition forces, was jailed in Nassau, along with seventy-six of his commandos. (The Bahamas had not yet been independent from Great Britain.) Magloire and his men had been arrested in March 1968 by the Bahamian police while training on Burrows Cay, off Grand Bahama, a major isle of the Bahamas archipelago. These 77 political prisoners symbolized resistance to the Haitian dictatorship and became the focus of our activities as we mobilized to save them from the ultimate fate.

Linden Pindling was undertaking his first high level diplomatic mission since he had become the first Prime Minister of the Bahamas the previous year. After the May 20 attack against Duvalier, he landed in Port-au-Prince to work out a deal with Papa Doc concerning his prized prisoners at Her Majesty's Fox Hill jail in Nassau. It could never be ascertained how much money the Haitian dictator had disbursed to his Bahamian guest, but Palace sources reported at the time that it was $250,000, together with a book by Duvalier entitled *Mémoires d'un Leader du Tiers Monde* (Memoirs of a Third World Leader).

We mounted a spirited campaign to save the "77 freedom fighters." We contacted various human rights organizations and worked especially with the International Rescue Committee, a human rights organization in New York, to help us save the patriots who were about to be delivered to Papa Doc. Certainly, they would have been executed on arrival in Haiti. A little pamphlet, with four bodies sketched on an 8 x 11 page hanging from execution posts, delivered a simple but powerful message: The Bahamian government is condoning murder. This was our response to a Bahamian court decision that had condemned four of our supporters of the murder of Antoine Dorlcé, the Haitian consul in Nassau. We organized a picket line in front of the Bahamas Tourist Office in Manhattan to protest the alliance of Papa Doc and Pindling. This was a serious challenge to the budding Bahamas tourist industry.

The Bahamas and several nations in the Caribbean were experiencing a tourist boom on the heels of events in two of the three major tourist markets at the time—Cuba, Haiti and Puerto Rico. In the 1940s and right through the early 1960s, Cuba and Haiti were playgrounds for North American tourists. Then, on October 22, 1957, Papa Doc, a dictator from the right, assumed power in Haiti, following the clouded election of September 22. And on January 1, 1959, Fidel and Raul Castro with Che Guevara swept into Havana from the Sierra Maestra and chased out the right-wing dictator Fulgencio Batista. A dictator from the right had been replaced by an unfolding dictatorship of the left. In general, tourists don't like social or political disturbance. Thus, they turned to more tranquil beaches.

Now, the scandal of jailed Haitian "freedom fighters" was threatening the budding Bahamas tourist industry. The Bahamian authorities understood the menace that "a band of malcontents" in Manhattan posed to their dream of turning the Bahamas into the new Havana with its casinos and call girls. Also, the American financiers of the new tourist developments weighed in favor of compromise. It would be better for the Bahamian authorities to displease Papa Doc instead of losing their newly discovered pot of gold. What is a paltry $250,000 compared to millions, even billions of dollars, to be gained from a looming tourist industry.

Prime Minister Pindling's government caved in under international pressure and sound reasoning. He agreed to the departure of all "the 77 freedom fighters" for whom we hurriedly secured visas to the United States, Canada, and France. The demobilization of the "Liberation Forces" had been completed. The Bahamas regained its composure.

Chapter 8

Closing Shop, New Direction: The Demise of Radio Vonvon

The US presidential election of November 1968 greatly affected the struggle for democracy in Haiti. Richard Nixon, the standard bearer of the Republican Party, had trounced the Democrat Hubert Humphrey, Vice President under Lyndon Johnson and formerly a popular Senator from Minnesota. The foreign policy of the United States was about to take a different course, especially regarding Haiti. That would become evident by the open embrace of François Duvalier by President Nixon's special envoy, Nelson Rockefeller, vice president under President Gerald Ford and a former three-term governor of New York.

During the summer of 1969, Rockefeller was received by hostile crowds while he toured Latin America and the Caribbean on behalf of President Nixon. The situation was particularly tense in Venezuela, where the Rockefellers had large interests in the oil fields. Papa Doc was going to make Rockefeller feel good about his heretofore disastrous mission, while exploiting the situation to his own advantage.

On July 1st, Duvalier organized the warmest reception in Port-au-Prince for Rockefeller. A crowd of thousands thronged the National Palace grounds and surrounding streets in a show of Haiti's love for Rockefeller and the US government. The photo of a Papa Doc with a broadly smiling Rockefeller from the second floor window of the Palace mirrored the secret pact between the two governments. No longer would President Duvalier be considered a pariah by the US administration. In fact, he was being rewarded for having been "the bulwark against Communism in the Caribbean" and a close ally of the United States. That goes back to Haiti's crucial vote at Punta del Este, Uruguay in 1962 when the United States engineered Cuba's ouster as a pro-communist state from the Organization of American States.

Two months after the famous photo of Papa Doc and Governor Rockefeller, it was no longer possible for *Radio Vonvon* to operate. The anti-dictatorship broadcast which had found favor with the Democratic administration of President Johnson was about to be silenced with the help of Papa Doc's newly found friends in the American government.

The first sign of trouble occurred when a pre-taped broadcast of *Radio Vonvon* was tampered with at WRUL, the radio station from which the broadcast originated. I was awakened by someone at a listening post around 6:05 who asked what was happening with the broadcast. Praises of Duvalier were being aired. I rushed to the station and burst into the studio as the broadcast was signing off. I asked for the tape. The operator looked somewhat puzzled. For, this was the first time I had come to the studios at Madison Avenue that early. I obviously looked disturbed. The operator did not speak Creole and probably did not know what had just been aired. I took the tape and disappeared. Once at *Radio Vonvon's* office, I made copies and dispersed them.

The same day I asked for a meeting with the manager of the station. I explained what had happened to our broadcast which was taped the previous afternoon. He looked surprised and disturbed.

Had the Haitian dictator's hand reached all the way from Port-au-Prince into the studios of Radio New York Worldwide on Madison Avenue? Later I was told that an internal investigation had been carried out and two employees of the station were supposedly dismissed. This would mean that at least two employees of the radio station were bribed by Duvalier's operatives in New York to sabotage my broadcast. Did the firing really occur? I had no way of knowing.

About a month later, the manager invited me for a discussion. He announced that beginning the following month he could no longer carry the Haiti broadcast. The station was changing its programming and the six o'clock spot we had occupied for more than four years would no longer be available. I never knew whether the tampering with our program was truly sabotage or an approved stratagem to get rid of us. The manager of the station could pretext that our broadcast represented a danger that wasn't worth the money. One way or the other, Papa Doc scored a victory. *Radio Vonvon* was silenced.

Other than WRUL, there was no other commercial radio station in New York with international shortwave capability. The board of the organization sponsoring *Radio Vonvon* decided that the political climate in the United States had become increasingly hostile to those who opposed Papa Doc. It would be foolhardy on our part to think that we could fight a policy of the US government allied to Duvalier. We closed shop in New York, as we devised other methods to combat the dictatorship. For a while, we continued intermittent broadcasting from Caracas, Venezuela. But that operation did not have the immediacy of the shows from New York. We ceased all operations.

———

After nearly five years of conducting revolutionary activities full time, I had to think about what I would do to support my family—a wife and four children of school age. We then lived in Roosevelt,

Long Island, at the border of Freeport. Late in 1965, I had moved my family from Chicago to New York because the weekend commute by air was getting too expensive, even prohibitive. Moreover, I missed having my family with me.

What were my options? Should I return to the University of Chicago to finish writing my PhD thesis? That would have taken at least eighteen months. After the PhD, I would have to spend time securing employment at a college or university. That could have taken an additional six to twelve months.

Someone mentioned that the New York Urban League, a nonprofit equal opportunity organization, had been advertising for minority writers. I was given a telephone number. I called and secured an interview. On questioning me about my journalistic experience, the interviewer found out that I had never reported for any public organ anywhere. At one point, he said, "Would you mind taking an exam?"

"I have no problem with that," I said.

He took me to a room, gave me a copy of the *New York Times* and pointed to the commentary page. It was a story by Tom Wolfe, if my memory serves me right. Anyway, the story was about the race to the moon and the billions of dollars it was costing. The interviewer told me, based on that commentary, I should write a brief reporting-style story, using no more than two quotes. After that, I was to write a short three-paragraph editorial to give my opinion. I had an hour for the assignment.

Before the hour passed, I had finished. In my editorial, I criticized the waste of resources to rush to the moon while we had myriads of problems to solve here on earth. Why wouldn't the authorities use some of the billions of dollars to create employment on earth, educate our children and solve other urgent problems?

I turned over my two sheets to the interviewer with a folder in which I had included my biography and a few clips from *Le*

Combattant Haïtien, the weekly newsletter I had been editing. He told me goodbye and promised to call.

The next day, I received a call from the interviewer. He said, "Who do you want to work for?"

"Anyone who will hire me," I responded. "I need a job."

"Will you consider the *Wall Street Journal?* They have seen your writing and the managing editor would like you to come for an interview."

"Yes, Sir, I am ready."

He gave me the telephone number of the *Journal* and the name of the managing editor. He added, "The rest is all yours."

After hanging up, my mind began to race. The *Wall Street Journal,* I kept repeating to myself. Yes, I knew about that paper. I had read it a few times, especially as I sat in some offices during my search for employment. To me, it was the newspaper of the Fat Cats, the big capitalists. How would I fit in that milieu?

The next day I was at 44 Broad Street, downtown New York, at the office of the *Wall Street Journal.* I told the receptionist I was in to see Managing Editor Ed Cony. Immediately I was ushered into his office. Mr. Cony, an amiable man, made me feel at home by asking questions about my family and how long I had lived in New York. He praised me for my academic accomplishments and teasingly said, "You are our second PhD candidate here. Fred Andrews [another reporter who eventually was hired away by the *New York Times*] is also a PhD candidate. There are not too many PhD candidates in the newsrooms of America."

Then, Mr. Cony got down to business. "Young man," he said, "what is your philosophy of the news?"

"My philosophy of the news," I repeated, pausing a few seconds, to assimilate the question and think about an appropriate answer. I responded, "It is Accuracy + Speed." I quickly added, "But I will not sacrifice accuracy on the altar of speed." Mr. Cony sat up straight in his chair and looked at me with some amazement, and said, "You know we have a beat for you. It's an industrial beat. I have looked at your writing. You won't be covering politics for us. Are you interested in the beat?"

"Yes, Sir, I am."

"Well, you are hired."

Next, he took me to the newsroom to show me the operations. He introduced me to two reporters who would become my mentors: Pulitzer Prize winner Stanley Penn and veteran electronics reporter Scott Schmedel, with whom I bonded immediately. Imagine, I was the only Black reporter in the whole newsroom.

A little more than a year after I had joined the *Journal*, an event caused some of my superiors to have muted respect for me. On April 20, 1971, I went to see my Bureau Chief to announce to him the death of the Haitian dictator. I told him that Papa Doc had died, but that there wouldn't be any announcement until the 22nd. He looked at me in disbelief and said, "You don't think we're going to publish such news, do you?"

"Oh, no, I am not telling you that because I expect you to publish it. I just want you to know, so you can be ready with a well-researched story when the information is made official."

I went back to my desk and I telephoned Virginia Prewett in Washington, DC, to tell her of the death of the dictator about whom she had written volume. Ms. Prewett was a veteran reporter for the defunct *Washington Daily News*. Over the years since I met her in 1965, I had provided her a few scoops. We had become friends.

This time, Virginia told me, "Ray, this is dangerous stuff. To announce the death of a president, even that of a hated one like Duvalier, without any official announcement, is beyond daring." Then, she exclaimed, "But, Ray, you have never lied to me." She asked a few questions to get more details. And she said, "Okay, I will do something about it."

On April 21, 1971, Virginia Prewett's column in the *Washington Daily News* broke the news that the Haitian dictator was dead, "according to a source that has never lied to me." She went on to write that the authorities were waiting for the 22nd to make the announcement and to proclaim his 19-year-old son Jean-Claude Duvalier his successor for life. Since the dictator had chosen "22" as his lucky number, as previously shown, it was fitting that his death should also occur on the 22nd of the month.

Although Papa Doc was dead a week prior to the official announcement, his body was kept in a frozen casket in a special room at the Palace. A man of occult powers, he had also chosen his mystical lucky day to depart from the scene that he had dominated for fourteen years. At least, that's the way he had it planned, and he made his will stick. Thus, people would continue to believe that he had not really died, or that even in death he continued to wield power. His close associates executed his will to the letter, thereby inheriting, they thought, some of the power of their mentor.

At about seven o'clock on the morning of April 22, 1971, I received a telephone call from my Bureau Chief at the *Wall Street Journal*. He was very excited as he told me, "Have you heard 10/10 News? . . . You give me goose bumps. They're announcing Papa Doc's death."

"Well, Sir," I responded calmly, "That's not news to me. I told you so two days ago. I had it from an impeccable source."

"Exactly, that's why I have goose bumps," he said, adding, "You did tell me two days ago. How soon can you get to the office? I want you to write a commentary for the paper about what's next."

"Yes, Sir, I will be there soon."

I quickly showered and rushed to work to write my first political piece for the *Wall Street Journal*. As I wrote that day, I kept hearing the words of Managing Editor Ed Cony when he hired me a year earlier, "You will not be writing political stories for us."

Instead of rehashing the brutal legacy of Papa Doc, I wrote about the struggle for power that was taking place around an inexperienced 19-year-old President-for-life. His mother, Simone Ovide Duvalier, and older sister Marie-Denise were considered the powers behind the throne. The sister was closest in temperament to her father. But the machismo culture of Haiti precluded her succeeding the old man. She had rushed home from diplomatic exile in Spain to be at her younger brother's side.

However, the Old Guard, called "Dinosaurs," maintained their hold on power. They included among others Papa Doc's most trusted bodyguard Gracia Jacques, Finance Minister Clovis Désinor, Interior Minister Luckner Cambronne, and Information Minister Paul Blanchet. Allied with Mama Doc, the Dinosaurs had planned a smooth transition with their group at the controls. They were suspicious of Dédé's husband, Max Dominique, the former Army colonel whose close collaborators had been executed by Papa Doc in June 1967.

Quietly, the Dinosaurs were planning a second exile for Dédé and her husband. That was the major revelation of my first political piece for the *Wall Street Journal*. In essence, I wrote that, although close to power, Marie-Denise was far from it and soon would be ousted. Less than six months into Baby Doc's presidency, there was a major upheaval at the Palace. Marie-Denise and her husband Max Dominique, as well as "Ti Simone" or Simone Jr., who was closer in age to her brother, were dispatched to a plush exile, this time to the Haitian Embassy in Paris.

The year 1971 solidified my reputation as a Haitian source to reckon with. In July 1971, my brother Leo and I allied with lawyer Georges D. Rigaud, psychiatrist Glodys St. Phard, and educator Clausel Théard to launch the *Haiti-Observateur*, the first commercial crusading weekly of the Haitian diaspora. Although based in New York, the *Haiti-Observateur* would become the voice of the dispersed diaspora yearning for news from the home front and also from other compatriots around the globe. In effect, the *Haiti-Observateur* would become the sequel to *Radio Vonvon*. Whereas broadcasting is regulated by the State, print journalism is a free agent. We launched an organ that could endure as long as it remained financially viable.

The headline of the first issue, July 23, 1971, caught the attention of my bosses at the *Wall Street Journal*. It read *La Tortue: Les Texans En Selle*. (Tortuga Island: The Texans In The Saddle) It was the story of a group of Texans led by James Pierson, who had gotten a concession to develop the Isle of Tortuga. Sitting on top of Haiti's northern coast, across from Port-de-Paix, that island was famous as a base for the pirates who, for two centuries, harassed the gold-laden vessels on their way to Europe. The film "Pirates of the Caribbean" was inspired in part by pirates based on Tortuga. Pierson intended to make Tortuga the rival of Grand Bahama, which itself was fast replacing Havana as a Caribbean playground and gambling haven for North Americans.

Innocently, I took a copy of our first issue to work and showed it to the managing editor. Recalling some of his high school French, he said, "But Ray, that's a great headline, a *Wall Street Journal* sort of headline!"

"Sir, you can have it," I said. "We only printed 3,000 copies. Anyway, we cannot be in competition with the *Journal*."

"What will you do when you find such great stories in the future?" he asked.

"I will give you first crack at it. As I say, I cannot be in competition with the *Wall Street Journal*. We are just a small community organ."

"Not if you keep coming up with major stories like this one," he said.

The upshot of it was that Stanley Penn was asked to follow through with the story for the *Journal*. Stanley Penn had won his Pulitzer Prize in 1967 for investigative work in exposing the link between American crime and gambling in the Bahamas. Now armed with a list of contacts in Haiti, even some in the underground, Stanley Penn went there to find out what the Texans were all about. In the process, he found much more than Tortuga Island. On his return to New York, he told me, "Man, you are really wired in." And he told the Bureau chief and others that I have solid sources.

Having left Haiti in 1961, I could not set foot there, because in 1968, I was condemned to death in absentia, following a kangaroo court trial ordered by Papa Doc. My citizenship was revoked. For eighteen years, I traveled the world with a Stateless document ("Re-Entry Permit") provided by the US Department of Justice. That was the punishment imposed on me by the Haitian dictator for daring to oppose his criminal enterprise. Although physically distant from the home front, I had vast underground connections. I trusted Stanley Penn and a few close journalist friends with my contacts in the country.

The biggest scoop that the *Wall Street Journal* got through me was the visit of Pope John Paul II to Haiti. Four months before the visit was to take place, I went to my Bureau Chief to alert him. He asked no question except to say, "Did you tell Stan?"

Eminent Haiti watcher by then, Stanley Penn was entrusted with the assignment. He had plenty of time to research the story. On March 9, 1983, when the Pope landed at the Port-au-Prince airport, the *Wall Street Journal* ran a major front page story on the visit. The Pope's declaration on landing that day would set the stage for open resistance to the regime. After kissing the ground, in front of Jean-Claude Duvalier and his wife Michèle Bennett, the Pope thundered, "Something must change here!" The pontiff criticized the opulence of the insensitive elite and asked for a better deal for the downtrodden. In effect, he became the champion of the poor. His hosts were taken off guard and looked dazed.

The Haitian government was not the only one which considered me a threat. The government of Joaquin Balaguer in the Dominican Republic also felt the sting of the *Wall Street Journal*. I was accused of wanting to destabilize the government of President Balaguer, a disciple of the late dictator Trujillo.

In the fall of 1976, Deborah Sue Yeager, a reporter for the *Wall Street Journal,* discovered questionable payments made by Phillip Morris Co., a US concern, to the President of the Dominican Republic and his Reformist Party. Not familiar with Spanish, Ms. Yeager could not successfully question the Dominican officials. The Bureau chief asked me to help with the interviews.

The first story about the scandal appeared with only the byline of Deborah Sue Yeager. I told the Bureau chief that this spelled trouble, because the Dominican officials will accuse the *Journal* of hiding behind a fake name to attack their government. They had not spoken to any Deborah Yeager, but to Raymond Joseph.

That same afternoon, the managing editor, Fred Taylor, called me to his office and handed me a letter faxed to him from the Dominican officials in Santo Domingo. They had accused the *Journal,* just as I had told the Bureau chief, of using a fake reporter to attack their government. The letter being in Spanish, Mr. Taylor asked me to get him a translation as soon as possible.

In half an hour, the translation was done. On reading the accusation of the Dominican government, Mr. Taylor, with a bemused look on his face, said, "You were right all along. So, you are a woman!" We laughed about it. From then on my name also appeared on the stories dealing with the Dominican scandal.

The Dominicans were intrigued about the messenger. Who is this Raymond A. Joseph? The name does not sound American. They went on a search. One morning, the daily *Ahora* in the Dominican capital, had a bold front page headline in red: *RAMON ES DOMINICANO.* (Raymond Is Dominican) The story went on to say that the *Wall Street Journal* reporter who knows so much about the Dominican Republic was born here of Haitian parents. And now he's working for the prestigious *Wall Street Journal* causing trouble for the Dominican government.

A week had not passed when I received a call from the Domini-can Consul General in New York. He invited me to visit him at the Consulate. I was warmly received. He complimented me on my achievements—from a *batey* of the *Ingenio Santa Fe* (the sugar cane work camp of the Sante Fe Sugar mill where I was born) to the *Wall Street Journal*! He was proud that one of theirs had made it to the top at the watchdog of the financial world.

Then, the real reason for the invitation was broached. His gov-ernment was ready to offer me Dominican citizenship. I graciously thanked him for such an honor. But I told him that I had a chance to choose when I turned 18, and that I had chosen to be Haitian. The look of disappointment on his face could not be disguised.

When my parents left the Dominican Republic in 1939, I did not have a birth certificate. Until now, the Dominican authorities refuse to provide birth certificates to Haitians born on their territory. The situation has worsened. In September of 2013, the Dominican Constitutional Court ruled to revoke the citizenship of Dominican-born Haitians retroactive to 1929. It's an international scandal.

Had I accepted the Consul's offer in 1976, I would be in limbo today. I would fall in the category of the thousands of children of Haitian parents born in the Dominican Republic who have been de-naturalized. Since the ruling is retroactive to 1929, the citizenship of José Francisco Peña Gomez must be revoked posthumously. The brilliant Dominican politician, born of Haitian parents in 1937, died in 1998. He was twice mayor of Santo Domingo, the Domini-can capital. The international airport of Santo Domingo bears his name. The Dominican government has come under pressure from various organizations, including the UN, the OAS and CARICOM, to reverse the discriminatory ruling which has turned the country into an apartheid State in the Americas. On October 22, 2014, the Inter-American Court of Human Rights condemned the Domini-can Republic for violating the rights of the Dominico-Haitians and urged that ruling of the Dominican court be annulled.

Since the election of President Jimmy Carter in 1976, I felt an urge to remobilize the opposition against the dictatorship. But I had to put a damper to my ardor, because of my familial responsibilities. Nevertheless, I felt that since the embrace of Papa Doc by Nelson Rockefeller, there was a policy change regarding Haiti. Eight months after his inauguration, President Carter tackled the dictatorship in Haiti. His ambassador to the United Nations, Andrew Young, delivered the message to the Haitian dictator. During a swing through the Caribbean, Young stopped in Haiti where he met with the young chief. No joint communiqué was released.

But in action and word, one got the gist of the conversation that took place. Unlike the lovefest of President Nixon's envoy Rockefeller with Papa Doc in 1969, there was no picture of an embrace of Baby Doc. An icon of the civil rights movement who had been a close aide of Martin Luther King, Ambassador Young carried a message of deliverance. During a press conference, he said: "We intend to share our experience that imprisonment of the voices of freedom of society, denying them access to their families, and treating them with brutality does not do anything to further the growth and development of a country."* Those words had a major impact. "Stop imprisoning the voice of freedom" became a refrain in the mouths of the critics of the Duvalier regime.

On September 21, 1977, Duvalier released 104 political prisoners and formally signed the American Convention on Human Rights. I considered this a victory, because before Ambassador Young had left New York for his Caribbean trip, he had received me and a group of victims of the regime at his office to enquire about the situation in Haiti. We fully briefed him and provided him a list of twenty-one political prisoners who were among those released. Under the Carter

---

*The Spokesman Review, Spokane, Washington, August 16, 1977

administration, repression was muted in Haiti and the flowering of a free press began.

By 1984, especially after Pope John Paul II's spectacular visit to Haiti the year before, I felt that I needed my independence to deal with unfolding political events on the home front. Also, the *Haiti-Observateur*, the weekly newspaper that I co-founded with my brother Leo, had expanded to such an extent that he needed help. Moreover, the launching of a well-financed competitor, the left-wing weekly *Haiti Progrès*, also meant that the *Observateur* needed new funding to modernize its operations. Otherwise, it would not be able to keep ahead of the competition which was trumpeting Cuba as an example for Haiti to follow.

I sensed also that some people in management at the *Wall Street Journal* would have liked to see me move on. My relationship with management was never the same after my 1982 testimony in Miami in a case of Haitian refugees vs. the Justice Department. I had joined the late Father Gérard Jean-Juste and lawyer Ira Kurzban in Miami who had brought a lawsuit on behalf of Haitian refugees in Federal Court. On my time off, I went to testify on behalf of the refugees. The judge was impressed with my testimony. He asked that I return the next day for further testimony. In fact, I was subpoenaed.

The next day happened to be a working day for me at the *Wall Street Journal* in New York. Early that day, I called my Bureau Chief to apprise him of my situation. He asked, "Where are you, anyway?"

"I am in Miami, under subpoena in a case of Haitian refugees vs. the Justice Department."

"Oh, I know all about it," the Bureau Chief said. "You know that your work is here. You should be up here now."

"I am under a subpoena, Sir." And the conversation ended.

The tone of the Bureau Chief was menacing, to say the least. Immediately, I figured what must have happened. The main government witness was Rudolph "Rudy" Giuliani, at the time Associate General, the No. 3 in the Justice Department. He had been in Haiti two weeks earlier where he met the dictator Jean-Claude Duvalier. He vouched for the freedom-loving government and against those seeking political asylum. I figured that Giuliani had called the *Wall Street Journal* to put pressure on me, because my testimony was damaging to his case.

Minutes after I spoke to the Bureau Chief, I contacted Ira Kurzban, the lawyer, and recounted the conversation I had with my Bureau Chief. He said, "We're going to fix things for their team. Anyway, there's nothing you can do to please your bosses at the *Journal*. You are under a subpoena and the judge is expecting you to appear today."

We arrived in court on time. But in light of the new development, we rehearsed on how to proceed. I took my seat at the witness box. At the first question of the judge, I said, "Your Honor, I don't think I can continue with my testimony, because I have been threatened by my boss at the *Wall Street Journal*. He told me that he knew everything about my testimony here and that my work is in New York."

The judge turned pink with anger. He looked sternly at the government lawyers and said, "Gentlemen, what do you have to say for yourselves?"

"Your Honor, may we approach the bench?" Giuliani asked.

"Fine," the judge replied. But he also asked the stenographer to continue taking notes.

From the witness box where I was seated, I followed the exchange between the judge and the lead government lawyer. The judge asked him to explain what had happened. Giuliani admitted that indeed he had called the *Wall Street Journal*. He wanted to ascertain whether I was truly a reporter there.

"You think he would come into my court room and lie about where he works," the judge retorted, adding "there is nothing in what you have said that couldn't be said publicly."

Turning toward me, the judge continued, "You will testify. If anything were to happen to you, the *Wall Street Journal* will be dragged into this court to explain. Go on with your testimony."

At that moment, I knew we had won our case against the Justice Department. I was emboldened by the judge. I continued to testify and returned to my job in New York the following day. My bosses didn't say a word. But their attitude toward me was no longer the same. I knew that they wished I would leave. But no one dared to fire me.

On my own accord, I was about to leave the *Journal,* more than two years after the Miami court case. I went to see my Bureau Chief to tell him that I was going on vacation. "If I am offered a good package, I may not return," I told him.

"Are you resigning?" he quickly said.

"No, I didn't say I am resigning. I said if you offer me a good package I may not return."

"Okay," he said, "I will call you."

No doubt the Bureau Chief wanted to discuss the news with his superiors and get their imput. That same day, he called me back to his office. This time I took my reporter's pad with me. He said to sit down. He closed the door. He began to tell me what he was offering. I kept writing. After he finished, he asked, "How about that for a package?"

"It sounds good," I said, "but I have to check with my lawyer."

When I left the Bureau Chief, I called my lawyer friend and unpaid adviser Ira Gollobin to tell him about the package I had been offered. He agreed that it was generous. He said I should be able to ask for something else, since management seemed predisposed to do anything to see me leave. He came up with a last demand, "Ask for health insurance coverage for a full year after you leave." It was done. The last week of August 1984, I left the *Wall Street Journal* in good standing.

Chapter 9

Preparing for a New Regime

Once I left the *Wall Street Journal*, I was no longer restrained from doing what I wanted to do—politically. I set out to organize the opposition to the tottering dictatorship of Jean-Claude "Baby Doc" Duvalier. I was, in effect, wearing two hats—that of co-publisher at the *Haiti-Observateur* and of political activist. I set out to do what I think had been my vocation: To build a coalition to challenge the dictatorship at home.

"The Haitian Fathers" were doing admirable work from their base at 333 Lincoln Place in Brooklyn, NY. For the most part, the group included the priests of the Holy Ghost Catholic Order that were exiled in August 1969 for allegedly plotting to overthrow the Duvalier dictatorship.

The expulsion order of the priests was indicative of the paranoia of the regime which displayed the nonsense of its action. The priests, all Haitian citizens, were charged with using their teaching posts at the elite *Petit Séminaire Collège St. Martial* to distribute communist articles harmful to the government and to the person of the Chief of State. One of the expelled teachers, Father Max Dominique (no relation to Colonel Max Dominique) was said to be affiliated with the

Haïti Progrès, a "right-wing party with leftist tendencies."* I developed a friendship with the superior of the group, Father Antoine Adrien, and with his associates Fathers William Smarth and Jean Yves Urfié. I convinced them that we should pull our forces together to give a final assault to the regime in Port-au-Prince. I reached out to various groups, including those in Canada and Europe.

After months of long distance telephone discussions, we met in New York in September 1985 and formed the *Rassemblement de l'Opposition pour la Concertation* (ROC) or "Platform for Dialogue." It was not a political party, but an organization which offered a setting for discussions leading to a common understanding in the face of a crumbling regime at home. An executive board was voted. I became secretary general and lawyer Jacques Brière Adolphe, executive secretary. Other influential members included former priest Ernst Verdieu, who represented Canada; Serge Gilles of the *Parti Nationaliste Progressiste Haïtien* (PANPRA) from France, representing Europe; and Professor Yves Volel, representing New York and the United States; Anna Baron was recording secretary; Lola Poisson and Manfred Antoine, advisers.

Inside Haiti, the weekly *Le Petit Samedi Soir* was publishing critical articles against the regime. A young Catholic priest by the name of Jean-Bertrand Aristide was gaining an ever larger audience to his revolutionary sermons. The *Haiti-Observateur* discovered him at the St. Joseph parish in Port-au-Prince soon after his ordination in 1982 as he began to denounce the Duvalier dictatorship. To dampen his ardor, his conservative superiors encouraged him to further his studies abroad.

When Aristide returned to Haiti in 1985, his campaign against the regime became the focus of his sermons. We followed him closely as he built his reputation at St. Jean Bosco, arguably the poorest parish then in the poorest part of town. St. Jean Bosco

---

The New York Times, August 31, 1969

became a center of attraction for congregants from far and wide who found in Father Aristide an uncompromising opponent of the regime. Indeed, he was playing a major role in preparing the people to rise up against the dictatorship. On September 11, 1988, Father Aristide gained an aura of invincibility when he escaped an assassination attempt during mass at his church. The church was torched and several congregants perished in the assault carried out by Namphy's military government. Preceding the United States' September 11, the Haitian September 11 at St. Jean Bosco remains sacred for *Lavalassians*, who go back religiously to the place of the crime for the sad remembrance and to demand justice for those assassinated on that day.

The Duvalier dictatorship always felt more at ease with Republican administrations. Thus, in 1980 when Ronald Reagan was elected, Baby Doc's government began a crackdown on the press which had become quite vocal following the election of President Carter in 1976. Several journalists were exiled after the assassination of Gasner Raymond, a fearless crusading reporter against the dictatorship. A new crop of journalists had landed in New York and elsewhere in the diaspora. Among the more prominent were Jean Dominique and his wife Michèle Montas, as well as Anthony Pascal, a.k.a. Konpè Filo, of *Radio Haiti Inter;* Pierre Clitandre, Jean Robert Hérard and Marcus Gracia of *Le Petit Samedi Soir.*

Their arrival in the diaspora was like new blood added to the pool. Instead of dampening the contestation to the regime, the expulsion of the journalists gave an added momentum to the struggle. Demonstrations were organized in front of the Haitian consulate in New York and at Dag Hammarksjöld Plaza across from the United Nations headquarters to denounce the brutal regime in Haiti.

A strongman of the regime, Dr. Roger Lafontant, popularized a slogan in a referendum held in the summer of 1985: *La Présidence à vie n'est pas négociable.* (The presidency for life is non-negotiable.) That was like a red flag to the opposition which responded with its own defiant slogan: *A bas le Président-à-vie.* (Down with the President-for-life.)

On June 22, 1985, we decided to carry the struggle to Washington, DC. In a new twist to our demonstration, we chose the 22nd to desacralize the date which symbolized Duvalierist power. We had a short silent vigil in front of the Haitian Embassy on Massachusetts Avenue in Washington. We lit twenty-two candles that were lined up on the sidewalk in front of the building. Then, we went to the State Department where we repeated the same ceremony. That was pre-9/11 (September 11, 2001) when security was lax. We went right up to the steps of the State Department to leave our 22 candles.

Weeks after this demonstration, we kept receiving reports that the Haitian opposition was using voodoo against Baby Doc's regime. A source at the Haitian Embassy told me that a counter ceremony was ordered by the Haitian officials at midnight the following month, on the 22nd. That was to undo what the opponents from New York had left by the sidewalk in front of the Embassy. The officials were convinced that the twenty-two candles were not left innocently. They even said that anti-government demonstrations are never staged at night. So, the June 22nd demonstration was a mystical hex placed upon the regime.

Three weeks after our first Washington demonstration, we planned another one, in broad daylight this time. Three members of our group—Anna Baron, Gérard Laforest, and I—arrived first, soon after 9:00 a.m. Without prior appointment, we went into the Embassy and asked to see the ambassador. We were told that the ambassador, Adrien Raymond, would not arrive soon. We will wait, we said, and sat down on a leather couch in the foyer.

One hour after we had been at the Embassy, a busload of our colleagues from New York arrived. With hostile placards to the regime, the demonstrators were doing their thing on the sidewalk across the street from the Embassy. At that point, some of the Embassy employees may have figured it out. The three of us inside are probably part of the group outside.

Finally, around 11:00 a.m., the ambassador entered the front door. In unison, the three of us stood up and said, "Good morning, Mr. Ambassador!" He did not stop. Neither did he acknowledge us. He rushed pass us and went up the stairs to his office on the second floor. As the ambassador passed, Anna Baron shouted, "Adrien, it's your cousin Anna—Anna Baron!" That had no effect on him.

About ten minutes after he had arrived, the ambassador sent someone to ask us to give him whatever documentation we had to deliver. We said we wanted to see the ambassador himself and that we could wait if he was busy. The person came back a few minutes later and told us the ambassador would not receive us. We should give him any material we have to deliver. By this time, the employees were convinced that we were part of the group outside vociferously denouncing the Duvalier regime. We did not budge. We said we will not leave without seeing the ambassador.

About an hour had elapsed since Ambassador Raymond had arrived and there definitely was a stalemate with no apparent break in sight. Suddenly, federal Marshalls entered Haitian territory, having been summoned by the ambassador. They quickly arrested us, slapped so-called democracy handcuffs (made of plastic) on our wrists.

As they hauled us out of the building to take us to a waiting paddy wagon, Anna Baron let out a yell of "Down with Duvalier" with all the power in her lungs. Pictures of Baby Doc and his wife Michèle on the wall appeared as if they were shaking. While being led out, I saw an individual with a bemused smile on his face behind the counter in a room next to the entrance of the Embassy. It was Lionel Délatour, a minister counselor at the time. Strangely, two decades later I will find myself collaborating with him during the interim government in 2004–2006 and long afterward during the presidency of René Préval.

We were taken to the municipal jail in Washington. Our lawyers went to work immediately. Within four hours we were freed—to the joyous acclamation of our supporters. They had come to the jail in front of which they had planned a vigil that night if we were not released. The bus ride back to New York, originally scheduled for 2:00 p.m., left Washington around 5:00. There was no gloom in our midst. On the contrary, we were going back triumphantly, knowing that the action in Washington would be a big boost to a demonstration we had planned in New York the next day.

All sectors of the opposition were invited to this show of unity against the dictatorship. The "Haitian Fathers" had mobilized the community for the peaceful demonstration which would turn out to be the largest ever held in New York by Haitians up to that point. The staging area for the march was the Dag Hammarskjöld Plaza (47th Street and First Avenue). By 9:00 a.m., about one thousand demonstrators were ready to march south on Second Avenue, to 42nd Street, then west on 42nd, with our final destination being the Haitian Consulate at 60 East 42nd Street, between Park and Madison Avenues.

Soon after we left the park and began to walk on Second Avenue, the Police knew they could not keep us on the sidewalk, as planned. We spilled onto the street, marching with banners unfurled and chanting, "Down with the Duvalier dictatorship," "Down with the President-for-life," "Democracy or Death."

As we got closer to our target, the crowd grew exponentially. By the time we reached Lexington Avenue, less than two blocks from our destination, the Mounted Police became edgy, because some unruly demonstrators were taunting the officers. When we reached the underpass at 42nd Street and Park Avenue, an unknown individual used a sharp instrument to dig a horse which jumped in the air and came crashing down with its front hoofs hitting heads, hands, and other human parts. As the Marshall of the march, I was immobilized by the baton of a policeman who held it with both hands as he stopped me. Seeing the baton coming, I stiffened my stomach muscles. The young officer's eyes almost popped out of their sockets as the baton bounced back. We were ready for all eventualities.

Yells, groans, and moans mixed with defiant slogans created an atmosphere of pandemonium. At that point, through a bullhorn, I invited the marchers to regroup at the staging point at Dag Hammarskjöld Plaza. I asked that they walk back on the sidewalks in small groups, not as marchers on the street. I also addressed a message to the Police, especially to the Mounted Police. I kept repeating, "We were demonstrating peacefully, and they loosened their horses on us. Yes, we were demonstrating peacefully."

As we made our way back to 47th Street and First Avenue, about half a mile away, word had reached City Hall that there was trouble in midtown with Haitian demonstrators. Ambulances had evacuated a few of the demonstrators who were badly injured. The cranium of an individual was broken; another had three fingers crushed. At least one pregnant woman aborted later as a result of the rough treatment in the ensuing brawl.

When almost all the marchers had regrouped at Dag Hammarskjöld Plaza, I mounted the platform erected for the occasion. A superb sound system carried the damning message with the recurring theme, "We were demonstrating peacefully, and they loosened their horses on us!"

Mayor Edward "Ed" Koch had dispatched his Special Adviser, James Harding, to come present his sympathy and apology for what had happened. Seeing officers on horses at the edge of the crowd, on First Avenue, I began shouting, "Here they are! They have no place here! They must go! Go! Go! Go! They must go!" And the crowd picked up the refrain, "Go! Go! Go! They must go!"

At that point, I saw Mr. Harding go over in the direction of the horses. And the horses with their riders disappeared. He had convinced the commanding officer that the presence of the Mounted Police at that juncture was a provocative act—which it was.

The stars of that day were the Washington jailbirds of the previous day. Others who spoke were Anna Baron and Gérard Laforest. After fully haranguing the crowd, we told them to go home peacefully. Meanwhile, the leaders of the march, including a member of the "Haitian Fathers," headed to the Police Precinct on 51st Street, between Lexington and Third Avenue, to file a formal complaint against the New York Police, the famous NYPD. This will be the basis for a class action suit on behalf of the demonstrators.

All those who had complained about being hurt that day, depending on the nature of their injury, got compensated. Compensation was as high as $400,000 for the individual whose cranium was broken to the $50 I received for the Police baton that hit my stomach. One famous case was that of Yves Volel, whose fingers were crushed when the hoof of a horse crashed on his hand.

Chapter 10

Baby Doc's Emancipation— And Fall

As Papa Doc sensed death approaching, in January 1971, he officially presented his 19-year-old son, Jean-Claude Duvalier, as his political heir. In a famous photo, the monarch put his right hand on his strapping son and said, "This is the young leader I promised you." In deference to the Constitution, Papa Doc dictated a change in the charter to his rubber-stamped unicameral parliament. The age to assume the presidency was lowered to eighteen years from forty.

Inaugurated April 22, the 19-year-old Jean-Claude, nicknamed "Baby Doc," was president in name only. His mother, Simone Ovide ("Mama Doc") was who really exercised power along with the old Duvalierist guards known as "The Dinosaurs."

After only four months in office, Baby Doc was forced to make a decision that would move against his elder sister and godmother, who had been his adviser. Marie-Denise Duvalier Dominique, 30 years old, had rushed to her younger brother's side when she learned that her father was near death. As previously mentioned, in June 1967, her father had exiled her together with her husband Max Dominique and her younger sister Simone Jr. to a diplomatic post in Madrid.

Upon her father's death, Marie-Denise assumed the title of secretary to the president. But the Dinosaurs considered her too ambitious to remain at her brother's side. Moreover, they feared the return of her husband, who might have wanted to avenge his comrades executed four years earlier. After an altercation with Minister of Interior Luckner Cambronne, Marie-Denise was exiled again, along with her husband and her sister to the Haitian Embassy in Paris.

Meanwhile, Baby Doc was being nudged by his close adviser Roger Lafontant to assert his authority. Lafontant, MD, the consul general in Montreal at the time, was on the phone almost daily with the president. Roger Lafontant was twenty years older and mentored the president. Jean-Claude often went on hunting trips with Lafontant who had been a fervent Duvalierist since his days at Haiti's medical school. Lafontant's influence on Jean-Claude was overwhelming.

In November 1972, eighteen months after his inauguration, Jean-Claude attempted to show his authority. In the absence of his mother, who was in Miami for medical reasons, Baby Doc fired Luckner Cambronne, the Minister of Interior and replaced him with Lafontant. That was a bold power move by the young leader because the Ministry of Interior is responsible for national security. Cambronne was Mama Doc's confidant. He was not only sacked, but exiled immediately to Colombia.

Mama Doc was livid when she learned what had happened in her absence. As soon as she returned to Port-au-Prince, she took control of the situation. In January 1973, she fired Roger Lafontant and replaced him with her trusted aide, Weber Guerrier. Lafontant was dispatched to New York as consul general. Baby Doc swallowed his lumps.

He swore off politics for the time being. He enjoyed the life of a playboy and left governance to mommy and her associates. Baby Doc did encourage the formation of an elite military corps known as the *Lèopards,* under the leadership of Colonel Acédius St. Louis. Mama Doc didn't object, because she was not fond of the *Tontons-Macoute* and their feminine counterparts, the *Fillettes Lalo.* Adroitly, the power of those repressive forces, created by Papa Doc, was being curbed, although they were not disbanded. Following in the footsteps of his father, Baby Doc was setting up his own force to continue with the repression that was the hallmark of the Duvalier dictatorships.

Jean-Claude had always been under the influence of a woman. In an April 1980 issue of the *Haiti-Observateur,* the upcoming wedding of Jean-Claude Duvalier to a 26-year-old divorcée named Michèle Bennett was announced. The article noted that the mother of two was formerly married to Alix Pasquet Jr., the son of a former Army officer. Pasquet Sr. had taken part in a mini invasion against Papa Doc in 1959. The rebels had even seized the *Casernes Dessalines,* the Army barracks next to the dictator's palace, before being defeated by forces loyal to Duvalier. Now the grandchildren of the man who was hacked to death by Duvalierist mobs were about to find residence at the Palace. Interestingly, the wedding was to take place on April 14, the birthday of Jean-Claude's late father.

The story caused a big uproar, because this was the first time that Mama Doc was learning about her son's plan to escape from her domination. The *Observateur* noted that the idea of Jean-Claude's marriage was taboo around the Palace. Three years earlier, the paper reported, Jean-Claude had confided to the *Sunday Times of London* that marriage was not for him. He was quoted as saying, "How can I marry? My mother is the First Lady of the country. If I marry there will be conflict." Nonetheless, Michèle's brother, Frantz Bennett, a friend of Jean-Claude, was quietly paving the way for his sister.

The feeling of being treated as a minor gnawed at the young chief for some time. For the first time, Baby Doc was about to exercise his authority of President-for-life, and his mother would be among the first to feel her son's sting. The week following the announcement

of the marriage bombshell, the *Haiti-Observateur* had another ominous headline: "Baby Doc Promises to Execute Those Who Oppose
His Wedding." Would that also include his mother?

First Lady Simone Ovide Duvalier realized that another woman
was about to eclipse her. It was an explosive situation, to say the
least. Things almost turned tragic when Mama Doc attempted to
spirit Michèle away. Army officers arrived at the residence of the
Bennetts in Pétionville, supposedly at the request of Baby Doc, to
escort Michèle to the Palace. Whereas Michèle had just been on
the phone with her beau and nothing of the sort was mentioned. A
quick thinking Ernest Bennett, Michèle's father, told them to wait
a minute.

He went into the bedroom to call Baby Doc. Had he indeed
sent the officers? No! Jean-Claude told him to keep them waiting.
Suddenly, a detachment of *Léopards*, the elite force of the president,
surrounded the Bennett residence and arrested all the soldiers on
mission. That's when Baby Doc had let out the threat of death
against those who opposed his wedding plans.

Apparently Jean-Claude's threat was not taken lightly. Mama Doc
was convinced that her son meant business. In the third week of the
saga, the *Haiti-Observateur* came with a more conciliatory headline:
"The Wedding of Jean-Claude: A New Date." A communiqué from
the palace, on April 29, 1980, stated that Baby Doc decided to unite
his destiny to that of Mrs. Michèle Bennett in Port-au-Prince on
May 27. And the people were invited to participate in the religious
ceremony which would take place.

The *Haiti-Observateur* had been banned in Haiti and was carried
out from its underground office in New York. But we couldn't miss
such an event as the wedding of the President-for-life.

Leo, who was editor of the paper, assured me that the underground would be fully represented and that the paper would not
miss a thing. I took upon myself the responsibility to provide the
photos. I called a photographer friend and offered him a week of

vacation in Port-au-Prince, all expenses paid. There was a catch to the offer: a major assignment. He would be covering Jean-Claude Duvalier's wedding. David Healey jumped at the unique opportunity of being part of history. "Awesome, I never covered the wedding of a president," he exclaimed.

When the young White American photographer went to the Haitian Consulate in New York to get his credentials, Dave was told that no photographer other than those of the major international television chains would be allowed. I sent him to a special source that provided him with a VIP pass for all the activities.

On arriving in Haiti, Dave met a friend from Guadeloupe who became his associate. She followed him around with three cameras around her neck, completing Dave's two. Being of short stature, Dave bought a lightweight aluminum ladder that his associate toted all over the place. This ladder provided him the best view wherever he went. At the cathedral in Port-au-Prince, no one was better positioned than Dave. He even covered the reception at Baby Doc's ranch in Croix-des-Bouquets, some eight miles north of the capital, where he photographed Baby Doc's herd of cattle that roamed the fields in a large enclosure.

The wedding took place on a Tuesday afternoon and the reception at the Croix-des-Bouquets ranch went on until the wee hours of Wednesday morning. We had told Dave that the photos should appear in the issue scheduled for Thursday. At 6:00 p.m., David Healey telephoned from Miami to say that he had landed from Port-au-Prince safely and that his connecting flight would arrive at JFK around midnight. We should find a photo lab in New York that could process the films on his arrival.

We picked Dave up at JFK and rushed to Modernage, a photo lab in downtown Manhattan where the technicians were waiting. By 4:00 a.m., we had all the pictures we needed. The front page photo told the whole story: Archbishop François Wolf Ligondé, right arm lifted, was blessing the new couple. The paper had fully covered what was for Haiti "The Wedding of the Age." Reportedly it was a three-million-dollar extravaganza in one of the poorest countries in the world.

———

The marriage of Michèle Bennett and Jean-Claude Duvalier was in great part responsible for the downfall of the Duvalierist dynasty. The citizens had gotten used to the young ruler's car-loving, playboy style. By the way, his penchant for cars played a big role in his decision to expand and pave two major roads. Under the Duvaliers, there was no accounting on how much money was spent. What the President or his wife wanted they got.

When Michèle entered the scene, all of a sudden, the taint around the Palace, as in skin color, became much lighter. Some old Duvalierist hands began grumbling about their "*noiriste,*" or Black power, revolution being hijacked by the mulattoes who surrounded the First Lady. The extravagances of Michèle Bennett even made the rounds of the international press, especially when she went on her million dollar shopping sprees to Paris or New York. She threw some crumbs at the people through her Michèle Bennett Foundation. Her name appeared prominently on her generous gifts, such as the Michèle Bennett Hospital in Bon Repos, north of Port-au-Prince. Without any accounting, the president's wife was spending money for whatever struck her fancy. And her propaganda machine burnished her image to the point that in 1981 the saintly Sister Theresa traveled to Haiti to extol the good deeds of the unusual First Lady.

A lavish party at the National Palace in a specially air-conditioned room became the symbol of the decadence of the regime. The temperature of the room was exceedingly cold, especially designed to allow Michèle and her guests to wear their mink coats in the tropics. Moreover, the party was televised. Giant screens, prominently placed in public parks, allowed the people to enjoy and participate vicariously.

The insensitivity of Michèle Bennett has become a reference for Haitians whenever they want to point out the extravagances of those who would like to emulate her. It is not to her honor that Sophia St. Rémy Martelly, Haiti's First Lady, was called "the new Michèle Bennett—revised and amplified." As it is said, those who fail to study history are bound to repeat its mistakes.

While the national press was muzzled, the *Haiti-Observateur* kept shedding light from New York on the excesses of the regime. This was to the great displeasure of the Haitian authorities. And Roger Lafontant approached the paper with a proposal for collaboration with the government. For a handsome fee, he wanted us to accept an editor chosen by the regime to join our staff. The offer was made to a staff writer at the *Observateur*, Firmin Joseph (who was not related to me).

We told Firmin that he had no authority to sign or accept anything in our name. This was important, because Firmin had called to say that Jean-Claude Duvalier's consul had shown him a briefcase full with $200,000 cash in exchange for *Haiti-Observateur*'s collaboration. Again, the regime was ready to make us millionaires in Haitian terms. At that time, one US dollar was still equivalent to five Haitian gourdes.

There was no way we would have let Firmin Joseph conduct negotiations for us. Firmin loved money too much and we had disavowed him in previous deals. As a businessman, Firmin did not have a good reputation so Leo decided to deal with Lafontant. Since the paper was an established institution in the community, we were ready to turn the whole operation to a team chosen by the government. But we asked for five million dollars.

This did not please the regime which wanted us to remain at the controls. We could not agree to that. Had Lafontant agreed to our price, we were ready to let the chosen editors of the government assume full control. They could use their own power of persuasion to convince the readers about their new line of thinking. We were ready to pursue other avenues. Apparently, our price tag was too steep. But in no way would we accept to become tools of a dictatorship. Thus, we remained a thorn in the side of the Duvalier regime to the end of the dictatorship on February 7, 1986.

Others apparently much closer to Baby Doc had tried to use the *Haiti-Observateur* for their own advantage such as Ernest Bennett, the father-in-law of the president. Soon after his daughter's marriage to Baby Doc, Bennett became the power broker to consult in matters of business.

He was involved in practically all business transactions in Haiti. And much money was being realized with several firms that had discovered Haiti as a cheap labor market. Haiti had become a textile manufacturing center. Some electronics firms had discovered the dexterity of Haitian fingers. And beginning in 1969, all the baseballs batted in the majors were manufactured in Haiti. Rawlings had moved its plant from Puerto Rico to benefit from Haitian labor. It is estimated that under Baby Doc, Haiti benefitted from about 80,000 manufacturing jobs which spun a cottage industry that supported nearly 400,000.

Among his new ventures, Bennett started an international airline service. Air Haiti was intended to become Haiti's international flagship. However, for the airline to be accepted, it needed the endorsement of the *Haiti-Observateur*. Thus, in May 1985, Bennett came to New York and asked to see me. Over coffee at a restaurant on East 42nd Street in Manhattan, I was meeting the closest ally of the dictator whose demise I sought.

Bennett was not on a political mission. Rather, he was all business and wanted to rope us in, especially since there was much money to be made. Bennett wanted to sign a contract with the *Haiti-Observateur* for long-term full-page publicity for Air Haiti. Cost was not a problem, he said, because he had ample financing for the airline.

I showed interest in his proposal, but I made a counterproposal. Considering that the newspaper is banned from circulating in Haiti,

I told Bennett perhaps he could help me get the *Haiti-Observateur* to the country. Immediately his mood changed. "A newspaper that is attacking and belittling my son-in-law all the time," he said. "You think I would take it upon myself to introduce it to Haiti. You must be kidding!"

"But, Sir," I responded, "if the paper begins to circulate in Haiti, we would have to tone down our attacks and change our approach somewhat. Certainly, we would stop using derogatory nicknames to refer to your son-in-law. Gone would be *Bonbonfle, Basket Head, Dry Fruit* and other such monikers."

"No, I cannot take that chance with you," Bennett said.

"Well, Sir, you want to use our services to leap over our head to speak to and woo our constituency, without our having anything in return?"

"What are you talking about?" he said. "You will have something big in return. You will be paid handsomely. It is a commercial deal, isn't it? I am ready to pay whatever you ask."

"But, Sir, we are not only a commercial newspaper. We are also a crusading organ whose mission is the democratization of our country. We just cannot betray our vocation, no matter the amount."

We parted without reaching a deal. The following week, the *Haiti-Observateur* published an article on the new airline that was dubbed *Le Tap-Tap Volant* (The Flying Tap-Tap). Tap-taps are colorful pick-up trucks converted into public transportation mini buses in Haiti. Not a flattering way to describe an airline with lofty ambitions. Accompanying the story was a cartoon in which a lad was throwing a toy plane in the air. That, more or less, spelled the death knell of Bennett's airline. Certainly, Haitians would not travel in a "flying tap-tap" which could put their life at risk.

Ernest Bennett was not pleased by the illustrated article which, apparently, had the desired effect as far as we were concerned. He hired a reputable law firm in New York to sue the *Observateur* in the Eastern Federal District Court in Brooklyn. The damage sought was $20 million. No doubt, he had reasoned that if he cannot use our services, he will ruin us financially.

We had no choice but to also hire a reputable law firm to defend us. Just to sign the contract, we had to disburse $10,000. We were prepared to engage the battle, not only on financial ground, such as the harm caused Air Haiti. We had envisaged the greater harm caused the *Haiti-Observateur* when the regime of Jean-Claude Duvalier, Bennett's son-in-law, blocked the entry of our newspaper on the Haitian market.

We relished the idea of counter-attacking by putting the dictatorship on trial in a US federal court. Certainly, our countersuit would have asked for monetary compensation much greater than $20 million. Punitive damages for denying our rights of free speech and for the reign of terror established in Haiti could have been in the hundreds of millions. Purposely, we waited until the first week of 1986 to announce Bennet's lawsuit against the *Observateur*. By that time we knew that the collapse of the regime would happen in a matter of weeks.

The political situation had been deteriorating ever since the visit of Pope John Paul II in March 1983. His declaration that "something must change here" was a boost to the movement to oust the dictatorship. But it took a tragic event in Gonaives, Haiti's birthplace of independence, to bring the dictatorship down.

On November 28, 1985, three students—Jean Robert Cius, Mackenson Michel and Daniel Israel—were gunned down by Duvalier's military. Their funeral at the Gonaïves cathedral on November 30 drew a mammoth crowd. It was like a signal for other cities, including Cap-Haïtien in the north and Cayes in the south. On January 27, 1986, the Palace of Justice in Gonaïves was burned down. The situation had gotten out of hand.

Abruptly, Ernest Bennett arrived in New York. He knew that the game was over and time was up. So, he was among the first to leave Haiti, ahead of the upheaval. Despite the adversarial relationship resulting from the lawsuit that he had filed against the *Haiti-Observateur*, Bennett felt no inhibition in calling me to ask for a favor. On meeting me, he couldn't be friendlier. He said, "Now that you are behind the counter and I am in front, I would like to ask you a favor. I would like to give an interview to the *Observateur*."

"No problem," I said.

Whereupon, Bennett said, "I have prepared it already. You know I am also a journalist. I have asked myself the pertinent questions and have also provided the answers. The interview is ready to be published, and I am willing to pay upfront for it."

"No, Sir," I said, "That is not how we operate at the *Observateur*. First, there is no payment for interviews. But most importantly, we ask the questions and the interviewee answers. We cannot accept an interview of the sort that you have prepared. We are willing to interview you right now, with our own questions." Bennett refused and that was the end of the conversation.

At that late hour, Bennett was trying to whitewash his son-in-law regarding the events in Gonaïves that would precipitate Baby Doc's fall. And he thought that the *Haiti-Observateur* was the perfect organ in which to do that. What gall! Even in their final days, the supporters of the Duvalier regime thought they could impose their will on anyone. They had perfected the techniques of corruption. Bennett probably could not understand how someone would resist his generous offer.

Why did Ernest Bennett feel so much at ease to contact me? He said his wife told him about me, that I am a fair person who would listen. That goes back to our elementary school days at the St. Augustin Episcopal School in Cayes. Aurore was my friend and she used to ask her parents to invite me for lunch during school break at noon. Her family lived a block from the school while I had to pedal four miles to my house. I was 12 years old the last time I saw Aurore. That was much water under the bridge.

The game was really up for Baby Doc and no whitewashing would have done any good. The Reagan administration, which had been pressuring Jean-Claude to resign for some time, made a premature announcement. On January 30, 1986, White House spokesman Larry Speakes broke the news of Baby Doc's resignation to a group of reporters on Air Force One. That happened while President Reagan was flying to Houston where he would be attending the memorial service for the Challenger astronauts.

How could the office of the President of the United States be so wrong in its estimation of the Haitian situation? Two hours later, while still in flight, Mr. Speakes retracted, saying events were "not as clear as we first thought." Knowing how closely I was following events, Terry Atlas of the *Chicago Tribune* reached me in New York for a comment. "The U.S. jumped the gun," I said.* No doubt, the embattled President-for-life had agreed to leave on January 30. But for security reasons, at the last minute he had changed his mind. He couldn't leave without proper arrangement.

Two weeks after my second encounter with Ernest Bennett and one week after the false alarm from Air Force One, Baby Doc was on his way out. A stratagem had to be found to get the President-for-life pass the security guards at the Palace. For, rumors were rife that Baby Doc was planning to escape and leave his faithful supporters to their fate. Anything could have happened, even an assassination attempt of the President.

Baby Doc had rehearsed thoroughly how to address the security guards. When, before daybreak, the door of the elevator from the presidential quarters opened on the first floor, the guards presented arms. Duvalier saluted and, in an amiable tone, said something like this, "You know my wife has not been well. In fact, she just came back last week from the hospital. Now again, I have to get her to the

---

The Chicago Tribune, February 01, 1986

airport, because a plane is waiting to fly her in an emergency to a hospital abroad. Thanks for your concern."

And he walked to the car which was already idling. He slipped behind the wheel of the BMW with his wife at his side. Thus, in the wee hours of February 7, 1986, Jean-Claude Duvalier drove from the Palace to the Port-au-Prince airport. In the back seat was his trusted aide, Army officer Prosper Avril. An idling US Air Force jet was waiting to whisk the couple to exile in France.

When Prosper Avril came back from the airport without the President, he was nervous yet calm. In addressing the guards, he said, "We are in trouble. When the President boarded the plane, I thought he was only going to kiss his wife goodbye. Next thing I know, the door of the plane closes and it taxies out to the runway and takes flight. He did not even tell me goodbye. Quickly, all of you, shed off your uniforms, because it is already open season on *Tontons-Macoute*, and you could be harmed if you are seen wearing the blue denim uniform." Pandemonium broke in *Macoute* ranks.

Chapter 11

The Bloody Road to Democracy

After three decades of a father-son dictatorship that reportedly caused about 30,000 deaths and hundreds of thousands of exiles, Haiti underwent a period of turbulence approaching anarchy. The four years following Jean-Claude Duvalier's flight were marred in blood and in a series of coups d'état intended to forestall the establishment of a democratic government.

Just as Prosper Avril had warned, the *Tontons-Macoute* and their supporters became the hunted instead of the hunters they had been for nearly two decades. The long suppressed sentiments of the victimized population exploded into unbridled violence. The *dechoukaj,* the literal uprooting of the remnants of the old regime, began with a vengeance.

There was not only the destruction and pillaging of homes of *Macoutes* and their followers, but also wholesale killing and burning of people—alive! The situation unsettled me. It reminded me of Papa Doc's public execution at the Port-au-Prince cemetery of the two remaining rebels of the *Jeune Haiti* movement. It also made me think of Fidel Castro's *Paredón* type executions in Cuba after his victory over Batista. When I found out that the major instigator of the abhorrent public violence was Jean-Bertrand Aristide, the priest of St. Jean Bosco, I felt real revulsion.

In October 1985 when the priest had assumed leadership of the Catholic Church–sponsored School of Arts and Trade in Port-au-Prince, he had at his disposal the chapel attached to the school. That's when he began to recruit the future leaders of the deadly *dechoukaj* movement. He was then working on his mini bible of violence titled *100 Vèse Dechoukaj—Va-t-en Satan* (100 Verses of Uprooting—Go Away Satan). It was a coarsely illustrated Creole booklet and officially circulated after February 7, 1986.

The messages of the "100 Verses" were direct, unequivocal, and clothed in biblical authenticity. Considering that the New Testament is generally peaceful in its prose, author Aristide turned to the angry prophets of the Old Testament, especially to Jeremiah. Always paraphrasing, he indicated what should happen to the enemies of the people. *"M ap fè pawòl mwen mete nan bouch ou tounen youn dife. Dife a pral boule yo nèt."* And he adds, *"L ap boule yo nèt, nèt, nèt!"* (Jeremiah 5:13). Actually, in the New King James version, the verse is 5:14 and reads as follows: ". . . Behold, I will make my words in your mouth fire, and this people wood, and it shall devour them." Aristide reinforced the message by adding "burning them totally!"

In another verse, Aristide paraphrases, "God, in his wrath, will chop them up while they're still alive." (Psalm 58:10b). Accompanied by explicit graphics depicting violence either with a machete, a baton or fire, unquestionably the priest had prepared his army of "holy thugs" for the destruction of the old order. Thus, after February 7, 1986, when a violent act called "necklacing" also referred to as *Père Lebrun* (Father Lebrun) made its official appearance, there was no question about its origin. Necklacing is when a gasoline-soaked tire is draped around the neck of a victim and lit. A most barbaric punishment!

As much as I had fought the *Macoutes*, I felt it was inhumane to inflict such horror on any human being. It seemed that the priest had ascribed himself the power of God. I knew then that I wouldn't have much in common with the so-called priest of the shantytowns, as Aristide was nicknamed by Amy Wilentz in her 1989 book *The Rainy Season: Haiti Since Duvalier*.

After Jean-Claude "Baby Doc" Duvalier departed, the *Conseil National de Gouvernement* (CNG), or National Council of Government, exiles that had fled Haiti more than a quarter century earlier were flocking back to the country from around the world. I didn't dare return immediately as many others did. I still had the death penalty, coupled with the cancellation of my citizenship by François Duvalier in 1968. I had to wait until the CNG publicly decreed the annulment of my death penalty and that of others before setting foot in Haiti. Otherwise, I could have been grabbed on landing at the airport and probably executed by those who follow the law strictly when it serves their purpose.

One month after Baby Doc's fall, my brother Leo and Georges Rigaud, the former underground leader, arrived in Haiti to open a bureau for the *Haiti-Observateur* in the Haitian capital. The newspaper, officially banned since its inception in New York in 1971, was coming out in Haiti for the first time.

Rigaud had fled Haiti in 1970 by seeking asylum at the Brazilian Embassy. From Brazil, he had joined us in New York. The resourceful lawyer that he was, he had maintained his contacts in the country. Away from the scene for sixteen years, Rigaud was able to pave the way for the *Haiti-Observateur*.

He found us the whole second floor of a major bank for our office. He negotiated lucrative advertisements from businesses intent on buying goodwill. Even the government wanted to be associated with us. The building housing the government newspaper *Le Nouveau Monde* was offered to the *Haiti-Observateur*. Rigaud advised us to politely decline. There was no way we would tie ourselves to any government.

The hostility against those who came from the diaspora was palpable soon after the fall of the dictatorship. There existed a feeling of betrayal on both sides. Most of those who stayed in the country and who, for survival, collaborated with the dictatorship, or resisted clandestinely, resented those who had escaped and who, supposedly, lived the good life abroad. This sentiment was expressed in the Constitution that received overwhelming approval on March 29, 1987.

By far, the most popular article of the new Charter was 291. It barred "fervent Duvalierists" from holding elective office for ten years. At the same time several other articles, such as 91, 96, 135, 157, 193 and 200-205, severely restricted Haitians who held nationalities other than Haitian from exercising certain civil rights. They could not be members of Parliament, president or prime minister. Neither could they be members of the Electoral Council. Granted, a transitory article provided a grace period of two years from the publication of the Constitution for holders of other nationalities to reclaim their original Haitian status. Beyond that window of opportunity, anyone still holding a foreign citizenship would be barred from occupying elective or high appointive posts.

———

Although the Duvaliers' dictatorship had departed, power was still in the hands of those who had been part of the Duvalierist system. Although the CNG had banned the *Tontons-Macoute* as an organization, many individuals were not disarmed. Paramilitary groups flourished.

When the people overwhelmingly approved Haiti's post-dictatorship Constitution, the military government was not at all pleased. The eminently democratic charter reinforced civilian rule, thereby curtailing the military. Moreover, as previously mentioned, it restricted "fervent Duvalierists" from holding certain posts. The military who took over after Baby Doc didn't want elections. That wouldn't happen until later under the presidency of Ertha Pascal Trouillot.

When the CNG failed in its attempt to control the civilian Provisional Electoral Council (French acronym CEP), it decided to wreck the first post-Duvalier democratic elections. As the polls were about to open at 7:00 a.m. on November 29, 1987, bands of thugs, some in military uniform, attacked the voters at several polling stations with guns and machetes. Reportedly, thirty-four people were killed and seventy-five wounded. The Argentine School on Ruelle Vaillant in Port-au-Prince remains the symbol of the massacre planned by the CNG. That's where the majority of victims were found in a pool of blood.

Three hours after the opening of the polls, the CNG cancelled the balloting throughout the country. General Namphy, who headed the CNG, blamed the Electoral Council for the situation, asserting that the Council violated the Constitution by inviting foreigners as observers of the process. Thus, left-of-center Professor Gérard Gourgue was denied victory. He had been leading in all the polls.

The international community quickly condemned the violent action of the CNG. The Reagan Administration, which had been shoring up the military government, suspended economic and military aid to the regime and called for expeditious free and fair elections in Haiti.

The CNG quickly organized an election on January 17, 1988. Only one major political party, the *Rassemblement des Démocrates Nationaux Progressistes–RDNP* (Rally of Progressive National Democrats), participated in the sham election that elevated Professor Leslie Manigat to the presidency. Inaugurated February 7, 1988, he was ousted four months later in a coup by the same General Namphy who engineered his rise. Leslie Manigat and his family as well as several of his ministers were flown to exile in the Dominican Republic.

I had disavowed my friend Leslie for trampling on corpses to gain the presidency. Throughout his 133 days in power, we remained at odds. We reconciled when he came to New York a few months later. For once, I heard Professor Manigat say he was sorry. He had planned to outmaneuver the military to start a modern democracy, he said. They outmaneuvered him.

He died on June 27, 2014, at age 83, after a long illness complicated by chikungunya, a mosquito-transmitted virus. There was an outpouring of praise for the eminent intellectual that he was. The Haitian flag was flown at half-mast on all government buildings, and on July 7, he was given a State funeral at which the President of the country gave a moving eulogy. Four former presidents attended the ceremony.

Since the collapse of the dictatorship, Haiti was on coup mode. Three months after Namphy's coup, on September 17, General Prosper Avril overthrew him in a bloodless coup. It is this same Avril who had accompanied Jean-Claude Duvalier and his wife to the Port-au-Prince airport in the wee hours of February 7, 1986, when the couple fled to France. An influential and trusted member of Jean-Claude Duvalier's Palace Guard, Avril had more control of the Army than anyone.

Meeting him privately at his residence, I proposed that he should use his influence to undertake local elections throughout the country. I promised to use my contacts in the United States to find sister cities for the Haitian counterparts that undertook the local democratic elections. He could have prolonged his de facto administration if he were to adopt the local election formula. He told me he would consider it. But, Haitian officials, especially the military, swear by centralized authority, to the detriment of democratization.

Instead of elections, Prosper Avril was settling in for a long stay. A year had passed since his ouster of Namphy and nothing was mentioned about local or national elections. The United States was concerned about the unfolding of a military dictatorship. In September 1989, President George H. W. Bush named Alvin Adams Ambassador to Haiti. At his send-off meeting at the State Department, the seasoned career diplomat showed his knowledge of Creole by citing a proverb: *Bourik chaje pa kanpe.* (A loaded donkey doesn't wait around.) He meant he was in a hurry to get to his post. The *Haiti-Observateur* made a headline of this and the nickname of Ambassador Adams became *Bourik Chaje.*

In Haiti, President Avril got the hint. He responded with his own proverb: *Bourik twò chaje kouche.* (An overloaded donkey just lies down.) In effect, he was saying he will not cooperate. Haitian political observers understood that Ambassador Adams was on a mission to get rid of Avril. The American ambassador was very popular with Haitians of all strata, because he spoke Creole fluently. Moreover, he was seen as an ally of President Avril's opponents.

Under much pressure from the United States, President Avril relinquished power on March 10, 1990, to General Hérard Abraham, a diplomat/soldier who had been foreign minister in 1988. Abraham knew that he was only in an interim capacity while Ambassador Adams met with a group of Haitian notables to press for a return to civilian rule. On March 13 agreement was reached to apply the Haitian Constitution. It calls for the Chief Justice of the *Cour de Cassation,* as the Supreme Court is called, to fill the vacancy in absence of the President. But the Chief Justice, Gilbert Austin, was a devotee of President Avril, who had named him to the post. His assuming the presidency was considered a continuation of Avril. An agreement was reached to name the most junior Justice to the presidency. Thus did Mrs. Ertha Pascal Trouillot become Haiti's first female President.

Chapter 12

The First Democratic Elections

After four years of turbulence, Haiti was about to have a break and it was a woman who would make the difference. Ertha Pascal Trouillot was not interested in power for personal advantage. She had a mission to accomplish, that of organizing the first democratic elections in Haiti. Unlike those who assumed power since the flight of Baby Doc in 1986, she reached out to those beyond her immediate entourage to succeed in her gambit.

That's how I entered government service for the first time. Georges Rigaud came to see me in early April 1990 with a proposition. He told me his former colleague Kesler Clermont was the new foreign minister. He would like me to take charge of the Haitian Embassy in Washington. He said Clermont believed I could open doors for the new government in the United States and bring it credibility. "I will tell Kesler that you have accepted," Georges said. "Don't hesitate."

What could I say when Georges had already decided for me. We had been working together since the 1960s when he and Hubert Legros, Sr. had organized the underground which defied Papa Doc's intelligence network. They had trusted me with their life when we chose to work together so intimately during the rule of one of the most cruel despots in Haiti's violent history. An astute observer of human nature, Georges would not be leading me into error, I was sure. So, I said, "If you say so, Georges, who am I to say no? Yes, I accept, and will make you proud. Tell Minister Clermont he can call me."

The following week, I flew from New York to Port-au-Prince to meet with the foreign minister and President Trouillot. I had met Clermont before, but this was the first time I would be meeting Mrs. Trouillot. When Clermont arrived with me at the National Palace, we were ushered immediately into the President's office. She looked much younger than her 46 years then. Standing erect, with a gentle smile on her face, she gave me a handshake and said, "So, you are the famous Raymond Joseph I have heard so much about."

I smiled and said, "Yes, I am Raymond Joseph."

She motioned us toward a couch in her office and she sat on an erect chair. She came directly to the matter at hand. She was delighted, she said, to learn that I had accepted to represent the government in Washington. The government could not have better representation. "I am counting on you," she said.

"Excellency," I asked, "What is your goal?" Looking her straight in the eyes, I added, "I need to know for sure what I am going to present to my interlocutors in Washington and how to defend the government in case that is needed."

"My goal is to organize free, fair, and democratic elections by November and to get out of here," she said, without any hesitation.

Foreign Minister Clermont interjected, "Excellency, could you not say elections by the end of the year and out of here by February 7, 1991?"

"Exactly, well put, Mr. Clermont," she said.

I sensed sincerity in President Trouillot. For her, the priority was the elections in record time. Based on what she said, she had only eight months to accomplish that. A major feat, I thought, especially since the country had been in disarray following the collapse of the three-decades-old Duvalier dictatorship.

I asked whether she would authorize me to invite unarmed international election observers to witness the process.

"Whatever you can do, so that we may have free, fair and democratic elections, you are authorized to do," she said emphatically.

"I will do my best, Excellency. You may count on me."

When I arrived in Washington in late April, I found out that all the Embassy employees had been there ever since the Duvaliers. In other words, I would be dealing with people who owed their allegiance to the dictators I had been fighting over the years. I was warned especially about the acting Chargé d'Affaires, Louis Harold Joseph. "He will be the banana peel under your feet," I was told by someone who declared himself my unpaid adviser. I nodded, but paid no attention.

I worked with Harold Joseph and the staff that I had found. I must admit that he proved to be one of the best professionals in the Foreign Service. Had I asked for Harold's dismissal, my work in Washington would have been much more difficult. Harold was a computer savvy professional with extensive connections in town. He became an outstanding deputy who made my task much easier.

In assuming any task, I always review the situation and set three or four goals to reach in record time. I have found out that meeting certain benchmarks in the beginning of an operation, modest though they may be, sets the stage for eventual success. When I took over the Embassy in April 1990, the government was facing three major challenges:

1. American Airlines, the sole US carrier linking Haiti to New York and Miami at the time, had cancelled all flights to the Haitian capital. That resulted from an incident where a would-be terrorist had fired a gun inside an AA craft on the ground in Port-au-Prince.

2. The government was totally broke.
3. And the weekends were replete with rumors of coups d'état against President Trouillot.

May 1st was Agriculture and Labor Day, an official Haitian holiday. That meant the Embassy was closed. I came to work anyway, and was alone in the building. Without employees around, I was uninhibited to carry out a sensitive conversation. I placed a call to American Airlines headquarters in Dallas, Texas, and asked to speak to the person in charge of flight operations to Haiti. I advised him that I would be putting charter flights on the routes between the United States and Haiti. The country could not remain isolated, I said. In those days, air travelers from the United States to Haiti had to use detours to reach Port-au-Prince. One could go to Montreal to make connection; travel via the Dominican Republic or Puerto Rico where transfer to Air France or other carriers was possible.

That same evening, I received a telephone call from Alvin Adams, the American Ambassador in Port-au-Prince. He asked whether I was serious about putting charter flights on the American Airlines routes. "Of course, I am," I said. "You must agree that Haiti cannot remain isolated as it is now." The ambassador said he had excellent relations with American Airlines. He certainly would be able to solve the problem. I should leave that to him. "Thank you, Mr. Ambassador," I said.

Within two weeks, the problem was solved. American Airlines resumed its flights to Port-au-Prince. I chalked that up as my first victory.

In my second week in Washington, I placed a call to the State Department and asked for a meeting with the Haiti Desk officer. I broached the subject of the government which had run out of money even to pick up garbage. "I know the State Department likes the Lady President," I said. "But how can she succeed if she has no money for the basics?" I was asked to have the government's Minister of Finance contact USAID. The upshot of the story is that more than $30 million in food and cash were made available to the government. I chalked that up as a second victory.

The third problem was more complex. How do I deal with the rumors of coups d'état surfacing every weekend against the President? Every Friday one would hear that "this will be her last week." I telephoned Ambassador Adams and asked whether he could do me a favor. I would like his assistance in getting First Lady Barbara Bush to pay President Trouillot a visit in Port-au-Prince as soon as possible.

"Why do you ask?" Ambassador Adams said.

"I want to stop those weekend rumors of coups d'état against my President," I said. "If Mrs. Bush pays her a visit, I am sure that will put a stop to the coup rumors. Certainly, the plotters will know that if they touch the Lady President, they will have to deal with the US President. I really think the visit will serve as a major deterrent."

"Ray, we can do better than that," Ambassador Adams said. "Why don't we have President Trouillot visit President Bush at the Oval Office?"

"That would be ideal," I responded, "but I know that the visit of a foreign head of state to his American counterpart is not something that happens overnight. Usually, it takes months of preparations, isn't that so?"

"Leave that to me," Ambassador Adams said.

On May 24, 1990, a mere four weeks after I had arrived in Washington, President Trouillot was welcomed by President George W. H. Bush at the Oval Office. At my suggestion, all Haitian media were invited to cover the event. For the first time, Haitian journalists of all stripes entered the White House. That was the event not to miss.

It was a major coup when photos of Presidents Bush and Trouillot appeared on the front pages of major newspapers and were splashed on television screens everywhere. From Washington, President Trouillot went to New York before returning to Haiti. All rumors of coups d'état evaporated. And President Trouillot went about governing the country. She delivered the elections on time, as she had promised. They have remained the gold standard by which Haitian elections are measured.

My question to President Trouillot about foreign observers for the elections was based on my observation of Haitians, especially those from *l'arrière pays,* or bush country, as city folks often refer to the peasants in the hinterland. In general, they are among the most hospitable people I know. When you visit Haiti's countryside, you are struck by the courtesy of the people. Visitors from town, no matter their color, are offered the best by the hosts. One would never have thought that those country folks possessed such fine cutlery and beautifully embroidered tablecloths, which are displayed on such occasions. The best linen sheets adorn the bed in the master bedroom which is offered to the visitor. Also, when strangers are around, the people are on their best behavior. It is no time to pick fights.

Based on that observation of Haiti's peasantry, I believed that if we had foreign eyes and ears throughout Haiti before and during the vote, everything would be normal. For, I was traumatized, just as many others were, by the tragic events of November 29, 1987. As previously mentioned, on that day Haitians were massacred, shot down like fowl or hacked to death with machetes, while they were in line waiting to cast their ballots.

I had vehemently denounced the election-day massacre. "Never again shall this happen in my country," I said on several radio interviews and in editorials in the *Haiti-Observateur.* I think that my forceful denunciation of the savage acts may have been instrumental in my being recruited to accompany the government in the awesome task of organizing the first democratic elections in Haiti.

With the full support of President Trouillot's government, I worked diligently with the Organization of American States on an accord which called for unarmed foreign observers in Haiti for the upcoming elections. On September 3rd, 1990, I signed the first accord which had been negotiated with the secretary general of the

Organization of American States, Baena Soares. At the time I was both Haiti's representative at the OAS and Chargé d'Affaires to the United States.

The secretary general, a seasoned Brazilian diplomat, was anxious about the signing of the document. Although Monday, September 3rd, was Labor Day, an official holiday in the United States, he called me at my residence and suggested that we go to the office to sign the accord. He had learned that my government had authorized me to sign. I concurred. Baena Soares opened the office himself and the two of us signed. The following day, we sat officially for a photo souvenir with our respective staff standing behind us.

President Trouillot had also called on the United Nations and former President Carter to send observers for the elections. On October 12, 1990, the UN adopted a resolution similar to that of the OAS. President Carter confirmed that the Council of Elected Heads of Government and the National Democratic Institute for International Affairs (NDI) would also send election observers.

Convinced that the upcoming elections would be fair, Jean-Bertrand Aristide made his move. With the support of Father Antoine Adrien, of the former Brooklyn "Haitian Fathers," and other associates, Father Aristide pushed aside Professor Victor Benoit, who was the candidate of the *Front National pour le Changement et la Démocratie–FNCD* (The National Front For Change and Democracy). The priest had gained much popularity as a proponent of the Liberation Theology movement of the Catholic Church which was called *Ti Legliz* (Mini Church) in Haiti. Fusing *FNCD* with *Ti Legliz,* there was no stopping Aristide. He coasted to victory in the presidential election of December 16, 1990. The people did not even wait for the vote count to be announced when they took to the streets on the morning of December 17 to declare Jean-Bertrand Aristide the winner. Later it was said that he had won with 67 percent of the vote.

In the presidential race of 1990, *Haiti-Observateur* had supported the candidacy of Marc Bazin, Father Aristide's opponent. The
priest-politician never forgave the newspaper for its free choice. At
his first press conference in January 1991, after Roger Lafontant's
failed coup attempt, President-elect Aristide singled out Rodrigue
Louis, a reporter of the paper, for retribution. The reporter had
asked a pertinent question regarding the Archbishop of Port-au-
Prince, François Wolf Ligondé. "In the spirit of reconciliation," he
said, "will you ask your followers to stop their pursuit?" The prelate
was being sought by Aristide's hordes to inflict him the punishment
of necklacing.

Aristide had targeted the Archbishop for execution, because in
a prophetic sermon on January 1st, 1991, the head of the Catholic
Church in Haiti had denounced "the Bolsheviks" coming to power.
He went on to mention the dire plight that the country would face.
"The situation will be so bad that people will eat rocks," the prelate
said.

Instead of answering the reporter's legitimate question about the
archbishop, the president-elect, speaking in Creole and in a threatening tone, said, "You are from the *Observateur*, are you not?" All
cameras turned toward Rodrigue Louis. "For a long time," Aristide
continued, "the *Observateur* has been observing me and I have been
observing the *Observateur*. Today I am asking the Haitian people to
observe the *Observateur* with me."

Aristide's inflammatory response to the journalist was a veiled
call for reprisals against him and the newspaper he represented. My
brother Leo, who was then in charge of the publication, recounted
on front page the menacing words of the president-elect, and concluded: "Since our vocation is to observe, Mr. President-elect, we
will continue to observe you. However, if a hair falls off the head of
one of our reporters, you will be held accountable."

The reporter was probably shaking in his boots after hearing
Aristide's answer to his question. To his credit, Rotchild François, a

Me and my brother Leo.

The National Palace before the earthquake.

Former President Ertha Pascal Trouillot at the White
House with me in the background.

Former President Ertha Pascal Trouillot
on her inauguration day.

François "Papa Doc" Duvalier in his 40s.

Wedding of Jean-Claude Duvalier and Michèle Bennett.

Former President Bill Clinton and me.

The day I presented my credentials to President George W. Bush: from
left to right, my son Paul, his wife Velma, my wife Lola,
President Bush, my daughter Jackie, my sons Pierre and Andre.

Wyclef Jean held by his godmother Laurette with his
mom holding his baby brother Sam.

Wyclef and his godmother Laurette visiting me
at the Ambassador's residence in Washington.

Former President Bill Clinton with Elizabeth Préval.

Grandpa with two of his grandchildren,
Julien and Gabriel.

The Jalousie shantytown before its renovation.

The ruins of the Sans Souci Palace in Milot.

courageous journalist, approached Rodrigue Louis after the press conference and offered to accompany him wherever he was going. The two walked out together. Immediately, Rodrigue went into hiding. Weeks later, when his car was defiled one evening with human excrements spread over it, we knew it was time to prepare his escape. The *Haiti-Observateur* obtained a US visa for him. He was spirited out of Haiti. He joined the staff at the weekly's headquarters in Brooklyn.

A few days after the December 16, 1990, electoral victory of Jean-Bertrand Aristide, I wrote a resignation letter to President Trouillot. I felt that my mission of helping with fair and democratic elections had been accomplished. Moreover, sensing what type of presidency was about to emerge, I knew that I could not collaborate with that team.

President Trouillot did not respond officially, but she telephoned me and said I should wait the arrival of her successor to tender my resignation. She said Washington is too important a post for me to leave at that juncture. The resignation, she continued, could also be misinterpreted by the newly elected president as a sign of discontent on my part, because he had won. I agreed to stay.

I did not go to Port-au-Prince on February 7, 1991, for the inauguration of the new president, as some people close to him had expected. Through my sources I had found out that plans were in the works to have me arrested on arrival in the capital. In their intimate circles, the close aides of the president-elect had discussed my alleged participation in the attempted coup d'état of Roger Lafontant against President Trouillot to derail the inauguration of President Aristide. On what basis did they reach that conclusion?

Late in the evening of January 6, 1991, a reliable source in Port-au-Prince had contacted me in Washington to say that Roger Lafontant had kidnapped President Trouillot at her home in the Christ Roi neighborhood of the capital. She was being driven in an armored car to the Palace where she would be forced to formally resign. I was also told that Lafontant had the backing of the Armed Forces.

Meanwhile, I received a telephone call from Fritz Longchamp who, at the time, headed the Haiti Office in Washington, a lobby that was heavily influenced by Father Antoine Adrien and his group, "The Haitian Fathers."

"What's happening in Port-au-Prince?" Longchamp asked.

"I don't know yet, but I will get back to you as soon as I find out," I said.

Immediately, I telephoned President Trouillot on her secure line. She did not answer. So, I presumed that indeed she had been kidnapped. I telephoned General Hérard Abraham, the commander of the Armed Forces, at his home. His telephone was engaged. I assumed that at least he was at home and not with the group heading to the Palace. My third telephone call was to US Ambassador Adams at his office. I figured that if the situation was indeed what I had been told, Ambassador Adams would be at his post.

"What's up, Ray?" the Ambassador asked, calmly.

"Is it true what I hear about Roger Lafontant's coup d'état? That he has President Trouillot with him and that he also has the support of General Abraham?"

"Yes, it is true that he has kidnapped the President and has entered the Palace with about a dozen men," the Ambassador said. "He doesn't have Abraham with him," he added. "The general is working with me. We could go up to the Palace tonight and arrest them all, but we don't want to break any lights. We are just waiting for morning to pick them up without any trouble. Don't worry about anything. You may go with that story."

I asked about the whereabouts of Father Aristide.

"Don't worry about him, he's safe and sound," the Ambassador affirmed.

On hanging up with Ambassador Adams, I called Fritz Longchamp to tell him not to worry about the president-elect. I knew that he was much concerned about the safety of the priest-president.

Then I placed calls to two or three newspapers, including the *New York Times* and a Mexican daily. I told them that the attempted coup in Haiti had failed and that I could be quoted as the source of the information. The first edition of the *Times* on January 7 carried the news. So did the Mexican daily. The news of the failed coup became the main event, even before Roger Lafontant and his associates were arrested.

In the morning of January 7, Aristide's supporters took to the streets with machetes, knives, and sticks. In a generalized frenzy, they killed more than seventy presumed *Tontons-Macoute* and people considered to be followers of Lafontant. Publicly, President-elect Aristide boasted that the people had defeated the *Macoutes* and caused the collapse of the coup. However, privately it was being said among Aristide's close aides that Raymond Joseph stole the victory of the people. How so? Long before dawn when the mobs took to the streets on the 7th, I had already announced the failure of the coup. On that basis alone, I was marked for arrest whenever I landed in Port-au-Prince. God knows what my fate would have been.

That initial action of President Aristide and his followers soured many, including some important sectors of the international community. He was seen as no different from the violent regimes that preceded him. Unofficially, some Washington officials told me the President-elect has chosen the wrong path. This would be evident shortly.

On inauguration day, I sent a congratulatory note in my name and that of the employees of the Embassy of Haiti to the Palace and the Ministry of Foreign Affairs. I stayed put in Washington. Later, I learned that President Aristide had remarked that I was tipped off about what was awaiting me. Information is a powerful tool. It had saved my life more than once.

On February 7, 1991, President Aristide showed his true colors. He misbehaved egregiously. Instead of receiving the presidential sash from President Trouillot, he had a Voodoo priestess place it over his head and shoulder. He asked the Justice Minister to serve warrant papers on outgoing President Trouillot for her alleged involvement in the Lafontant coup. She rightly refused to accept them. Against military regulations, he ordered a realignment of the Army at the top. That is the prerogative of the Commander of the Armed Forces.

Most telling to me, however, was his incendiary remarks in the course of his inaugural speech. One of the proverbs he evoked signaled that his presidency would be characterized by misery and destruction. *"Wòch nan dlo pral konnen* **doulè** *wòch nan solèy,"* he thundered. ("Stones in [the freshness of] the water will now know the **pain** of stones in the sun.") To me, it meant that he was about to spread Haiti's misery and poverty at all levels. Haiti's "haves," enjoying the freshness of the water, will be like the "have-nots," also suffering under the hardship of the sun. President Aristide could have been more positive by saying: *"Wòch nan solèy pral konnen* **dousè** *wòch nan dlo."* ("Stones in the sun will now know the **freshness** of stones in the water.") By his words and actions on the first day of his ascension to power the President had set the stage for confrontation. I wanted out of the Embassy as soon as possible.

On April 4, not yet two months in power, President Aristide ordered the arrest of his predecessor for her complicity in the Roger Lafontant coup. International pressure on Aristide, including a telephone call from President Bush, brought about her release the next day. But she was kept under house arrest. On April 11, the US Embassy in Port-au-Prince issued a statement expressing surprise at the continued status of President Trouillot. And Aristide's government protested against interference in Haiti's internal affairs. Obviously, US relations with the new government were anything but friendly.

Since I had already written my letter of resignation, I kept reminding the Ministry of Foreign Affairs of my status by signing my weekly reports *"Chargé d'Affaires démissionaire."* (Interim Chargé d'Affaires) The government acted as if I were non-existent.

My reports were not even acknowledged. Then, a sensitive situation arose which required that I speak directly to the director general at the Ministry of Foreign Affairs.

A few days after the incident surrounding Mrs. Trouillot's arrest, I received a telephone call from a person in Canada who said he represented the "Group Mercoux," which was helping the government solve the perennial problem of electrical blackouts. The person asked if I was not aware of the problem that the government faced in securing about three million dollars to buy electric turbines that would quickly ease the power shortages.

Yes, I knew about the problem of constant electrical blackouts, but I was not aware of the government's search for funds and the rebuff it had encountered. However, I was not about to discuss any such matter over the telephone with someone I did not know. He said he was working with the ministries of Public Works and Foreign Affairs in Haiti. "Okay," I said, "Have them contact me directly."

Immediately after I ended the call with the person from Canada, I telephoned the Ministry of Foreign Affairs. The minister being absent, I asked to speak to the director general, Jean-Marie Chérestal. He was delighted that I had called to confirm the *bona fide* of the Canadian contact. Could I do something, he inquired. I asked him to send me a memo authorizing me to undertake any action for a quick disbursement on the part of USAID. For, as Chérestal explained, the Swiss and Canadian governments, which were implicated in the dossier, had placed restrictions on making any disbursement.

By this time it was late Thursday afternoon. I told Chérestal that Washington is a town that operates on a Tuesday to Thursday schedule, with Mondays and Fridays being "iffy days." Meanwhile, there was a Monday deadline for the Haitian authorities to act. Otherwise, they would lose the turbines to Kuwait whose cash was readily available.

Once I knew that it was a legitimate affair, I did not wait for the authorization note from the director general. I called the State Department which referred me to USAID. I explained the predicament of the government which was in a bind for three million dollars. I reasoned with my interlocutor that this was a great opportunity for the United States to show that the American government was ready to work with the new Haitian government, especially since rumors had spread that Washington was hostile to the new president.

The USAID official told me exactly what I had explained to Chérestal. Time was against us, because nothing could be accomplished on such a short notice. As for the amount of money involved, that is very little and could be found in Port-au-Prince, he said. But to get things done by Monday was a major challenge. I referred him to the Foreign Office in Port-au-Prince to follow through.

Sometime on Tuesday, Chérestal spoke to me and said, "Mr. Joseph, you are a real patriot." I asked why such a compliment. He told me that the Americans had released the funds to the Haitian government that morning. Unfortunately, Kuwait had paid for the turbines the day before.

"You will tell me I am a patriot only privately," I responded. "There is no way you will repeat that publicly." I added, "I really feel bad that I was not involved in the negotiations much earlier. Consider how I feel when it's a foreigner who is contacting me about the plight of my government. We did not have to lose such a great opportunity to solve the electricity crisis." I never received the authorization that I had requested from Jean-Marie Chérestal to undertake the negotiations with the US officials in Washington. Probably, his superiors did not want to go on record as having requested anything from me.

Early in April 1991, I received a communication from the Ministry of Foreign Affairs to the effect that "the President has regretfully accepted your resignation." Since there was no indication as to whom I should turn over the responsibilities, I sent a note to the Ministry inquiring "to whom should I give the keys?" I never received a response.

The following day, my deputy, Louis Harold Joseph, came to show me a letter the Ministry had written to him asking that he get the keys from me.

"Fine," I said, "I will clear my desk soon."

"Oh no, Chargé," Harold told me, "Take your time. Do it in a week or more."

After an audit and a final report, I cleared out of Washington and returned to New York. Before I left, Etzer Racine, a former consul general in New York who had joined my staff in Washington, told me that I would be the ideal person to stand up to the whims of the new president who had started his administration on the wrong footing. "You can already see their style," Racine said. "They are branding anyone who opposes them with the *Macoute* etiquette. I count on you to stand up to the priest-president, because they cannot pin that etiquette on you."

But they did. That's another story.

Chapter 13

Squandered Opportunities: Aristide's Presidency

A s the first president to be popularly elected in a democratic post-Duvalier election, Jean-Bertrand Aristide represented a break with the dictatorship and its remnants. But in action and word, the Catholic priest of the Salesian Order had lost his way from the very beginning of his rule. He never succeeded in ushering in the era of democracy that was expected. On the contrary, his administration must be characterized as one of squandered opportunities.

On leaving Washington, I went back to the *Haiti-Observateur* in Brooklyn with the determination to counteract the new president. Even before my return to the paper, my brother Leo had begun to warn the new leader about his unpopular decisions which could spell greater trouble down the road. For example, before President Aristide ordered the arrest of President Trouillot, the paper had warned against that decision. The *Observateur* was accused of manufacturing the information. Nonetheless, President Aristide went on with his plan and arrested the former president, as previously mentioned. We know the rest of the story. As predicted by the *Observateur*, President Aristide had to back down and release Mrs. Trouillot.

Based on the saying that a picture is worth one thousand words, I asked one of our cartoonists to draw the face of Jean-Bertrand Aristide on the body of a scorpion that was stinging itself. It's in the nature of the scorpion to poison itself whenever it runs out of options. To accompany the drawing, the following legend appeared at the bottom of the cartoon: *Observera bien qui observera le dernier.* (The last observer will have the best view.) It is a parody of the French saying *Rira bien qui rira le dernier.* (The last laugh is the best laugh.) That was our response to the president-elect's threat to the reporter of the paper at the January press conference: "I have been observing the *Observateur* for a long time. Now I am asking the people to observe the *Observateur* with me!"

Although the cartoonists usually signed their work, that time the *Haiti-Observateur* assumed full responsibility. So, it was an unsigned cartoon—and for good reason. The new authorities had begun to use thugs against their critics. When we first published a half page of the cartoon, we received threatening calls in New York from the fanatics of *Lavalas,* as Aristide's party is called. True to their name, the *Lavalassians* (from flood, or torrent) felt insulted that their leader was presented as a suicidal scorpion. They were ready to tear us to pieces. That did not deter us from continuing with the cartoon which became a regular occurrence on the pages of the weekly. We used it as fillers whenever there was a dead spot in a page, reducing it to a quarter of a page, an eighth, or even a sixteenth.

After the general uprising which forced President Aristide to flee Haiti on February 29, 2004, the scorpion was published for the last time on front page, with all eight feet up. The legend, in Spanish, said, "*Se murió El Scorpion.*" ("The Scorpion is dead!")

Another famous cartoon that I inspired was the rooster that had lost its spurs. When President Aristide went to the United Nations General Assembly in New York in September 1991, the *Haiti-Observateur* published the cartoon of a rooster without its spurs in the edition that appeared September 25. The legend, in Creole, stated: *Tonnè! Sapatonn mwen rache!* (Damn it! My fighting spurs are gone!) It was a warning of impending doom for the president who faced a major plot to oust him.

The president must have been on Cloud 9 after his extravagant show-off at the UN where he displayed his linguistic prowess by citing phrases in several languages, including Creole and Hebrew. On landing in Port-au-Prince on September 27, President Aristide sent word from the airport, apologizing to the Diplomatic Corps that was waiting his arrival at the Palace. The diplomats could leave, because he would not be arriving on time. Instead, he went to *Cité Soleil,* the sprawling shantytown north of the capital, to be acclaimed by the masses that were totally devoted to him.

Aware, finally, of the plot to oust him, President Aristide was preparing for war. He made the infamous speech in which he unleashed the masses against the bourgeoisie. "*When the heat of the sun is too much under the soles of your feet,*" he said, "*lift up your heads to the highlands!*" And in a recurring refrain, in a staccato style, he shouted, "*Ale-ba-yo-sa-yo-merite!*" ("Go-give-them-what-they-deserve!") He also made reference to "*the smart instrument, which smells so good when it burns!*" There was no mistaking the instrument to which he alluded. The forthcoming aroma of *Père Lebrun,* the burning tire around the neck of victims, seemed to have sent the priest-president into a trance. Obviously, President Aristide had ordered the slaughter of the bourgeoisie.

The September 27 speech sealed President Aristide's doom. The Army decided that he had overstepped his bounds. He must go. For, in effect, he had declared civil war in the country.

Although General Raoul Cédras, who headed the Army at the time, would bear responsibility for the coup against Aristide, the lead instigator and organizer was Colonel Joseph Michel François. He was commander of the Police unit at the "Cafétéria," the police station in downtown Port-au-Prince. The late Colonel Philippe Biamby, an aide of General Cédras, was the third member of the triumvirate that assumed responsibility for the coup. They said the democratically elected president had become a terrorist who threatened the peace of the country.

On the night of September 29, the President was captured at his private home in Tabarre, but not before he allegedly ordered the assassination of Roger Lafontant in his jail cell at the National Penitentiary. And not before his goons had captured Pastor Sylvio Claude in Cayes. The popular leader of the *Christian Democratic Party of Haiti* (PDCH) was tortured and necklaced, *Lavalas-style.*

General Cédras acted forcefully to spare the life of President Aristide. Then, President Carlos Andres Perez of Venezuela dispatched an aircraft to Port-au-Prince to transport the deposed chief to safety in Caracas. Venezuela, in accord with the OAS charter, was determined to reverse the coup against President Aristide. Recently, the hemispheric organization had adopted a resolution protecting elected presidents against military coups. Aristide would have been the first to benefit from that governance insurance policy.

Venezuelan troops under the command of a general were ready to return President Aristide to Port-au-Prince on Friday, October 5th. A meeting of the OAS Permanent Council was scheduled for Wednesday evening, October 3rd, in Washington to put the finishing touches and the seal of approval on the Venezuelan invasion plan of Haiti. But the September 27 speech of President Aristide urging his partisans to "go-give-them-what-they-deserve" caused the derailment of the hasty return of the democratically elected president-turned-terrorist.

The *Haiti-Observateur* was the only publication that had published President Aristide's Creole speech in its October 3rd edition. Some diplomats in Washington who were alerted to the incendiary speech contacted the paper that same day and requested an English translation in a hurry. We obliged. When the deliberators took their seats at the OAS main hall that Wednesday evening, a copy of the speech was in front of every delegate. On reading the speech, it was obvious to all that a return of President Aristide to Port-au-Prince at that time would have resulted in a major bloodbath. The democratically elected president needed to be schooled in Democracy before returning to his rightful place in Port-au-Prince. The Venezuelan invasion plan was put on ice.

The stay of President Aristide in Venezuela would not be for long. By March 1992, he arrived in Washington, where he remained until October 15, 1994. Some say he went to Washington to be schooled in democracy before he could be returned to Haiti. Nonetheless, he was widely considered—and treated—as the legitimate President of Haiti.

President Aristide used that legitimacy to undertake a campaign for his return to power in Port-au-Prince.

With his legitimacy, President Aristide assumed control of millions of dollars in royalties from international telephone companies doing business with Haiti. He also consolidated the issuance of passports to Haitian citizens living abroad at the Embassy of Haiti in Washington.

Flush with cash, unrestricted and unaccounted for, the president was well poised financially to press the military triumvirate in Haiti to vacate power. One of Aristide's actions against Haiti was the declaration of an embargo to force out the military. I had denounced the embargo, arguing that it would hobble Haiti's economy for years to come. But the exiled President made his will stick.

Meanwhile, Haiti's military mounted a sophisticated contraband operation with the help of their Dominican neighbors to frustrate the embargo. While the population suffered the impact of that measure, the leaders of Haiti and their supporters hardly felt its effects. To strengthen their grip, the military hid behind puppet civilian presents. In the three years of Aristide's exile, three provisional or acting presidents were installed: Joseph Nérette, Marc Bazin, and Emile Jonassaint.

Through the *Haiti-Observateur*, I campaigned forcefully against the return of President Aristide at any cost. I alienated some powerful bodies, such as the Congressional Black Caucus and Pan Africa, that were totally devoted to the Haitian president. It was Congresswoman Maxine Waters (Democrat of California) who spearheaded the fight on behalf of President Aristide. I held to the position that an eventual return of Aristide would result in political disaster.

The election of President Clinton in November 1992 was a boost to those who were clamoring for the return of the president to Haiti. An audience with President Clinton at the Oval Office was secured for President Aristide in March 1993. His partisans went wild, because to them this meant that the return was imminent. However, having been fully briefed about Aristide, the recently inaugurated President Clinton was not yet ready to undertake the risky task of deploying US troops to return the priest-president to Port-au-Prince.

Meanwhile, President Aristide decided to intensify the flow of Haitian refugees to the United States. After his overthrow in September 1991, there was a debut of boat people leaving Haiti. By 1993, the numbers increased as thousands took to sea. They were coming to the US to be with Aristide. That's when the exiled president surreptitiously began financing boat building operations in Haiti.

His underground supporters recruited passengers, some of whom were paid, to travel to the United States. The people were trained to denounce the deteriorating political situation in Haiti since the overthrow of their *Father Titid*, as the priest was affectionately called. Now they wanted to join him in America. Most of those would-be newcomers to the United States ended at the Guantanamo Naval Base where their increasing numbers became a political hot potato for President Clinton. There were thousands of Haitians housed in two tent camps at the base located at the eastern tip of Cuba. When questioned, they said they would go back to Haiti when President Aristide returned.

All kinds of strategies and tactics were being used to build support for President Aristide's return home. In that light several attempts were made to get me to some public meetings where the president was officially invited. I always found a reason not to appear, because I knew of the plan devised for President Aristide to throw his arms around me publicly, as if he had finally found a long lost brother with whom he was making up. Mind you, Aristide was being advised about how to deal with his opponents, how he should show himself as a bridge builder; that it isn't true that he holds grudges. Since I was among his lead critics, he wanted to show that he could work even with me. But I knew him to be a chameleon.

I almost got roped in when the Caribbean American Chamber of Commerce and Industry (CACCI) hosted him in New York. CACCI's president, Grenada-born Roy Hastick, had invited me to be a charter member of CACCI in 1984 when we first met at the New York office of Governor Mario Cuomo at the World Trade Center. That was even before the formal launch of CACCI in 1985. For years I was an active CACCI board member. Roy presumed that since my president was coming to town at the invitation of CACCI, I certainly should be there in my capacity of a board member. I told Roy that I would like to come but as a journalist from the *Haiti-Observateur*. If I went as a board member, I would be sitting on the dais, probably next to Aristide, because I'm one of his compatriots. It would have been a great photo op, as if he were in intimate conversation with me.

The event was closed to the press, he told me. In that case, I declined the invitation. Aristide had refused to meet me when I was in Haiti while he was a priest at St. Jean Bosco. Twice, he told friends who tried to set up a meeting for me that he has nothing to do with a "reactionary." My being anti-communist didn't sit well with him. Now, as president-in-exile, he wanted to meet me on his own terms, in a way that would show him as a conciliator. If he really wanted to meet me, he would have done so when he went to Brooklyn to visit Benjamin Dupuy, the chief editor and publisher of the *Haiti-Progrès*, the leftist weekly that wholeheartedly embraced his cause. Considering that the *Haiti-Observateur* was also based in Brooklyn, the president could have killed two birds with one stone by stopping at the office of our weekly at the Brooklyn Navy Yard.

The pressure for President Aristide's return to Port-au-Prince was such that President Clinton caved in. Former Majority Whip in the US House of Representatives and CEO of the United Negro Fund, the late Congressman William H. Gray, replaced career diplomat Lawrence Pezzullo as coordinator of the "Haiti Working Group" at the State Department. It was a clear signal that the powerful Afro-American political establishment had succeeded in forcing the Clinton administration to change its policy regarding Aristide. In his book, *Plunging into Haiti: Clinton, Aristide, and the Defeat of Diplomacy*, Ralph Pezzullo, the son of the ambassador, deals amply with the blunders of the Clinton administration in equating Aristide with democracy and dispatching more than 20,000 US troops to reinstate "democracy" in Haiti.

Randall Robinson, founder and CEO of Trans-Africa, decided to stage a twenty-seven-day hunger strike to force the Clinton administration to make a decision about the Haitian refugees and to return President Aristide to Haiti. He obtained what he sought. All the refugees would no longer be lumped into the "economic" category. Interviews at sea would attempt to differentiate those fleeing political persecution. More yet, President Clinton ordered that an invasion plan of Haiti be readied, in case the military who had overthrown the president refused to vacate power on their own.

Robinson lost thirteen pounds during his hunger strike. But his sacrifice was not in vain. His wife, Hazel Ross-Robinson, was an adviser to President Aristide. Her consulting firm, Ross-Robinson & Associates, reaped $1.3 million for lobbying activities. Records of US Justice Department reveal that from 1991 to 2004, President Aristide paid a total of $18.2 million in lobbying fees.*

The most spectacular sign of the impending return of President Aristide was his visit to the Pentagon, September 21, 1994, to receive a 21-gun salute. Surrounded by top US officials, the former anti-imperialist firebrand was honored by the "imperialist" High Command, including Defense Secretary William Perry and General John Shalikashvili, chairman of the Joint Chiefs of Staff. He said "thank you." He had surrendered publicly to those he had vilified so furiously when, in a sermon at St. Jean Bosco, he declared, "Capitalism is a mortal sin." The show at the Pentagon was like his graduation after completing his major in Democracy. I maintained, however, that he had failed the "Democracy 101" course. That became evident when he returned to power in Port-au-Prince.

The Clinton administration deployed about 23,000 troops in operation "Uphold Democracy," that is the return of Jean-Bertrand Aristide to Haiti. On October 15, 1994, flanked by US executive and congressional officials, as well as by dignitaries of the Organization of American States, President Aristide landed in Port-au-Prince. The military who had overthrown him, personified by Raoul Cédras, Philippe Biamby and Joseph Michel François, had already been flown to exile in Panama and Honduras.

A month before the triumphant return of President Aristide, US forces had landed in Haiti to set up the security apparatus to receive the man who symbolized democracy. On the actual day of the return, Haitians had cleaned up the capital. The supporters of the President swept the streets clean and freshly painted their dwellings, even the shacks of the vast *Cité Soleil* shantytown. There was no

---

*Source: http://www.haitipolicy.org/lobbying7.htm

doubt that the people wanted their "savior" back, even if he had to come in the belly of the *Zwazo Mechan* (Wicked Birds or Vultures), as Aristide and the Haitian leftists used to call the Americans.

========

As soon as President Aristide set foot in the country, he began plotting for a long stay in power, perhaps for life, even indirectly. Using his executive powers, in January 1995, he decreed the dismantling of the Armed Forces, including the rural constabulary. It was an act of vengeance because the Army had overthrown him three years earlier.

This unconstitutional action left the country unprotected. A Police force in its infancy was not yet ready to provide security to the citizens. This was of no concern to the anti-imperialist firebrand, because his protection was entrusted to the American military. That responsibility would be transferred later to United Nations troops.

To fill the vacuum that he had created when he illegally disbanded the Armed Forces, President Aristide set up private militias that eventually turned into the infamous *chimères* (shadowy gangs) that caused havoc in Haiti. Their distinctive names paralleled their actions. Among them, *Lame Dòmi Nan Bwa* (Sleep in the Woods Army), *Lame Bale Wouze* (Clean Sweep Army), *Lame Wouj* (Red Army) and *Lame Sadanm Ousenn* (Saddam Hussein Army). They had carved out sections of the country where they operated under the command of local warlords. Unlike the Army, which had a structured chain of command and a central authority, the "gangs" that sprung up under Aristide were not coordinated. Their commanders were local chiefs who imposed themselves by sheer force. The most feared of these "armies" was the self-proclaimed *Lame Kanibal* (Cannibal Army) which ruled Gonaïves, the capital of the Artibonite region in north-central Haiti, where independence was officially declared on January 1, 1804.

Aristide's disbanding of the Armed Forces had nothing to do with reform of the corps. There could have been reform by dealing with the rotten oranges, not by throwing out the whole basket. Three military officers—Raoul Cédras, Philippe Biamby and Michel François—were blamed for the coup. They and their close aides should have been removed. After World War II, the defeated Nazi Army was not disbanded, but reformed. That helped bring order to Germany. But in Iraq, where the Army was disbanded, the insurgency flourished. The United States had to rebuild that army. The lingering security problems in Iraq are in great part the result of the shortsighted policy of disbanding the Iraqi Armed Forces.

Without being apologetic for the excesses of the Haitian Army and its rural branch, the *Police Rurale*, we must admit that a certain order was kept in the country. That same Army had provided security nationwide for the democratic elections of December 16, 1990, won decisively by Candidate Aristide. The officer in charge of providing the security net for those elections was Colonel Cédras. He had carried his duties so admirably that on the day of his inauguration as President, Jean-Bertrand Aristide catapulted him, against all norms and regulations, to become head of the Armed Forces.

Although the Constitution forbade it, President Aristide began preparations to run for reelection in 1995. The charter provides for two five-year non-consecutive terms for president. Aristide argued that his first term had been aborted after he was in power for only eight months. But, as already shown, the international community, especially the United States that had brought him back with 23,000 troops, asserted that he never lost presidential recognition—and prerogatives—during his three years in exile. He had to abide by the Constitution. Whereupon, President Aristide designated René Préval, his first prime minister in 1991, to run for president. As self-styled president of the *Lavalas Family* Party, Aristide is the supreme authority in choosing candidates for various posts, especially for president. In effect, he set himself up as a party dictator and it remains so till now. Behind the scene, Aristide controlled the State's apparatus.

On September 12, 1996, the US State Department dispatched armed security to Haiti to disband the security detail that President Aristide had left to protect President Préval. Joseph Moïse and his deputy Milien Romage were immediately dismissed. More than twenty others were let go from the security detail during the course of a week. And US security personnel, in civilian clothes, provided protection for President Préval until he had reorganized his own Palace security.

There was never an official explanation of this show of force by the American authorities. However, unofficially, it was said that an assassination of President Préval was being planned by the security detail left behind by Aristide. If successful, the plot had called for major demonstrations by the people who would have asked for the return to power of their beloved *Titid*.

Three years into Préval's presidency, he was still not in full control of security. The assassination attempt on his sister, Marie-Claude Calvin, attests to that. In the afternoon of January 12, 1999, Mrs. Calvin, who was her brother's personal secretary, was leaving work at the Palace when assailants on a motorcycle peppered her vehicle with bullets. Her chauffeur was killed and she suffered several wounds, fortunately none fatal. She was flown to Cuba for immediate care. The ambush, it should be noted, took place only one block from the Palace.

President Préval was thwarted in conducting an investigation into the circumstances surrounding the attempt against the life of his sister. Privately, it was said that the assailants had the protection of the real power in Haiti—President Aristide.

Another example of President Préval's limitations was his inability to conduct an investigation into the assassination of Jean Dominique and his security guard Jean-Claude Louissaint. A crusading journalist, Dominique was the President's friend. On April 3, 2000, as he arrived at his Radio Haiti Inter station, he was peppered with bullets and died instantly. The spectacular crime remains a mystery, although it was perpetrated in broad daylight in the courtyard of the station, on the well-traveled Delmas Boulevard. Thus, even after four years in office, President Préval was hamstrung in conducting an investigation into the murder of such an eminent personality. I am told that President Préval was warned that such an investigation could destabilize his government.

Who would have thought that Jean Dominique, affectionately nicknamed Jean-Do, would have met such an ignominious fate under a *Lavalas* government? He had fought against the dictatorships of the two Duvaliers and the military that succeeded them. He had gone into exile twice and had last returned to Haiti when President Aristide was brought back in 1994. His powerful advocacy in behalf of *Lavalas* made him an architect of the regime. But in his popular broadcasts over Radio Haiti Inter, without actually naming names, Jean Dominique had begun to forcefully criticize the excesses of the *Lavalas* authorities, especially of President Aristide. It was rumored also that the fearless radio personality would be a presidential candidate in the upcoming elections that were to consecrate a second victory of the former priest turned conniving politician.

People close to Aristide, including his former chief of Police and Senator Dany Toussaint, were suspects in the killing of the popular broadcaster. But nothing could be done against them. Some say that President Aristide had never forgiven Jean Dominique for his broadcast of December 16, 1996. The fearless journalist had denounced corruption and accused Aristide of embracing Haiti's "big oligarchy" which he said was responsible for the country's ills.

President Aristide could have pushed to have the crime solved when he assumed power again in 2001. That was never done. Neither did President Préval do anything when he became president a second time in 2006. In 2014, under President Martelly, the investigation into the assassination of Jean Dominique was reopened.

Some people close to President Aristide have been indicted, but most are abroad, away from the reach of Haitian Justice.

On April 30, 2014, the Argentine Police arrested Markington Philippe on an Interpol warrant for his participation in the murder of Jean Dominique. Philippe, considered a key witness in the assassination, had been living for many years in Argentina where he sought refuge. At the request of the Haitian authorities, he was extradited to Haiti where he arrived on June 21. Officers of the Judiciary police grabbed and handcuffed him as he deplaned. As of writing, no trial had been held.

When Aristide was reelected to succeed his puppet president in December 2000, he reportedly won with 92 percent of the vote. However, disillusioned by their former idol, the majority of Haitians had boycotted the vote. Voter participation had been estimated at less than 10 percent in the elections for Aristide's second coming. The international community, led by the United States, withheld economic aid to the regime.

Then the president began finding resistance in his own camp. Eventually, the gangs that he had set up to provide security in the absence of the Armed Forces spelled his undoing. The assassination of Amiot Métayer, leader of the *Cannibal Army* in Gonaïves, added fuel to a rebellion that was simmering for a while. Métayer had disappeared September 20, 2003, when he was supposedly lured into a meeting by an alleged representative of President Aristide. Two days later he was found dead with his eyes yanked out. The picture, splashed on the Internet, became a warning to other gang leaders who had become powerful local warlords, independent of any central authority. In other words, Aristide had lost control of the armed groups he had sponsored.

Several of the warlords defected and joined the violent opposition led by underground officers of the disbanded Haitian Army. With the civilian Group 184, or G-184, in the lead, the days of President Aristide were numbered.

The lavish preparations for the celebration of Haiti's 200th anniversary of independence on January 1, 2004, in Gonaïves, were marred by violence. Of the eminent foreign guests invited to the event, only South African President Thabo Mbeki came, but he failed to attend the official ceremony. His helicopter reportedly came under fire from undisclosed sources. Apparently, President Mbeki was aware of the delicate situation, because a South African navy ship was in Haitian waters during his stay in the country. And a South African cargo plane loaded with arms bound for Haiti was stopped in Jamaica and returned to South Africa. Definitely, President Aristide was under siege.

On February 29, 2004, President Aristide was whisked out of Haiti ahead of street battles that would have proved bloody in Port-au-Prince. The rebels were closing in from the Plateau Central area, Haiti's highland region to the east of the capital. US troops, under a UN mandate, came ashore to reinstate order. Three months later, the Americans relinquished leadership to the United Nations. Until now, the UN peace mission, named MINUSTAH, is in Haiti. In June 2013, UN Secretary General Ban Ki Moon named a Trinidadian diplomat, Sandra Honoré, to be the civilian head of the force whose largest military contingent is composed of Brazilians.

President Aristide was forced out by a popular uprising. The international community had saved him from certain death. Forget the accusations of kidnapping by the United States, Canada, and France. There is plenty of evidence that President Aristide was preparing his escape. But he feared the negative fallout from his followers who would consider him a coward. Hence, the propaganda campaign to make a victim of the man who brought upon himself the wrath of some of his former staunch supporters.

I wrote a column, March 12, 2004, in the *New York Sun* where I mentioned the complicity of President Aristide in his alleged kidnapping. Three weeks before his "kidnapping," his in-laws landed in Miami. They had a house in the Sunshine State. On the Wednesday prior to the "kidnapping," the two underage daughters of the Aristide couple, together with their French nanny, left Port-au-Prince with a one-way ticket to Miami to join their grandparents who had ample time to prepare their nest.

Then in the wee hours of February 29, a well-dressed President Aristide and his wife Mildred Trouillot arrived at the Port-au-Prince airport aboard a vehicle of the US Embassy in the company of the Chargé d'Affaires Luis Moreno. Several suitcases were loaded on the US Air Force jet idling on the tarmac. The couple boarded for an unknown destination, which happened to be Bangui, the capital of the Central African Republic. That was courtesy of the French government which had coaxed the leadership of its former colony to receive, if momentarily, the eminent visitors. So, I contend if there was a kidnapping, President Aristide was complicit in the elaborate plot.

Chapter 14

The Power of the Haitian Vote in America

While Haitians were having problems at home setting up a democracy they were making headway in America. In the 1960s, many Haitians fled to America by the thousands as a result of the Duvalier dictatorship. Many of them landed in New York. They showed no interest in the politics of their new land. In fact, the politics they had left behind had soured most.

Fiercely nationalistic, Haitians needed to settle in and undergo a change in mentality before they could get involved in the politics of their adopted country. At first they were reluctant to change their nationality. For many, their coming to America was supposedly for a short stay. The immigrant wave of the '60s comprised mainly professionals and intellectuals fleeing the increasingly repressive Duvalier dictatorship. They intended to go back home as soon as the political situation changed. There was a joke at the time about those who were more politically inclined and who refused to undo their suitcases. They were ready to take the next flight back home. Each winter was their last one and they often mentioned selling or giving away their winter coats then.

As the seasons changed and the years piled up, the visitors began to settle in. They bought property, started families, became American citizens and turned certain neighborhoods into Haitian enclaves. Embracing politics again, they were about to make their major impact in the 1989 election of David N. Dinkins, the first African American mayor of New York City.

Dinkins made a concerted effort to reach out to Haitians. The *Haiti-Observateur* conducted interviews with him and published his photos in the company of leading Haitian figures. When the paper endorsed him, his photo with me adorned the editorial page. The results were telling. David Dinkins won about 97 percent of the Black vote, including that of Haitian Americans. He defeated Rudolph Giuliani by a mere two percentage points. Haitians who had voted in bloc proudly claimed that they were responsible for the historic victory of New York's first Black mayor. Few people commented on that boast.

The next vote of the Haitians was not at the ballot box. It was with their feet and chants when they shook the Brooklyn Bridge on April 20, 1990. On that day America witnessed a mammoth demonstration by Haitians. Reportedly 75,000 to 100,000 Haitians and their friends left Cadman Plaza in Brooklyn Heights on their way to Federal Plaza in downtown Manhattan, with placards denouncing what they perceived as racist, the Food and Drug Administration (FDA). They chanted "We won't take it no more." That was their defiant challenge to the FDA which was dubbed "Federal Discrimination Administration." The FDA had banned Haitians from donating blood.

In 1981, scientists of the Center for Disease Control and Protection (CDC) diagnosed a new disease which they called Gay-Related Immune Disease (GRID). As the name indicates, homosexual men were its first victims. By 1982, GRID had become AIDS, or Acquired Immunodeficiency Syndrome, a mysterious, sexually transmitted fatal disease. Four groups were targeted as being at-risk: Homosexuals, Hemophiliacs, Heroin addicts, and Haitians.

The new "4H Club" got much press, to the detriment of Haitians. Soon Haitians were accused of being at the origin of the epidemic that was devastating America. So-called scientists were competing to solve the enigma of how the disease entered the United States. Some theorized that it came from a Haitian who was bitten by an infected ape in West Africa before returning to Haiti. Somehow he had intercourse with an American homosexual who came back with the disease to the United States. Others alleged that a Haitian infected with the disease traveled to New York or Miami and through sexual relations with homosexuals had spread the disease. There even was the theory of a profligate airline steward who contracted the disease during an escapade in Haiti and brought it back to the mainland.

To protect America from infected Haitians, the FDA issued a ruling in 1983 banning Haitians who had emigrated after 1977 from participating in blood donations. By March 1990, the ruling was generalized to cover all Haitians and their foreign partners. Haitians of all stripes and categories felt insulted and decided to challenge the FDA. Haitian health professionals, including reputable medical doctors, as well as community activists, demanded a retraction from the FDA.

The issue became the theme for many a sermon in Haitian churches. For the first time since the 1960s when Haitians began their mass migration to New York, they showed an unusual solidarity. Immediately after the demonstration, the FDA retracted by lifting the ban on blood donations by Haitians. In America, especially in New York political circles, Haitians had gained new respect.

Nonetheless, the harm was already done. Haitians, and Haiti itself, would pay dearly for the racist so-called scientific breakthrough. In school, Haitian students had to contend with a moniker other than that of "boat people." They were now taunted as AIDS carriers. Many young Haitians were declined friendships or dates on the basis of their nationality. Haiti, itself, suffered the economic fallout of the discriminatory AIDS policy of the FDA. Tourists who, timidly, had been rediscovering the country after the violent years of Papa Doc, began to shun the country.

Back to Mayor Dinkins. Once in office, he paid little attention to Haitians, except for a few low-level appointments. However, he would need them again for his reelection. For his rematch against Rudy Giuliani in 1993, Dinkins thought that he could take a ride on the popularity of President Jean-Bertrand Aristide, then living in Washington.

On a visit to New York, the Haitian community gave the exiled President Aristide a raucous reception at Central Park. The national press reported that 15,000 had come to hear their idol. But *Haiti-Progrès*, a mouthpiece of the exiled leader, boosted the numbers to 75,000. Mayor Dinkins received President Aristide at City Hall and presented him the key to the city. Moreover, the Mayor declared, "We are *Lavalas*"—adherents of Aristide's party.

The Mayor and his advisers made a major mistake by fully embracing Aristide. When I asked for an interview with Mayor Dinkins, I was rebuffed. Not even Bill Lynch, an old acquaintance who was the Mayor's campaign manager, deigned to return my call. Since I was a reputed opponent of President Aristide, City Hall decided to treat me as an enemy. My support was no longer necessary as in the 1989 election. After Aristide's Central Park noisy reception, City Hall thought that the majority of Haitians were supporters of the popular exiled chief. Therefore, he will deliver the Haitian vote to Mayor Dinkins in the upcoming rematch against Giuliani.

The Giuliani camp made a move that would prove fatal to the re-election of Mayor Dinkins. I received a telephone call from Giuliani's office requesting an interview with the *Haiti-Observateur*. I was invited to his headquarters on Madison Avenue for a tête-à-tête with the candidate. During the interview, I did not mince words. Among the questions to the candidate was his treatment of Haitian refugees in Miami in the early1980s when he was the No. 3 at the Justice Department.

"I remember you well, Mr. Joseph," Giuliani said. "I was then working for the Reagan administration, executing policy. Do you think I will follow Reagan's policy here in New York, such a diverse ethnic city? Please, give me a chance to address your constituents. I will show you what I'll do."

Rudolph Giuliani almost made me lose my job at the *Wall Street Journal* when I testified in 1982 on behalf of Haitian refugees in federal court in Miami. Now, here was the new Giuliani who needed the support of Haitians and who was meeting me again under different circumstances. "Give me a chance," he pleaded, "I will show you what I can do for all New York citizens."

I published the interview and wrote an editorial in which I recounted my frustration in not being able to secure an interview with Mayor Dinkins. In conclusion, I wrote, "Of the two candidates the one who thought Haitians have something to say in this election is Rudolph Giuliani. May the better one win."

In the November 2, 1993, Dinkins-Giuliani rematch, the challenger defeated the mayor by almost the same percentage by which he had lost to him in 1989. The actual numbers, after 100 percent of the precincts were counted, came to 903,114 (50.7 percent) for Giuliani and 858,868 (48.3 percent) for Dinkins. In 1989, Dinkins had won 97 percent of the Black vote, but in 1993, it fell to 90 percent. By only 44,246 votes Mayor Dinkins had failed to concretize his reelection bid. By then, Haitian American voters were estimated at around 50,000.

The following Monday, November 8, Mayor-elect Giuliani was coming to Brooklyn Borough Hall. The *Haiti-Observateur* was invited to his press conference. The mayor's office had specified that I should come with my staff and to remain after the press conference. The mayor-elect wanted to meet with me privately.

After the general press conference, Mayor Giuliani motioned to me to go into the Borough president's conference room. On seeing the majestic conference room of the Borough president, he cracked a joke. "I think I should move in here," he said, "it's much better than what we have at City Hall." He invited us to sit down.

"I wanted to thank you personally," he said, "for having allowed me to address your constituency. The preliminary election results show that the Haitian community voted for us overwhelmingly. I want you to know that the doors of City Hall are open to you. Thanks very much."

Mayor Dinkins and his advisers had failed to realize that the thousands who had welcomed Aristide to New York were in majority nonvoters, many of whom were illegal newcomers. The Haitians who had settled in New York since the 1960s were tax-paying citizens and homeowners who felt that Mayor Dinkins had failed them. Moreover, they were for the most part readers of the *Haiti-Observateur* and not particularly fond of Aristide. They understood the nuances of our editorial. Although it was not a full-fledged endorsement of Giuliani, it leaned toward him. He was the candidate who had reached out to us.

A few months after he was inaugurated, Giuliani began to show that he was indeed a defender of illegal immigrants. In a story in the *New York Times*, June 10, 1994, entitled "New York Officials Welcome Immigrants, Legal or Illegal," Deborah Sontag quoted the Mayor as saying, "Some of the hardest-working and most productive people in this city are undocumented aliens. If you come here and you work hard and you happen to be in an undocumented status, you're one of the people who we want in this city. You're somebody that we want to protect and we want you to get out from under what is often a life of being like a fugitive, which is really unfair."

The Mayor went further. In 1996, he sued the federal government on behalf of undocumented immigrants. He wanted to uphold a 1985 executive order of former Mayor Ed Koch that protected the illegal immigrants. That executive order forbade government employees from snitching on undocumented immigrants who sought government benefits from the city. Giuliani's lawsuit asserted that the new federal requirement to report illegal immigrants violated the 10th Amendment. He ordered his lawyers to forcefully defend the rights of the undocumented. When he lost in court, he appealed all the way to the Supreme Court, where he lost again in 2000.

In the fourth year of his mayoralty and only four months before facing the voters to renew his mandate, Mayor Giuliani faced a major crisis with the Haitian community that could have wrecked his campaign. In the wee hours of August 9, 1997, Abner Louima, a 30-year-old Haitian immigrant, was arrested in Brooklyn following a fight at the Rendez-Vous nightclub on Flatbush Avenue. Louima was severely beaten and led to the 70th Police precinct in East Flatbush where he was crudely sodomized with the handle of a plunger. He was rushed to Coney Island Hospital where an angel was waiting.

Magalie Laurent, with assistance from her husband, sounded the alarm. The Haitian nurse called Louima's family to tell them about what happened. Then she placed calls to the Internal Affairs Bureau of the Police and to New York-1 television. By her action, she broke the silence that surrounded the case at the hospital. The sodomized Haitian immigrant dominated the news and he became a cause célèbre. On August 29, thousands of Haitian demonstrators marched to the 70th Precinct and to City Hall, calling for justice for Abner Louima and punishment for the NYPD brutes.

In May 1999, Justin Volpe, a 25-year-old police officer from Staten Island, admitted his guilt in court. He was sentenced on December 13, 1999, to thirty years in prison without the possibility of parole. In 2012, he got married while in jail. It has since been reported that Volpe will be released in 2025, four years before serving his full thirty years.

Charles Schwarz, another police officer who had helped Volpe, was sentenced in 2002 to five years in prison for perjury. The convictions of Thomas Bruder and Thomas Wiese, two other police officers implicated in the case, were overturned in 2002. They had earlier been convicted of obstruction of justice. They failed in their attempt to be reinstated into the police force.

On July 30, 2001, a settlement was reached with New York City and the NYPD for $8.7 million to be paid to Abner Louima. After legal fees, Louima collected approximately $5.8 million. He moved from Brooklyn to Florida. In 2003 he visited his grandfather in Thomassin, in the house where he was born in the mountains beyond Pétionville. On that occasion he announced the set-up of the Abner Louima Foundation, whose primary goal is education for the children of that community.

From the outset, Mayor Giuliani acted forcefully and diligently to address the criminal scandal that rocked the city, even the nation. The sodomized Abner Louima became a symbol of police brutality that could no longer be ignored. Mayor Giuliani, well known for his strong support for the Police, asked that those responsible be punished.

The four policemen involved in the attack were immediately relieved of their duties. Within a week, the whole leadership of the 70th Precinct was replaced. On August 19, ten days after the attack on Louima, the Mayor created the Task Force on Police/Community Relations. He appointed thirty-three notable New York City residents to the civilian group entrusted with finding ways to improve relations between the police and the communities they serve. I was named to the Task Force to represent the Haitian community.

After six months of work, which took Task Force members to all five boroughs and into several police precincts, nineteen specific recommendations were made to the Mayor and the NYPD to improve police-community relations. A very important finding of the Task Force was the composition of the Police Force compared to the population. The Task Force noted that although 61 percent of the city's population is not White, the police force was 68 percent White, and many of the officers resided in the suburbs. Thus, residency in the city was recommended for police officers. This would result in more African Americans, Latinos and Asian American/Pacific Islanders on the force. That would change the perception of city residents who would identify with those entrusted with enforcing the law.

More than a decade after the Task Force report, at the end of 2010, the percentage of White police officers had dropped to 53 percent while that of minorities increased to 47 percent, a gain of 8 percent. However, in top-tier positions, the increase was only 4.5 percent, or about half of the overall gain in minority representation in police ranks. While some progress has been registered in the diversity of the NYPD, much work remains to be done to fully diversify the force and to make it more minority-friendly.

Under Mayor Giuliani, New York experienced a revival and security improved greatly. Despite criticism leveled at the Mayor for his handling of the homeless issue and the squeegee experts who made life miserable for drivers at stop signs, Haitian homeowners applauded Giuliani. He had maintained contact with the Haitian community through a weekly column in the *Haiti-Observateur*. In 1997, at the paper's 26th anniversary gala at the Grand Prospect Hall in Brooklyn, Mayor Giuliani spent one hour at the affair, dining with us, and appeared very relaxed among a constituency that he was meeting for the first time. Certainly, the Haitians he had met that night were not the stereotype "boat people" and AIDS carriers who should be shunned.

The reputation of the Haitians as a pivotal bloc was underscored that evening. Prior to the arrival of the Mayor, Ruth Messinger, the Democratic candidate facing Giuliani in that November race, showed up also. She came to salute the assistance. The two candidates almost bumped into each other as Messinger's party was leaving and Mayor Giuliani and his entourage were arriving.

A sector of the Haitian community tried, unsuccessfully, to inject the Abner Louima case into the mayoral campaign by putting words into Louima's mouth. Supposedly, while he was being assaulted, some of the police officers had yelled, "This is Giuliani's time." But Louima retracted that statement.

The Mayor went on to score a 60 percent victory in the November 1997 election in a city that is six-to-one Democratic. He almost doubled his take of the Black vote—to 19 percent, up from 10 percent in 1993. Were it not for term limit, Mayor Giuliani could have been elected a third time, because on 9/11 he had shown his leadership in time of crisis. On that fateful September day in 2001, the Mayor had rallied the city in the face of the terrorist attack that rocked New York and the nation.

Michael Bloomberg, sensing the popularity of Mayor Giuliani, changed his Democratic Party affiliation to run as a Republican in the election of 2001. Two months after the tragedy of the World Trade Center, Bloomberg coasted to victory against the Democrat Mark Green. The new Mayor also embraced the Haitian community. He continued the policy of the Mayor Giuliani's weekly column in the *Haiti-Observateur* to keep in touch with the Haitian community. When he went for reelection in 2005, he blanketed the Haitian community with Bloomberg ads.

An adept politician, Bloomberg sensed the mood of the electorate in the wake of the financial crisis of 2008. He lobbied, successfully, to change the two-term limit policy on the mayor's mandate. With his unsurpassed financial war chest, he won narrowly his third term in 2009—under an independent label this time. In a way, the vote of the Haitian community had allowed the Republicans to dominate New York politics for nearly two decades. But in 2013, Haitian American voters embraced Democrat Bill de Blasio.

The Giuliani lesson should not be lost on the Republicans who have come under the heavy influence of the Tea Party. Unless the Republicans embrace key ethnic blocs and address issues relevant to them, they could remain a minority party for the foreseeable future. The demographics of the United States are clearly unfavorable to politicians who fail to understand the dynamics of ethnic bloc voting.

During the early years of their immigration to New York, a great number of Haitians settled on the Upper West Side of Manhattan, from 72nd Street up to the border of Harlem at 110th Street. The Haitian Bookstore of Jacques Moringlade at 84th Street and Amsterdam Avenue became a focal point for political debaters. As gentrification spread through Manhattan's Upper West Side, the Haitians were pushed out to Brooklyn, Queens, New York's Rockland County, especially Nyack and Spring Valley, as well as to the Oranges in New Jersey.

When it was launched in July 1971, the *Haiti-Observateur* became the organ to unify the dispersed community. Besides maintaining the flame of nationalism in the new immigrants, the paper sought to accompany them as they eased their way into their new environment. In the process, the *Haiti-Observateur* became the main reference of the community in need of guidance. The introduction of English columns and a regular English editorial every week were a deliberate attempt to prepare our constituency for the inevitable. Life in the United States was becoming permanent and we had to adapt to the new reality.

It was a time of conflict for Haitian families whose children, born in America, were straying from the disciplinarian mode of their parents. Haitian neighborhood centers proliferated and served as unofficial counseling clinics for the newcomers. The paper also ran advice columns and became home for lawyers in search of new clients. For twelve years the *Haiti-Observateur* remained the sole written voice of the community.

Little by little, the paper was drawn into American politics. Editorially it pushed the candidacy of Una Clarke who became the first woman of Caribbean descent to be elected to the New York City Council in 1991. It became involved in the Congressional campaigns of Major Owens, Edolphus Towns, Gregory Meeks, and Charles Rangel, all New York Democrats. In 1994, when George

Pataki, a Republican senator from Westchester, ran for governor, he came to Brooklyn in search of the Haitian vote. One of his operatives, Harold Doley III, used his Haitian connections to pave the way for Pataki, who served three terms as governor.

Sometime in the early '70s, I had alerted the Caribbean Action Lobby (CAL) to the upcoming power of the Haitian voting bloc. CAL's founder, New York State Senator Waldaba Stewart, had invited me to address his group at a function in the Poconos. He was concerned about the aloofness of the Haitian community in respect to the larger Caribbean community. I explained that the language barrier was to blame. Whereas the West Indians, as most islanders were called, are English speakers, Haitians speak Creole and French and don't feel at ease in meetings where English dominates. Since they relied on their French and Creole media, they tended to follow their advice on what to do, especially when it came to politics.

At the time, there were two reputable broadcasts serving the Haitian community in New York: *L'Heure Haïtienne* (The Haitian Hour) which aired on Columbia University's WKCR-FM at 6 a.m. on Sundays, and *Moment Créole* (Creole Moment) on WLIB [AM] at noon, also on Sundays. (WLIB was the sister station of WBLS [FM], both Black-owned by Inner City Broadcasting Corporation, which was started by Percy Sutton, a former president of the borough of Manhattan.) Meanwhile, the *Haiti-Observateur* was the only written organ involved with American politics. Its endorsement of a candidate was priceless.

While Haitians helped to elect others to office, they showed little unity in electing one of their own until 2007 when Mathieu Eugene, MD, was the first Haitian-born American to be elected to the City Council. In a primary election for the New York Assembly in September 2014, the old demon of division reared its head when two women of Haitian ancestry, Rodneyse Bichotte and Michèle Adolphe, vied for the seat of veteran Assemblywoman Rhoda Jacobs in the 42nd Assembly District in Brooklyn.

Rodneyse Bichotte, female Democratic leader of the 42nd District, was considered a shoo-in against her main challenger Leithland Rickie Tulloch. Mr. Tulloch didn't have the name recognition of Bichotte, who had run before for Ms. Jacobs's seat. At the last minute, Michèle Adolphe sued to knock Bichotte out of the race on the basis that years earlier she had been registered in Illinois. It was really petty for Adolphe to attack Bichotte since she had served her community and become a female leader of her district. It did not show solidarity amongst Haitians in politics. As a minority group in the United States, Haitians should show soldarity amongst themselves. This is the only way Haitians will advance. A judge rightly threw out the case and Bichotte won with 51 percent.

Certainly, Haitians at home and in the diaspora need to reflect on the motto that helped them gain independence: *L'Union fait la Force* (In Unity there is Strength).

Chapter 15

At the Embassy in Washington

Following the ouster of President Aristide on February 29, 2004, an interim government was installed to administer Haiti for two years. In line with the 1987 Constitution, Boniface Alexandre, Chief Judge of the Supreme Court, assumed the presidency. But the government was run by a retired United Nations official, Gérard Latortue, as Prime Minister. In the absence of a Parliament, a group of Haitian notables had called on Latortue in Boca Raton, Florida, to manage the government in the turbulent period following the second ouster of President Aristide.

Latortue called me in New York and said the new government wanted me to take charge of Haiti's Embassy in Washington. It was then staffed by *Lavalassians,* as the supporters of President Aristide are called. Time is of the essence, he said, so I would assume the post as Chargé d'Affaires until I am upgraded to Ambassador.

In October 2005, President Alexandre named me Ambassador. I presented my credentials to President George W. Bush. The Alexandre-Latortue team worked harmoniously. For the first time since the post of prime minister was created in 1987, these two executives exemplified how the administration should operate. Latortue was the Chief Executive Officer who ran the government on a day-to-day basis and Alexandre, the Chairman of the Board, was the guarantor of the Constitution and the ultimate voice in international relations.

At the outset, the interim government faced a major problem. The emergence of gangs under President Aristide had given Haiti a violent reputation. The *chimères,* as they were called, roamed around freely, always leaving a trail of desolation. Their "Operation Baghdad" was turning some parts of Haiti into major battle zones. Their main bastion was *Cité Soleil,* a shantytown in the northern outskirts of Port-au-Prince. With a population of 250,000, *Cité Soleil* had defined the whole country of about nine million. Stories about kidnappings were constant in the US press. Invariably they were connected with *Cité Soleil* where the gang leaders had their fortresslike headquarters. *Cité Soleil* had become a no-man's land where lawlessness ruled.

Haiti was not necessarily the most violent country in the region. Considering US-tourist investment in several Caribbean isles, reporting on violence in most countries of the region is often suppressed in the media. On the other hand, little investment was made in Haiti, which got the brunt of the scrutiny into violence. Haiti had much work to do to change its image.

The gangs that sprung up after Haiti's Armed Forces were disbanded in 1995 had to be reined in. I alerted Prime Minister Latortue of the presence in Brooklyn, NY, of a superb candidate for Police Chief. Mario Andrésol was a former Army officer trained in Ecuador and among the first to join the Police force in 1995 when Police Chief Raymond Kelly of New York helped to set up the new Haitian Police. Kelly was appalled to learn that Andrésol was not in Haiti. "Don't they know that he's among the best?" Chief Kelly told me during an informal conversation at Gracie Mansion, the official residence of New York's mayor.

Prime Minister Latortue was excited to learn the whereabouts of Mario Andrésol. A meeting was set up while the Prime Minister visited New York during the first week of July 2005. By July 18, Andrésol became the new director general of the Police, replacing Léon Charles, a former Coast Guard officer who had assumed the leadership of the Police in 2004 after the departure of President Aristide. Charles had come to the attention of the decision makers for his behind-the-scenes role in saving the Coast Guard from annihilation when the goons of President Aristide were planning to attack the Coast Guard. There was a smooth transfer of power from Léon Charles to Mario Andrésol.

In line with the Creole proverb that *De Towo pa gouvènen nan menm savann* (Two bulls don't rule in the same compound), Latortue asked that I take the former Police Chief under my wings in Washington. Thus Léon Charles joined the staff of the Embassy as a minister counselor in charge of security matters. He was a superb collaborator. His mastery of Spanish and English made him a valuable asset in a milieu where those two languages dominate the diplomatic discourse.

Andrésol had his detractors, especially since he had targeted some drug kingpins who were close to President Aristide. He had been framed and even jailed for a month in August 2001 for his alleged participation in a bogus coup. On his release, he had left Haiti to escape assassination. In 2012, Chief Andrésol denounced the return of some former drug lords who had been exhibiting themselves in the company of high officials of the Martelly government. He vowed to deal with them as he had done in the past, despite their acquaintances. Undoubtedly, this explained the strong pressure to force his resignation.

The results obtained by Andrésol as Police director were so eloquent that the Senate twice approved his three-year reappointment to the post. The total of the Police Force, which stood at about 2,500 in 2004, rose to nearly 10,000 in 2010. Andrésol was supported in his modernization program of the Police when President Préval assumed the presidency in 2006. Hopefully, the training and programs instituted under his leadership will be maintained as the Police force is beefed up to between 16,000 and 20,000. Moreover, I believe that the Haitian Police should be dedicated to community policing and safety.

A major accomplishment of the Alexandre-Latortue team was the establishment of multi-floor buildings to house government offices in each department, as our mini states are called. The consolidation of operations in one all-purpose building was intended to facilitate services to the constituents, cut operations cost, and allow for better interchange among various government institutions.

Under the interim administration, the Central Unit for Economic and Financial Investigations, or UCREF, was set up to shed light on financial shenanigans that occurred under President Aristide. In two reports, UCREF established that millions of public funds were diverted to private companies tied to Aristide and to his foundation. Ira Kurzban, the lawyer of the former president, disputed the reports and denounced a witchhunt against his client. By its action, however, the Alexandre-Latortue administration sent a clear message that corruption would not be tolerated, especially in the highest spheres of State.

Most importantly, within two years, the interim government organized the elections which resulted in René Préval's reelection in May 2006. I felt some satisfaction that the two interim governments that I served in Washington, including that of President Trouillot, had accomplished their mission on time. It is noteworthy that since the overthrow of the Duvalier dictatorship in 1986, only two interim governments have organized elections to the satisfaction of most.

———

When I came back to the Embassy in April 2004, Gisèle Dépestre was the only one still there of the employees that I had left in April 1991. Mrs. Dépestre is a veteran who was first posted in Washington in 1961. She served in Italy and New York before she came back to Washington in 1983. Even after her retirement in 2006, she remained an asset to the Embassy on a part-time basis. The retirement package for State employees, especially those who choose the Foreign Service as a career, is so meager that a life of poverty awaits Haitian government retirees. Certainly, that policy breeds corruption in employees who use their position to amass a nest egg for an uncertain future.

All the other employees had been named by the *Lavalas* governments of Presidents Aristide and Préval. My reputation as an opponent of *Lavalas* was well known. In a meeting with the staff, I reassured them that I was not on a witch hunt. They had nothing to fear of me.

Of their own accord, two top-echelon employees left immediately. A third left a few months later. I fired only two employees, one of whom I had hired. The other, Ms. Maricile (a pseudonym), was let go eighteen months after my arrival and following several warnings about her behavior. Through the *teledyòl,* the Haitian grapevine, I was warned in a Creole proverb: *Bat chen, tann mèt li!* (Strike the dog, wait for its master!) The teledyòl is the preferable diplomatic mode of communication for cowards. The message is usually coupled with a menacing Creole proverb. In other words, she was powerfully connected and I was bound to suffer the consequences of my temerity. "If this employee must come back to this Embassy, she might as well be named Ambassador," I responded through the grapevine.

Months later, her brother became a high official in President Préval's government. Then I received a note from the Foreign Office stating that I owe Maricile a full year's salary, because she had been dismissed illegally. I responded that the Ministry has the complete file. She was fired for cause and the record shows that. A week or so later, an amount was credited to the Embassy's account equal to the sum I supposedly owed her. I called the director general at the Foreign Ministry for an explanation. I was told the money represented what was owed to Maricile. "I have no memo stating this," I said. "I will wait for it before making any payment."

The memo arrived the next day. I instructed my secretary to transfer the funds to the Consulate where Maricile had been reassigned three months earlier. I also asked the secretary to send an accompanying statement with the note of the Foreign Ministry to her new boss, the consul general, explaining the purpose of the funds.

The consul called me later to say how my former employee was bragging about my being a fair person. She even said that I was not really responsible for her firing; that it was a plot concocted by people at the Washington Embassy who did not like her.

No doubt, I had gained the fairness reputation from my early days at the Embassy in 2004. When I found out that the employees had not had a raise in ten years, I met with the Embassy's accountant to discuss salaries. I asked the accountant to figure out how much cash it would take to give the employees a raise of 5 percent, 10 percent, 15 percent, 20 percent, up to 25 percent. On receiving the accountant's report, I discovered that with the available funds, I could give a 25 percent raise. I ordered that this be done.

The employees were not the only ones who were satisfied with my monetary decisions. The three ministries with which I dealt directly—Foreign Affairs, Interior, and Finance—must have been astounded about the change observed in transfer of funds from the Embassy to the Treasury. The Embassy generates funds mainly through the passport unit, which is an operation of the Immigration and Emigration Office in Port-au-Prince, itself under the Ministry of Interior and Territorial Collectivities. All Haitian citizens abroad, even those in the Dominican Republic, next door to Haiti, obtain their passports from Washington. This practice began while President Aristide was in exile in Washington from 1992 to 1994. On his return to Haiti in October of that year, he continued to manage that source of revenue from Washington.

When I arrived at the Embassy in 2004, about $60,000 monthly was being transferred to the Haitian Treasury from the Embassy passport operations. On orders from the presidency, huge amounts were paid to concerns in the United States. One such organization, The Steele Foundation, a bodyguard company in San Francisco, was receiving $134,000 monthly. That amounted to $1.6 million a year, ostensibly to provide protection to President Aristide in Haiti. Immediately I discontinued that payment.

I also began an investigation of some of the consulates that were notorious for withholding payments of passports whose applications were sent to Washington. The situation was explosive, because more than 5,000 passports were waiting in Washington to be delivered. Citizens had been waiting for months for their precious documents, but the managers of the passport unit had refused to issue them without the payment held by some of the consulates.

It was an embarrassing situation. The Haitian media, especially in the United States, were reporting about the scandal. Our investigation revealed that the two most lucrative consulates—New York and Miami—were particularly guilty of withholding funds. The situation was unbearable, especially in New York. With the help of the consul general, an investigation was undertaken. We discovered that one consul with powerful political connections back home had siphoned off nearly $250,000.

After a thorough investigation, which also involved the Foreign Ministry, the consul was fired. But not before he had signed a document acknowledging his debt to the Haitian government for the stolen funds. Order was restored in both Miami and New York. Then I asked the managers of the passport unit in Washington to work overtime to issue all the passports that were held up. At the same time they had to keep up with new demand. The employees were paid overtime for that work.

A new policy was instituted. Passport requests from continental United States and Canada should be returned within two weeks—three weeks at the most for problem cases. Urgent requests for which payment for express delivery was made should be honored within forty-eight to seventy-two hours. If an individual traveled to Washington to obtain a passport, it should be treated as an extreme emergency, deserving of the fastest treatment. If all documents of the individual are correct, the passport should be issued within two hours.

In the aftermath of the clean-up operation, the financial situation changed positively. On the second month of my arrival at the Embassy, the transfer to the Treasury amounted to $250,000. That translated into $2.9 million in my first year. The amount increased steadily every year until I transferred more than $5 million in 2009, the last full year I was in office, a far cry from the approximately $700,000 when I arrived in 2004.

It is possible to run a sound administration, devoid of shenanigans. The words of the French proverb are indeed applicable when it comes to sensible leadership: *Le poisson pourrit par la tête.* (The fish begins to rot at the head.) The monthly financial report, in three copies, went to the Ministry of Foreign Affairs, that of Interior and Territorial Collectivities (Homeland Security) and to the Ministry of Economy and Finance, which also received the transferred funds.

Since most of the money was generated by the passport unit, in reality Interior could have demanded to have direct oversight over the transfers. There was never a problem with Interior for the funds transferred to Finance. However, at one point a new director general at the Ministry of Foreign Affairs asked that I transfer the funds from consular operations directly to his ministry instead of to Finance. Other than revenue from passport operations, some funds are collected for consular services, such as issuance of mandates and visas, wherever applicable.

I inquired of the Finance minister whether there was a change at the level of the ministries to that effect. He asked me whether I had a written request from the director general. No. It was a verbal request.

Whereupon, the Finance minister said, "Ask him to send you a formal request, indicating to whom the check should be addressed or to what account should the funds be credited." He added, "I can bet you won't hear a word from him." Indeed, the director never responded to my request, but our relationship became strained ever since. I continued to transfer all funds as I had been doing. Subsequently, I learned that some consulates had complied with the director's directive.

———

As relative peace began to take hold in Haiti, my task of representing the country became easier. The idea of Haiti being hostile to foreign investment had to be addressed. Most people probably don't know how the idea of Haiti's hostility to foreign investment developed.

After the defeat of the French over 200 years ago, stringent laws made it impossible for foreigners to acquire property in Haiti. "Haiti is not for sale, wholesale or retail," is often repeated by Haitian super nationalists. This attitude even affected Haitian-born citizens who had chosen another nationality and country to facilitate life in. The xenophobic slogan must be countered. I proposed, somewhat sarcastically, that we rent—not sell—parts of Haiti. Fortunately, some of the anti-foreign laws have been changed. Now, foreigners, in partnership with Haitian citizens, can possess land.

There was a period, not long ago, when Haiti made a play for outside investment. On the death of his father in 1971, Jean-Claude Duvalier, who became President-for-life at the age of nineteen, was surrounded by some sharp thinkers who saw the need to change course from the oppressive dictatorship of Papa Doc. Soon after taking power, Baby Doc made a memorable speech in which he said, "My father made the political revolution, I will make the economic revolution."

The regime opened up to local and foreign investment, especially to the value-added industry, the *maquiladoras,* or free trade manufacturing, made famous in certain Latin countries like Mexico.

Haiti attracted several companies interested in taking advantage of a skilled and inexpensive labor force only 800 miles from Florida shores.

Things changed after the 1986 revolt that forced out Duvalier into exile. As previously mentioned, the *dechoukaj* (uprooting) movement following Baby Doc's flight resulted in untold destruction. A leading figure of that movement, the Catholic priest Jean-Bertrand Aristide precipitated the flight of the foreign investors. In a memorable statement during one of his fiery sermons, he said, *Kapitalis se youn peche mòtèl.* (Capitalism is a mortal sin.) All investors being capitalist, they saw the writing on the wall, because the revolutionary priest of the poverty stricken St. Jean Bosco parish was the most popular voice in Haiti at the time. Several companies, including baseball maker Rawlings, shut down their operations and migrated to neighboring countries.

By the time I arrived in Washington in 2004, Haiti was producing very little for the foreign market. Haiti's textile manufacturing force had dwindled to about 20,000 workers from 80,000 in 1985. In the 1940s and '50s, Haiti vied with Cuba and Puerto Rico for North American tourists. By 2004, tourism had greatly declined. Haiti had even disappeared from all international literature on tourism, a situation that is yet to be remedied. The number of hotel rooms atrophied to about 1,000, compared with 50,000 in the Dominican Republic, next door.

If Haiti wanted to attract investors again, an appeal to them should be tailored in an attractive package. If investors were repulsed by the damaging statement "Capitalism is a mortal sin," I felt that a welcoming statement should be devised and expounded: "Haiti is open for business." Interestingly, President Martelly included this sentence in his inaugural speech in May 2011. Since then, the phrase has become like a mantra in the mouth of Haiti's Prime Minister Laurent Lamothe in his attempt to attract foreign investors.

But for that appeal to bear fruit, the government must provide a secure environment to do business and cut back on red tape that impedes the timely establishment of new companies. Above all, Haiti's judicial system must be reformed and become truly impartial.

Government's seizure of Haitel Telecomunication International, S. A. is the wrong signal to investors. Established in 1998 by Franck Ciné, a Haitian American citizen, Haitel was the first cellular telephone company in Haiti. The case of Haitel reached a Federal Court in New York, because rulings of the Haitian courts in favor of Ciné were ignored by the executive branch.

Dispossessing citizens of their land, without proper compensation, can only lead to a destabilizing atmosphere impeding investment. Such is the current situation in *Ile à Vâches* (Cow Island), a pristine piece of real estate in the south, near Cayes, whose population is estimated at 17,000. The Martelly government had declared the 20-square-mile island eminent domain. It contemplated turning it into an attractive tourist development. But anti-government demonstrations kept potential investors away.

Until the State resolves the question of land rights, Haiti will have much difficulty to attract investors. The case of the Haitian Academy University in Lafiteau on the National Road No. 1 illustrated the risks involved in doing business in Haiti. In 1979, enterprising educator Marie-Pologne Jacques René and her husband Grégoire René established the Haitian Academy in Brooklyn to offer alternative first-rate education to immigrant children. The school obtained national accreditation. After the fall of the Duvalier dictatorship, in 1986, the Renés moved their operation to Haiti. By 1991, they opened a modest campus in Lafiteau, some 20 miles north of Port-au-Prince. The school added a university section and offered degrees in medicine and agriculture.

In June 2014, the property of the Academy was invaded on orders of Bernard Martinod, a Frenchman who resides in Haiti. Armed with a bogus court judgment, Martinod grabbed the property that he had coveted for some time. Since Grégoire René died in 2013, Martinod assumed that the widow was no longer a match for him. Moreover, he had the support of corrupt judiciary officials.

Alerted to the situation, Mrs. René, in Brooklyn at the time of the invasion of her property, rushed to Haiti. Indeed, the 24-acre property had been seized, including 20 buildings and the private plots where her husband and father are buried. She appealed to a higher court which nullified the judgment dispossessing her. One month later, Bernard Martinod erected a wall blocking entry to the Academy.

Meanwhile, Martinod had already begun the destruction of the establishment, starting with the library. His plan for the property called for the establishment of a French village. Martinod still holds on to 144 acres of land adjacent to the Academy, land which the Renés had bought for a reforestation project and further development. The liberator of Haiti, Jean-Jacques Dessalines, must be turning over in his grave!

The government should be applauded for revamping the rules to allow on-line registration of new corporations within a month, instead of the seven months it took in the past. However, it will be difficult to attract foreign investment as long as the country is ruled by "legal bandits" who are protected by a corrupt Judiciary, itself under the dictates of the President of the Republic.

Chapter 16

Haiti is Open for Business

When I evoked the slogan "Haiti is open for business" in 2005, I took action to make it a reality. The Republican-controlled US Senate was moving slowly on a bill to give Haiti preferential tariffs on textiles. With strong sponsorship from Senator Mike DeWine (Republican of Ohio), the Senate had approved the "Haiti Economic Recovery Opportunity" (HERO) Act in 2004.

The chairman of the Ways and Means Committee of the House at the time felt that the Senate had overstepped its prerogatives. Such legislation should have obtained first the imprimatur of Ways and Means, which failed to follow suit. The Haitian private sector, led by entrepreneur Jean Baker, had worked feverishly to get HERO approved. Their labor would not be in vain. I built on their momentum to push for something else, the more modest "Haitian Economic Partnership Empowerment" (HOPE) Act. I concentrated all my effort on getting the approval of Ways and Means first.

The campaign to get approval of the HOPE Act required a vast coalition. The Haitian private sector found strong backing from Minister of Commerce Fritz Kénol as they undertook their lobbying effort in Washington. I worked with the Congressional Black

Caucus, the Catholic Bishops Conference, the Evangelical churches, and various Haitian Diaspora associations. Pop star Wyclef Jean and many others were mobilized to make HOPE a reality. In turn, they worked on their constituencies which targeted their representatives in Congress asking their support for HOPE.

By June 2006, I knew I had succeeded in getting Congressional approval of the legislation, although that was not publicly known. For some time I had been speaking with Representative William "Bill" Thomas (Republican of California), Chairman of the Ways and Means Committee. I told him that he should leave a legacy by which Haitians will remember him. I knew that he was retiring from Congress after nearly twenty years representing more than one district in California. I received a telephone call for a meeting with the Chairman. I asked Minister Counselor Carole Préval to accompany me. I wanted a witness to corroborate what would be discussed. The Congressman asked Angela Allard, a key staff member of Ways and Means, to be there.

Chairman Thomas made sure that I understood the rules concerning what he was about to disclose to me. "Ambassador, I know your background," he began. "If the press finds out about what I am going to tell you, it will be off the table."

"I am no longer an active journalist," I responded, "and certainly not a conduit for any press organ, not even for the one I helped to found years ago." We all smiled.

Then, Chairman Thomas said that Haiti probably deserves more than what he was able to secure for us. "That's the best I can offer now," he said. The bill covered only five years. It contained many restrictions as to where Haiti could buy the fibers used in textiles manufactured under the advantageous tariffs proposed. Countries like China where the fibers would be cheaper were out. Moreover, we would start losing some of the advantages within three years, unless otherwise renewed.

The Chairman said something else: "You know we will have Congressional elections in November [2006] and it is very possible that the Democrats may win and take control of the House. They could oppose the HOPE Act that I am offering you, so that they may come with their own legislation to take credit for themselves."

I nodded, without commenting, and we said goodbye.

As soon as I sat in the car, I told Carole Préval to excuse me, because I could not wait until I arrived at the office to make a special telephone call. It was to Congressman Charles "Charlie" Rangel of New York, the ranking Democrat on the Ways and Means Committee. I knew that if the Democrats were to win, as Chairman Thomas indicated, Charlie would become the Chairman of Ways and Means. So, I wanted to break the news to him and also tell him what I was offered by Chairman Thomas.

"That bill with all the restrictions, and only for such a limited period," Congressman Rangel said.

"Yes," I said. "But the Chairman also said that you and the Democrats will oppose it."

"Oh, no, I won't oppose it," Rangel said. "Take it and I will bring you Democrats to pass it. But when we get in, we will give you a better HOPE. Go ahead, take it."

That is how I knew that HOPE was in the bag. I had assurances from both the top Republican and the ranking Democrat concerned. Thus, when President Préval told me that he heard that HOPE was in jeopardy and that we risked losing it, I told him firmly that the bill would be approved by Congress. But that would not happen before the upcoming November legislative elections in the United States.

"Are you sure?" he asked.

"I am certain, Mr. President."

"Work on it," he concluded. That was one of the first conversations I had with the President who was inaugurated on May 14, 2006.

———

President Préval, an agronomist by training, was the only president to complete his two five-year terms and return to his hometown of

Marmelade. After his first term in 2001, he started an agricultural experiment in Marmelade with a bamboo farm, developing an industry of bamboo furniture. In 2006, peasant groups drafted him to run again under the label *Lespwa* (Hope).

Préval's 2006 win was disputed, because he had scored 48.7 percent, shy of the 50.1 percent required to forego a rerun. His closest competitor, Professor Leslie Manigat, had won only 12 percent of the vote. To forestall widespread violence on the part of Préval's supporters, a compromise was found to include a large number of blank ballots into the mix. That provided the two top candidates a percentage of the blanks based on their original percentage. Thus did Préval's percentage jump to 51.15 percent while Manigat's edged up to 13 percent.

President Préval was under much pressure to replace me as ambassador. Rumors were persistent that Lionel Delatour would be named ambassador. Mr. Delatour of *CLED* (French acronym for Center for Free Exchange and Democracy) is a brother of Tourist Minister Patrick Delatour and an ally of Elizabeth Débrosse Delatour, the widow of his brother Leslie Delatour, himself a former minister of Economy and Finance. Moreover, Mrs. Débrosse Delatour was a financial adviser to President Préval and his unofficial fiancée. They have since gotten married. It was a foregone conclusion that Lionel Delatour would be the next Haitian ambassador in Washington. Having some contacts in Congress, Lionel Delatour boasted about his ability to deliver the HOPE Act as soon as he got in.

President Préval was not swayed by the arguments on behalf of Lionel Delatour. This was evident when all conditions had been met for the passage of the HOPE Act in November 2006. As expected, the Democrats had trounced the Republicans in the legislative elections. But the Republican Congress would remain lame duck until January 20, 2007.

On Thanksgiving Day 2006, I received a telephone call from Elizabeth Débrosse Delatour, asking me to book hotel rooms for

President Préval and a party of about twenty. The objective of the trip was a final push of lobbying for the passage of the HOPE Act.

"I don't think it's necessary," I said perfunctorily. But what could I do if the president had decided to come to Washington?

I found out that at the last minute, Lionel Delatour was intent on getting credit for the passage of the HOPE Act. In that light, he argued that President Préval's presence in Washington for a last round of lobbying among some of his Congressional contacts would seal the deal. Apparently, he had convinced Elizabeth who, in turn, obtained the president's approval for the hasty trip.

I told Elizabeth how difficult it will be—and also expensive—to secure rooms in Washington at that late hour. For, this was the last Congressional session of the Republicans for some time and all sorts of groups were descending on Washington for a final lobbying campaign among their Republican contacts in Congress. Scarce hotel rooms were at a premium. She said to do the impossible and not to worry about cost.

After a disappointing search for hotel rooms in Washington, I contacted the consul general in Boston. I knew Max Charles had excellent relations with top executives at the Marriott Hotel chain. I told him to do his outmost to find us a presidential suite and twenty rooms at one of Marriott's prestigious addresses in Washington. In less than an hour, Consul Charles had accomplished his mission. The presidential suite was at $10,000 daily and the regular rooms at $1,000. Elizabeth told me to seal the deal. I booked.

Late that same Thanksgiving day, I received another phone call asking me to find a telephone number for Senator Mike DeWine, the Ohio Republican who was defeated in the recently held elections. President Préval wanted to speak to him. The senator was home in his state and I did not have a home number for him. While I was making contacts to reach him, Elizabeth called me again to say not to worry, because the American ambassador, Janet Sanderson, had found the number for President Préval. Elizabeth also said to cancel all hotel reservations, because the president is not coming to Washington anymore. She added that Senator DeWine had advised against the trip.

At that point, I opened my heart to her. Had President Préval come to Washington, I said, we could have lost HOPE, because of his recent trip to Cuba. The press would have certainly dwelt on his visit there and would have been asking about Comandante Castro, especially about his declining health. HOPE would have lost out, because several anti-communist Republican legislators from textile states in the South who were already opposed to HOPE would have found an additional reason to vote against the bill.

Later I learned that Senator DeWine was forceful in discouraging President Préval from coming to Washington. He had said that everything was done for HOPE to pass. If a last minute hitch were to develop, he would take care of it. Indeed, there was a last minute threat to block HOPE from two Republican Senators: Elizabeth Dole of North Carolina and Lindsey Graham of South Carolina. They proposed to block any bill that would have HOPE as a rider. Senator DeWine responded that he would block any bill that did not have HOPE as a rider.

Senator DeWine's threat carried more weight, because he did not need to curry favor with his colleagues anymore. He would be out of office on January 20, 2007. He could afford to be reckless, if needed. But Senators Dole and Graham would still be in office and could not alienate their colleagues by their opposition to HOPE. In a bipartisan vote, the Senate overwhelmingly approved HOPE in December 2006. And the House followed through.

――――――

When President Préval was elected in 2006, I found out that he was told that I only knew how to deal with Republicans. In fact, some of my detractors even called me "Republican Ambassador" behind my back. They explained that I had served in Washington under the presidency of two Republicans: George H. W. Bush, or *Bush père,* in 1990–91; and again in 2004 when George W. Bush, or *Ti Bush,* (Bush Jr. in Creole) was in office. As if an ambassador's job is not to represent his president and defend the interests of his country! By action, I demonstrated that my relations knew no political or ideological bounds.

President Préval must have been impressed during his first visit to the United States in March 2006, even before he was sworn in on May 14 of that year. At the Embassy, I saw the President huddling with some of the employees in intimate chats. Later I would learn about some of the conversations. Invariably, the President would tell them in Creole, "So, you are still here?" The employees told me they responded that I had no chips on my shoulders and that I was perfect to work with.

One of the employees was considered a buddy of the president during the latter's exile in Washington in 1992–94. He was entrusted with driving Préval's teenage daughters to school during their two years in Washington. He told me about his comments to the president concerning me, "He's going nowhere, but here. You cannot find anyone better." I reflected for a long time about Louissaint Louis's appraisal of me. Here was this clerk in the passport unit who is also a professional chauffeur whose services I often used. Unbeknownst to me, he had a close relationship with the Chief of State. Had I been an arbitrary boss who belittled or harassed my subordinates, the president would have had his report about my behavior in the most unorthodox way.

On that first visit, President Préval experienced my long diplomatic reach. In preparing the president-elect's visit to Washington in March 2006, his office had included in the agenda an official time to meet President Bush at the White House. I returned the agenda with a correction: "Meeting with the National Security Council Adviser at the White House." The staff of the President-elect didn't like the change, because they thought I was operating in an anti-*Lavalas* mode, and that I was about to derail the visit with President Bush.

That would be clear by what President Préval told me once he arrived in Washington. His visit here, he said, would have no sense if he did not see President Bush. I concurred and assured him that he will see President Bush. But I explained that there are diplomatic sensibilities in the manner he will meet the US president. There was still a sitting president in Haiti—Boniface Alexandre. Based on protocol, there is no way President Bush could officially receive him in the Oval Office. But he would have an opportunity to converse with the president, I said. Of this I was 100 percent certain.

The diplomatic work to make that happen had already been done. I had no doubt that the meeting would take place as previously discussed. Other anomalies during that first trip of President Préval to Washington escaped the glare of the public or even of members of the presidential delegation. Since Préval had not been sworn in as president yet, he could not be given Secret Service protection, as required by US law for a dignitary of his rank. State Department security was arranged for him during his stay, and common mortals don't know the difference.

At the appointed time we arrived, properly escorted, at the White House. We were led to the office of the National Security Adviser. On entering the office, I noted the number of chairs for the delegation. There was an extra one. It was placed next to the chair President Préval would occupy. The National Security Adviser was seated juxtaposed to the entrance of the room. Two minutes had not passed, when he abruptly stood up. "Here is President Bush," he said. We all stood up. President Bush strolled into the room and, acting surprised, he said, "President Préval, you are here." And the conversation was engaged.

President Préval even made President Bush laugh heartily. He told an anecdote about a departing president who gave three letters, marked 1, 2, and 3, to his successor and told him what to do with them. When you have your first crisis, open the first letter, then the second on your second crisis, and the third on the third crisis. The first letter said, "Blame your predecessor." The second said the same thing. And the third said, "Prepare to pack up to leave." Everybody laughed.

It was a courtesy, a sort of get-to-know-each-other-visit, not one for any substantive discussion. It was also a photo-op meeting. And the photo of the two presidents together was taken. On leaving the White House, President Préval asked me how he would get the photo-souvenir before leaving town the next day. I told him not to worry, because one way or the other he will have the picture. I called my contact at the White House and asked that the photo be emailed to the consul general in Miami. Then I called Ralph Lator-tue, the consul general, and told him to surprise President Préval when his flight lands in Miami. Knowing that the president is a computer buff, I told the consul to take him to the computer room at the VIP lounge and show him the photo. It can be printed and given to him.

Everything went as planned. President Préval landed in Port-au-Prince properly equipped with his photo taken together with the American Chief of State. That was the answer to those who had said President Bush would not receive him, because he had not been inaugurated yet. It was also a rebuke to those who were spreading rumors that the ambassador in Washington was sabotaging the president elect's first visit to the US capital.

I don't know whether President Préval wanted to know for sure if my relations in Washington were solely Republicans, as some people asserted. On one of his trips to the Federal capital in 2007, he asked whether I could arrange a meeting for him with Senator Hillary Clinton. Of course, I said yes. It happened that the senator's agenda was full and her scheduler said it might be impossible. I left my telephone number for the senator to call me.

Someone from Senator Clinton's staff did call and acknowledged that her schedule was indeed full, but that she would come even to the hotel to see President Préval. Or we could meet at her office after 5:00 p.m. President Préval said we will go to her office. That day we had several meetings in Congress. By 1:00 p.m., I noted that the president looked haggard. I told him we should cancel the next meeting on the list, because he should rest in preparation for the meeting with Senator Clinton. President Préval asked, "Ambassador, what will we do about the meeting already scheduled?"

"Leave that to me," I responded.

I told the Secret Service agent in charge of the security detail that we were changing the agenda and the president was going to his hotel after the 1:00 p.m. meeting. That's what was done. I called the office of the senator that we were to see at 2:00 p.m. to cancel. I explained that President Préval was not feeling well and that he would be going to his hotel for rest. We are sorry that we have to cancel. Of course, that was all right. The president was grateful for the way I handled the situation.

At 5:00 p.m., we were at Senator Clinton's office on Capitol Hill. The Senator was very happy for the visit. She managed to be photographed with each member of the delegation. That was a smart move on the part of her staff, considering that she would later be announcing her candidacy to the presidency. President Préval was satisfied of the meeting with Senator Clinton. If he had any doubt about what I could deliver, he found out otherwise. The welcome I was given by Senator Clinton and her staff was all that the president needed to be fully edified.

A few weeks later, President Préval was coming back to Washington for a summit of Caribbean Chiefs of State. Before he left Port-au-Prince, his office had called to know whether I could arrange a meeting for President Préval with former President Clinton. I said I would. I called the New York office of President Clinton and arranged for a face-to-face in Washington during a visit of the former president to Capitol Hill. The meeting was scheduled for a Thursday at 5:00 p.m. That Thursday morning, as President Préval was having breakfast with some members of his delegation, he looked at me and said, "Ambassador, I have to be in Miami tonight for a very important meeting. My flight leaves at 5:30."

"But, Your Excellency," I said, "you have a meeting with President Clinton at 5:00 p.m. on Capitol Hill. What are we going to do?"

He looked at me with the air of a debonair, and said in Creole, *Wa debouye w!* (You'll sort it out!)

Everyone was looking at me to see what my reaction would be. I just looked at the President and said nothing. I don't know what President Préval was thinking. He must have remembered how I handled the Senate situation weeks earlier.

I excused myself and went to another room. I telephoned President Clinton's office in New York and asked to speak to the scheduler. I explained that something had happened and President Préval must be in Miami that evening. His flight is leaving Washington at 5:30. I know that President Clinton wants to see President Préval, and since President Clinton is flying in his private plane into Reagan National Airport, couldn't we arrange for them to meet at the airport? President Préval is flying out of Reagan. I can arrange for a conference room at the airport.

"We'll call you back, Mr. Ambassador," the scheduler said.

About fifteen minutes later, I received a call from the scheduler. "All done, Mr. Ambassador," she said. "President Clinton will arrive at 4:00 instead of 5:00, as was previously scheduled. A meeting at 4:15 or thereafter is feasible."

I went back to the room where the breakfast was still in progress. As I walked in, the conversation stopped. All eyes were riveted on me, for they did not know why I had excused myself so abruptly earlier. Addressing the President, I said, "Your Excellency, the meeting with President Clinton is at 4:30 at Reagan National Airport. A conference room will be ready for us. And you will have plenty of time to make your Miami flight."

"How did you do that, Mr. Ambassador!" Elizabeth exclaimed. "You must be a miracle man!"

"No, I am not a miracle man," I responded. "I am just doing my job."

President Préval looked stunned. Everyone was in awe. I knew I had scored a home run.

Just before we left for the airport we learned that the Miami flight was delayed by half an hour. That was a bonus. There was no need for the presidents to rush through their meeting. We arrived at a building of the old National Airport where a conference room was set up for us. About five minutes after we had arrived, President Clinton also arrived. He gave President Préval an accolade as that reserved for a long-lost friend. Then he shook hands with everybody and said, "Okay, Okay, you all. You may sit down, because I have nothing I'm going to discuss with the president that you cannot hear."

I said to myself, President Clinton is about to send a message that he would like all to hear. Indeed! He said, "Mr. President, I cannot tell you how happy I am to see you as president again. Because I know when you were president the first time, Aristide didn't let you do anything that you wanted to do. Now that you are president in your own right, how can I help?" We all looked at each other and internalized what was said.

President Préval responded immediately that there were about 500,000 children out of school and that it was a priority for him to find funds to send them to school. That was the gist of the conversation. President Clinton promised to help, but he needed more information and a plan of action.

After the meeting, as we shuffled out of the room, President Préval turned to me and said, "Ambassador, now Clinton is mine."

"Your Excellency, you may have him."

Since then, I don't know how the education project evolved or what transpired between Presidents Clinton and Préval and their staffs. Indeed, basic education is sorely neglected in Haiti. In his inaugural speech in 2011, President Martelly listed Education as one of the "five E," along with Energy, Environment, Employment, and "Etat de droit" (French for the Rule of Law) as the priorities of his administration. To finance his education program, President Martelly unilaterally imposed a $1.50 fee on every money transfer made to Haiti. Unfortunately that laudable project has come under much criticism, for lack of accountability of the funds collected.

Chapter 17

Presidential Honor . . . and
a Congressman's Shame

A few days after the earthquake, President Obama ordered that Temporary Protected Status (TPS) be granted to undocumented Haitians living in the United States. That status is usually granted by the American president to undocumented citizens of a country facing major natural disasters or political turmoil. This allows those living illegally in the United States to obtain documentation, such as Social Security cards and work permits, enabling them to work without fear of deportation. Normally, TPS is granted for eighteen months. But some countries in Central America and Africa had TPS renewed for their citizens for ten years. I had attempted to obtain that status for Haitian citizens following the three major hurricanes in 2005 but was unsuccessful.

When President Obama was inaugurated, I renewed my request. I wrote a letter to the new Homeland Security Secretary, Janet Napolitano. The lobbying was intense, with various organizations, US legislators, notable personalities and newspaper editorials calling on the Obama administration to do the right thing by Haitians.

The requests did not only go to Secretary Napolitano, but also to President Obama. All to no avail!

The US authorities feared that if TPS were declared for Haitians, it would be like a signal for them to renew the boat trek to the United States. The administration envisioned being overwhelmed in a manner that had forced the Clinton administration to detain would-be Haitian refugees in camps at the Guantanamo Naval Base in Cuba for repatriation to Haiti.

It took a killer earthquake of major magnitude to finally get the President of the United States to treat Haitians as others had been treated.

Haitians were not treated fairly by Democrat and Republican administrations when it came to immigration status. During President Obama's first term, his administration did not allow Haitians to benefit from the "Family Reunification Parole" (FRP) program which was granted to Cubans in 2007 and also to others. That program permits close family members who have already been approved to immigrate to come to the United States where they can wait for their green card.

After the earthquake, a major campaign was undertaken to obtain FRP status for 106,000 Haitians already cleared to come to the United States. Advocacy lawyer Steven Forester in Miami noted that 11,715 of these were children and spouses of US citizens or residents who must wait from two-and-a-half to twelve years before they can immigrate.

Editorials in major publications, entreaties from elected officials at the municipal, State and Federal levels did not sway the administration. "Haitians felt betrayed," said Forester.

Unexpectedly, on October 17, 2014, two weeks prior to a very competitive race for governor in Florida, the Department of Homeland Security (DHS) announced that early in 2015 it will begin to implement a Haitian Family Reunification Parole (HFRP) program. This was a political move by the Obama administration intended to corral the Haitian vote for Charles "Charlie" Crist. A former Republican governor of Florida, Crist left the Republican Party to endorse President Obama for reelection in 2012. The power of the Haitian vote had forced a policy change in Washington to the benefit of thousands of Haitian families.

═══════

For the traditional Union address to the nation, on January 27, 2010, the White House invited me and my wife to a reception at the White House. From there I was driven to Capitol Hill where I sat in the box reserved for First Lady Michelle Obama and her guests. I was seated exactly behind her and when she walked in, she turned around to shake my hand. I kissed her on the back of the hand and spoke briefly with her. She motioned to her secretary and told her to take my information. The television cameras were on us throughout the brief encounter. During President Obama's speech, the cameras again focused on me when the president mentioned the tragedy in Haiti.

That evening and the following day, Haitian friends and acquaintances were calling to say how honored they felt by the way Haiti was treated through me. One thing that the public did not see was the handshake that President Obama gave me afterward in the holding room at the Capitol where he congratulated me for the way I represented Haiti during its most tragic hours.

Nonetheless, there was some criticism of President Obama from Haitians at home and in the diaspora, because he did not visit President Préval after the earthquake as some other Chiefs of State had done. They noted that President Nicolas Sarkozy was the first French president to visit Haiti since Haitians had defeated France's elite troops more than two centuries ago. The Port-au-Prince visit in April 2010 of Mrs. Obama and Mrs. Jill Biden, the vice president's wife, softened the criticism somewhat. But Haitians were still unsatisfied. Yet, President Obama had honored President Préval by inviting him to Washington two months after the earthquake.

I was speaking in California the weekend prior to the president's arrival in Washington. But I remained in contact with my staff in charge of preparations to welcome President Préval and his party that were arriving Monday evening, March 8. Someone on the staff told me that reservations for the president and his party were made at the Marriott Wardman Hotel.

"But President Préval is a guest of President Obama," I said. "He should be at Blair House," the official residence reserved for guests of the US President. I told the staff person that I would call her back.

I placed a call to the White House and spoke to the appropriate person about President Préval's visit, at the invitation of President Obama. I asked whether Blair House was available. It would be ready by Tuesday at 3:00 p.m., I was told.

"For how many?" I inquired.

"Fifteen rooms, Mr. Ambassador."

I said thanks. I called back the staff person at the Embassy and said, "Listen, book the President and his party at the Marriott just for Monday night. Ask for an extension till Tuesday 3:00 p.m. Then, the whole party will be moving to Blair House." I put my staff in contact with the Blair House welcoming committee to work out the details. Thus, President Préval got the treatment to which he was entitled.

The meeting at the White House with President Obama was one of the most elaborate. There was a select audience at a joint press conference of Presidents Obama and Préval and many photo-souvenirs. But one of the most fruitful meetings was the one I had set up for the movie star Sean Penn with President Préval at Blair House. Somehow they clicked immediately and President Préval told him, "I really like you and what you propose to do in Haiti."

After Penn left, the President said, "He's a good one. It was a great meeting." That same week, Sean Penn was honored by my wife Lola Poisson at a fund-raising event in Washington. The following week Penn was back in Haiti where he had set up a camp for the displaced of the earthquake at the Pétionville Golf Club, a camp that became a model of efficiency.

———

Although Préval chose the label *Espwa* (Hope) to run when he was reelected in 2006, many *Lavalassians* believed that the time had come to reassert their authority. After all, Préval had been President Aristide's first prime minister in 1991 and had been tapped by his former boss to run for president in December 1995. But the new President Préval had emancipated himself from Aristide in many ways. A clear signal was his decision to keep almost intact the diplomatic corps set up by the interim government. Many of the diplomats were known for their opposition to Aristide.

Some *Lavalas* legislators decided to force President Préval's hand and I would be the first to feel their sting. There's no question that they wanted my scalp. In August 2006, a mere five months after President Préval was sworn in, I received the visit of some parliamentarians. Heading the delegation was Congressman Sorel François, then president of the Foreign Affairs Committee of the Lower House of Parliament. His business card indicated that he was *Lavalas*, the party of exiled President Jean-Bertrand Aristide.

Certainly, Congressman François knew about my past as an opponent of the *Lavalas* regime. However, if he had done his homework, he would have learned that my fight was not with *Lavalassians* per se, but with *Lavalas* as a philosophy to run a country. What better testimony than my dealings with the staff at the Embassy for more than two years!

But Congressman François was on a fishing trip. He was convinced that I had embezzled funds, not unlike other officials that he probably knew. As president of the House's Foreign Affairs Committee, he was undertaking an internal investigation and he needed my cooperation. He had no introductory letter from the Foreign Affairs Ministry, of which I depend. I could have refused any cooperation on the basis that I am not authorized by my superiors to discuss anything with him. I reasoned, on the other hand, that he might think I was refusing to deal with him because I had something to hide. Moreover, I said to myself that he legitimately heads the Committee as proven by his business card. Also, as a *Lavalassian*, if I did not cooperate, he could interpret it as continued hostility to *Lavalas*.

"How can I help?" I asked.

He said he was looking for documents regarding some disbursements. He was also interested in certain bank accounts. I provided him about thirty documents which covered a wide range of financial transactions. As I usually did for visiting dignitaries, I invited the congressman and his colleagues to lunch. Ambassador Duly Brutus, Haiti's Permanent Representative to the Organization of American States and Foreign Minister under Martelly, had joined us. We had a pleasant moment together. The delegation returned to Haiti.

To my great surprise, three weeks later, I heard Congressman François, who preferred to be called Congressman Sorel, on *Radio Caraïbes* in Port-au-Prince. He was making wild accusations, such as the disappearance of $250,000 from the Embassy's account. More importantly was the deposit of $1.9 million in a non-governmental account. Obviously, he had discovered what he thought was occurring under my stewardship in Washington. I began receiving calls from friends in Haiti who told me that I was in deep trouble, because in his disclosures to the press, the congressman said he had documents to prove his assertions.

I did not lose one minute of sleep about the matter. But unlike diplomats who usually deal privately and through diplomatic channels with such matters, I often prefer to confront my accusers head on. Perhaps my journalism background predisposes me to react that way, especially when corruption or embezzlement is alleged.

I called *Radio Caraïbes,* one of the stations on which the accusations were made, and asked for my right to respond. I began by saying that I was astounded to hear Congressman François' accusations. I thought we had developed good rapport during his visit to Washington. We had broken bread together at a restaurant. I thought he knew how to read financial statements. That is why I gave him some documents that he needed for an internal investigation he said he was conducting. If I knew he was going public with the documents, I would have taken care to explain things to him. And if he did not understand some of the transactions, he should have had the decency to call me for clarification and explanation.

Regarding the $250,000 that he said had disappeared from the Embassy accounts, apparently the congressman had passed the addition test, but failed subtraction. Otherwise, he would have seen the authorization of the minister of Finance asking me to use $250,000 to pay a bill for Police equipment. He only needed to deduct the $250,000 from the account. It has disappeared to nowhere.

As for the $1.9 million going into a non-governmental account, that is a serious accusation. The congressman seems to ignore simple banking rules. For nearly half a century, the Embassy of Haiti had its accounts at the venerable Riggs National Bank in Washington, DC. But Riggs had run afoul of Federal regulations when it got involved in some corporate and international scandals. The bank was forbidden from doing international transactions. (Riggs paid a substantial fine and eventually was merged into PNC Financial Services. The name of Riggs disappeared in the Greater Washington metropolitan area, as its branches became PNC.)

We had to close our Riggs accounts and open new ones at Wachovia National Bank. On closing the accounts, Riggs issued a $1.9 million check, which represented the balance of the Embassy accounts, in my name and that of co-signer Marie-Claude Malebranche. That sum was deposited at a new Wachovia account. But Congressman François did not know what Wachovia meant. We also had to close our Wachovia Bank accounts for reasons given by the bank that were not totally clear. The only information we received was that Wachovia is also forbidden to do international transactions. I warned the congressman about making rash judgment. For his information, I said, we now have our accounts at Citibank.

It is logical that deposits can no longer be made at Riggs Bank. Neither can we issue checks on Riggs, because the account is closed. If Congressman François were really interested in finding the truth, he would have inquired about the destination of the transfers made from the Embassy account. He would have found out that funds from the Embassy were being transferred monthly to the same account that the Ministry of Finance provided us at the Central Bank in Port-au-Prince. The only difference is that funds no longer originate from Riggs. It is that simple.

The day following my radio defense, I began receiving calls from friends and acquaintances in Port-au-Prince congratulating me on my performance. Now it was all out war. The congressman felt that I had insulted him publicly. Privately, he said he would drag me in front of his committee at a formal hearing to air his findings and shut me up for good, even force me to resign or be dismissed in shame. Publicly, he refrained from pursuing me. Apparently, he had learned his lesson, at least partially. I knew the congressman had no authority to call me directly to testify. His only recourse was to summon my boss, the foreign affairs minister, and request that I accompany him before the committee.

That is exactly what happened. To add a semblance of impartiality to the witch hunt, the Consul General Felix Augustin in New York was also summoned. After the congressmen returned from their four month recess, in January 2007, Foreign Minister Jean-Rénald Clérismé was summoned to appear with me before the Lower House's Foreign Affairs committee.

Meanwhile, I had asked my financial team at the Embassy to prepare full financial documentation covering the period since I arrived at the Embassy in April 2004. I had a black loose-leaf tome weighing about two pounds that covered everything. My wife said she would not allow me to go into "the lions' den" alone. So, she accompanied me to Port-au-Prince and followed the proceedings from the section reserved for spectators. The consul's wife, Monique, had also accompanied her husband to Port-au-Prince. It was the show of the week and the press was out in force.

As expected, questions to the foreign minister and the consul lasted about forty-five minutes. Then, the inquisition began in earnest and went on for about two hours. Among the most pertinent questions was what authorization did I have to dispose of passport funds to carry out unauthorized business?

That question gave me an opportunity to expose the chaos and mismanagement that existed before I took over the Embassy. All the consulates under my jurisdiction—and perhaps elsewhere—had not received any funds for about three months. That meant employees received no salaries and bills were left unpaid. A stream of threatening letters from creditors caused a collective depression on the part of our financial staff.

At the same time, I noted that the passport account was flush with more than $2 million. I asked the Ministry of Foreign Affairs to consult with the other ministries that have oversight over the money and to give me written authorization to liquidate the debts of all the consulates and missions in the United States. At the same time I asked all the consulates and missions to make formal requests for funds to the Embassy, accompanied by supporting evidentiary documentation.

As soon as I received the written authorization from the Foreign Ministry, I asked my secretary and the Embassy accountant to execute various requests that we had received. By that action I had kept our diplomatic and consular offices opened. Then I threw a rhetorical question at the panel of congressmen: "In my place, Honorable Congressmen, what would you have done?"

A congressman dared to say, "Well, we have many of our school teachers that go for months without being paid."

"Oh yes," I responded, "You are talking about what happens in Haiti, where you have an uncle, an aunt, any relative, to feed you, to give you a place to rest your head. Yes, you may even have a benevolent judge to ask that you be allowed some time to pay your rent. But we are talking about the United States of America. You cannot scratch your head to the landlord when the first of the month rolls around. There is no mango or avocado tree from which to pluck your fruits. The markets don't provide credit. You definitely cannot compare apples with oranges. You should know that when you send diplomats to represent our country abroad, they should not be made the laughingstock of the host country."

I also took the opportunity to show, with figures to boot, that financial order had been restored at the Embassy. So much so, that the transfers to the Treasury had more than quadrupled from what they were when I took charge in April 2004.

I felt on top of my game. I pointed to the black loose-leaf tome that I had brought with me and, looking directly at Congressman François, I said, "Mr. Congressman, was it not I who gave you those few documents that you have in your hand when you came to Washington? Do you think I would have provided you the rope with which I would be hanged? Well, Sir, you see this book here. It has all the financial documents. I will turn it over to my minister. If he wants to share some of the information with you, it is his prerogative. But I want you to know that you are dealing with someone who is an enemy of corruption." I handed the black loose-leaf tome to Minister Clérismé.

I was moved almost to tears when a congressman, spotting white hair, stood up and asked his colleagues, "Do you know who that white-haired man sitting in front of you is? Have you heard of *Radio Vonvon*? You were probably too young to know. For sure, most of you were. Go ask your father or mother about *Radio Vonvon*. This is the man who fought for us to be able to be here today debating freely."

Later, I learned that he was the congressman representing Corail in the Grand'Anse Department. He was someone who had lived through the years of the Duvalier dictatorship. He had emigrated, just as I had to, in order to escape certain death. When he shook my hand after the hearing, I could only say, "Thank you! Thank you!" Witnesses of our struggle for democracy are everywhere, including in Parliament.

In Haitian circles rumors often are more harmful than the reality. Those who expected that the House Foreign Affairs Committee would have nailed me began to spread false information. Thus, I received a telephone call from New York while I was still in Haiti to tell me that *Radyo Panou* (Our Radio) had announced my arrest at the Port-au-Prince airport. The boss at *Radyo Panou,* the *Lavalassian* Jude Joseph (no relation) was gloating about the fact that finally I was exposed for the hypocrite that I am. "He is not as clean as some contend," he stated.

On leaving Port-au-Prince the day after the session in Parliament, I flew directly to New York. Without announcing my visit, the next day I asked a friend to drive me to *Radyo Panou*. I told the receptionist to let Mr. Jude Joseph know that Ambassador Raymond Joseph was in to pay him a courtesy visit. It took him about ten minutes to show up. He was, no doubt trying to think of what he could say to me. After all, he had just celebrated that he thought I was in jail.

Until I resigned in August 2010, I never heard complaints or accusations from anyone.

Chapter 18

President Martelly:
Turning the Clock Back

Half a century after the rise of the Duvalier dictatorship, the new leadership in Haiti is bent on turning the clock back to that era. The Duvalier regime appears as the model to emulate.

In 1957, François Duvalier assumed the presidency through an election. Half a century later, Michel Joseph Martelly also ascended to the presidency through an election. The Duvalier election, backed by the military, was supposed to usher in the era of the middle class. As for Martelly, backed initially by the lower classes, his presidency was touted as one of change. However, a pattern reminiscent of the emergence of the Duvalier dictatorship is troublesome.

The idea of an omnipresent chief is being nurtured. One day the president is distributing automobiles or motorcycles to partisans. The next day he is inaugurating a new road started by his predecessor but for which he takes full credit. A Creole literacy class is graduating and the president is delivering the certificates. A major hospital built by a non-governmental organization is considered an accomplishment of the president and he promises more hospitals. A well-oiled publicity department makes sure that the president is given credit for every good thing that happens in Haiti. It was ludicrous in January 2012 to read about President Martelly being responsible for the renewal of Temporary Protected Status (TPS) for Haitian immigrants living illegally in the United States when President Obama was responsible! The supposed accomplishments of President Martelly in only one year in office were legion.

Journalist Frantz Duval, writing in the Port-au-Prince daily *Le Nouvelliste* made an apt observation. While an international football (soccer) match was being broadcast live on television, a text at the bottom of the screen flashed all along: "Thanks to President Martelly."

President Martelly demonstrated his omnipotence during the national carnival held in Cap-Haïtien in February 2013. Although a committee was entrusted the organization of the carnival, the president banned certain musical groups from participating. He even took to the air to assume responsibility for banning the group Brother's Posse of the popular musician Don Kato. The president found objectionable the lyrics of one of the most popular carnival songs of the year. All the same, the trendy tune pushed the song into No.1 position on the charts, as it was being hummed by almost everyone. The song, in Creole, entitled *Aloral* (Orally), was a biting criticism of the propaganda machine of the government. In other words, the president is lying about his accomplishments.

Other traditional carnival favorites, like *Boukman Eksperyans* of Lòlò (Theodore Beaubrun) and *Ram* were not authorized to participate in the national fiesta. The lyrics of their songs failed the official test. In the case of *Ram,* the video accompanying the music showed a lady who resembled First Lady Sophia Martelly indecently stuffing herself. Not a subtle criticism of the alleged voracity of the president's wife, who is known for pillaging State funds.

Senior adviser and singer Morse gave no reason for his resignation six weeks before the carnival. He created a carnival song insinuating that he disagreed with the grab-all policy of the First Family. By April 2013, when Marie-Carmelle Jean-Marie, minister of Economy and Finance, resigned and denounced irregularities and the loss of support for fiscal restraint, Morse broke his silence and said he also had resigned to protest against corruption in high places.

President Martelly judging morals is interesting. He must have seemingly suffered from amnesia. At one time, President Martelly was a bawdy musician and carnival participant who also unleashed salty lyrics that won him acclaim. In one of his most depraved songs, he once used the crudest language against President Aristide, denouncing his *Lavalas* political party as "s . . . t." He did not spare even the president's mother, as he termed President Aristide himself a "mother f . . . . r."

Obviously, President Martelly knew the power of carnival songs to rattle the authorities. Thus, he took it upon himself to usher in an era of censorship, not unlike what was in vogue under the dictatorship of the Duvaliers, father and son.

In the process, the president opened himself to criticism from the public, and especially from the press, which vowed not to be saddled again with a new dictatorship.

In that sense, the 2013 national carnival opened an era of generalized confrontation, pitting the Executive branch against society at large which disavowed the actions of the Chief of State.

Paying no attention to the Constitution, President Martelly imposed his new style of government on the nation. In addition to father and mother, another presidential family member, 23-year-old son Olivier Martelly, formed a powerful trio. Nepotism notwithstanding, the younger Martelly was officially named adviser to the president for sports. As such, Olivier Martelly crowded out the minister of youth and sports.

In an interview to the daily *Le Nouvelliste* (June 13, 2012), Martelly Jr. mentioned various sports projects under way and to come. He inaugurated two small soccer stadiums in Gressier and Verrettes, localities distant from the capital of Port-au-Prince. He also announced two others in the works for Jérémie and Thomonde, still farther away from the capital. Then it will be the turn of St. Louis in the south and Cayes-Jacmel in the southeast region.

All of it, he said, was part of a well-defined plan that will extend to about ten cities. Sports, he noted, should be decentralized and extended to the youth throughout the country. A noble idea, indeed! (As of September 2014, twelve of these mini stadiums had been built.)

It was not known for sure how much funding was put at the disposal of the president's son. Several press reports mentioned as much as $25 million. There was no acknowledgment or denial by the government. At a presentation in Washington to legislators of the Congressional Black Caucus in September 2013, Haitian Senator Steven Benoit, a critic of President Martelly, denounced that Olivier Martelly was spending more than $1 million to build a store in a ritzy neighborhood of the capital. "Where is the source of that money?" he asked. Embezzlement is alleged.

When it was pointed out that in his official capacity of adviser to his dad, he was stepping on the toes of the minister of sports, Martelly Jr. explained, "Being responsible of sports for change, [being] sports adviser and also son of the President of the Republic, I maintain very good relations with the minister of sports, as well as with several other ministers."

He had daily contacts, he said, with the sports minister to discuss what was being done for the youth and how he could provide support. Obviously, Olivier Martelly, by presidential fiat, became the tsar overseeing the work of the minister of sports—and perhaps of other ministers. One could even say that Martelly Jr. became a rival to the prime minister who, constitutionally, oversees the work of the ministers.

In a cabinet reshuffle in January 2013, the third such change in twenty months of Martelly's presidency, the minister of sports was replaced by Magalie Racine, who previously served as the First Lady's private secretary. The minister of sports had proved uncooperative with the presidential sports tsar. Definitely, Mrs. Racine was a more pliant minister. (In the fourth cabinet reshuffle in April 2014, former Army officer Himmler Rébu replaced Magalie Racine as minister of sports.)

President Martelly may have long-term plans for his son. In line with Papa Doc's thinking, he seems to be preparing a "young leader" for the Haitian people. Few had believed that Baby Doc Duvalier could have stepped into his father's shoes as President-for-life. But when Papa Doc felt his days coming to an end, he said that he was preparing a "young leader for the people."

With the power that he exercised over his close aides and the country as a whole, the dictator changed the existing Constitution to lower the age for president from forty to eighteen. As previously mentioned, at nineteen, the inexperienced "young leader" was foisted on the Haitian people by the dying monarch.

In the 21st century, when democracy is flourishing even in the most arid of soils, only a major upheaval would allow the creation of a new dynasty in Haiti with President Martelly's son succeeding him.

By issuing decrees to put his wife and son in charge of public funds, President Martelly provoked widespread criticism. Two young lawyers, Newton Louis St. Juste and André Michel, accepted to represent Enold Florestal who sued the wife and son of the president, charging them with embezzlement of public funds, corruption and usurpation of titles. The president responded by saying that the poor lawyers are jealous, because his then 22-year-old son already had more money than they could ever aspire to earn.

The scandal caused a split in government ranks, pitting the chief prosecutor in Port-au-Prince, Jean Renel Sénatus, against his superior, Minister of Justice Jean Renel Sanon. The chief prosecutor learned through a radio announcement that he had been fired "for insubordination and grave administrative errors." The prosecutor fired back, declaring that the minister had ordered him to arrest thirty-six individuals, including lawyers Newton St. Juste, André

Michel, and Mario Joseph. The latter is a well-known civil rights advocate who also represents former President Aristide.

Within three months, Prosecutor Sénatus said, Minister Sanon had issued seventeen orders that were illegal. "If my resistance to execute illegal orders is considered insubordination," Sénatus continued, "I plead guilty." Meanwhile, he denounced high level officials who were plotting to use the justice system as a personal tool to carry out their vendetta. In effect, he showed that justice in Haiti remained subservient to the whims of the Executive.

When, on August 20, 2013, Francisco René was sworn in as Port-au-Prince's chief prosecutor, the tenth such prosecutor in twenty-six months since Martelly's presidency, there was no longer any doubt about the intentions of the government.

Liane Piere-Paul, president of the Haitian Media Association took offense and put out a statement that denounced the threat to fundamental rights won in a long fight against the dictatorship.

By July 2013, the lawsuit against President Martelly's wife and son turned into tragedy. Investigative Judge Jean Serge Joseph had breathed life into the complaint of those who dared to confront entrenched power. On July 2nd, the judge asked that the president lift the immunity of several high level officials of his administration that should appear in court on the matter. Included among them were cabinet ministers, beginning with the Prime Minister, the Finance Minister and that of Interior. Also included in the list to appear was the Governor of the Central Bank. By his action, the judge appeared to have concluded that some high level officials of the government were involved in financial shenanigans to the detriment of the State.

Immediately, the judge became a target of the Executive branch. Judge Joseph was asked by the government to vacate the case. But he was in no position to acquiesce to the orders of the President and the Prime Minister. The chief prosecutor for Port-au-Prince had previously appealed the case to a higher jurisdiction. This was a stratagem to remove Judge Joseph from the case. Notwithstanding the intricate judicial nuances, the Executive branch was adamant. Judge Joseph must squash the case. Or else.

According to Samuel Madistin, a respected lawyer and former senator, the judge was summoned to a meeting by the Executive on July 11 during which he came under unspecified threats. Madistin said the intense mental pressure and alleged verbal threats had their effect. At 3:00 a.m. on July 13, Judge Joseph was rushed to the Bernard Mevs Hospital in Port-au-Prince in critical condition. Around 8:00 p.m. that Saturday evening he died at the hospital, victim of a stroke, according to doctors there.

As should be expected, the sudden death of the 58-year-old judge placed the Executive branch in a very delicate position. Accusations of "political assassination" were hurled at President Martelly and Prime Minister Lamothe. Unknown to most, the judge held Canadian citizenship. Thus, his body was flown to Canada for an autopsy. To squash rumors that he had been poisoned, the office of the coroner in Quebec acknowledged that the judge had succumbed to a stroke. Four months later a full report of the coroner's office confirmed the earlier finding. Nonetheless, doubt persisted as to the reason for the stroke causing the death of a relatively young person who did not suffer from diabetes or high blood pressure.

An unusual diplomatic flap had delayed the funeral of Judge Joseph. For unknown reasons, the widow of the magistrate, Rachelle Acéla Joseph, was denied a visa by the Canadian Embassy in Port-au-Prince. With pressure from undisclosed sources mounting, the Canadian officials in Haiti finally relented. Days before the rescheduled August 11, 2013, funeral of Judge Joseph in Montreal, the widow was granted a visa. Thus was she able to join other members of the family who were already waiting in Montreal. The Haitian government chose not to be represented at the funeral.

Meanwhile, legislative and judiciary investigations were under way to ascertain whether the President and the Prime Minister had met with the judge to pressure him to drop the case against members of the First Family. Both the President and the Prime Minister vehemently denied that they ever met with the judge. But that would not have been the first time that President Martelly had denied being involved in blatantly illegal actions in which he was the principal actor.

A five-member Senate investigative commission made public its findings on August 6. After hearing more than fifteen individuals, including the judge's wife, brother, driver, bodyguard, as well as some government officials, the commission concluded that the two top government officials had lied to the commission and the nation.

The July 11 meeting indeed took place at the law office of Gary Lissade. Two weeks later, an investigative commission of the Lower House issued a more extensive report than that of its Senate counterpart. The same conclusions were reached.

Interestingly, the President and the Prime Minister forbade their chauffeurs and bodyguards to appear before the commissions. The executives gave the impression that they had something to hide. They could have had their bodyguards testify about their whereabouts on July 11 at the time they were said to have been at Gary Lissade's office. Certainly, it would have been in their best interest to squash the rumors.

Meanwhile, neighbors of Gary Lissade in the Bourdon neighborhood of Port-au-Prince had already attested to several government vehicles in the area at the time of the alleged meeting of the judge with the President and the Prime Minister. Moreover, Lissade, the president's adviser, had given Judge Joseph his calling card with his private number. And the card still existed.

The Senate commission turned its report over to the Superior Council of Judicial Power (French acronym CSPJ), the organization mandated to supervise the courts and sanction the judges, if needed. For, it had been corroborated that the chief judge of the judicial corps, Raymond Jean Michel, was the one at the wheel of his vehicle when he drove Judge Joseph to the law office of Gary Lissade. The report called for the dismissal of the chief judge whose case should be turned over to a civil court for prosecution. The Prime Minister and the Minister of Justice should be dismissed and brought to trial. Gary Lissade, accused of being an accomplice, should be tried as such.

Regarding President Martelly, the Senate commission called for his impeachment. The report was turned over to the 99-member Lower House, where the Congressmen were urged to begin impeachment procedures against President Martelly.

On September 6, 2013, a thirteen-member investigative commission of the Lower House presented a resolution for the impeachment of President Martelly to the full House. On September 9, the legislative year closed and the Congressmen went on official leave until the second Monday of 2014.

The Senate, though permanently in session, cannot by itself impeach the President. Yet, on September 24, 2013, it held an unusual session where seven senators voted to do just that—to impeach the President. Nine abstained. A staunch supporter of President Martelly, Senator Edwin "Edo" Zenny, left the room before the vote. The most forceful defender of the Executive, Senator Wencesclas Lambert was in New York accompanying Prime Minister Lamothe at the UN General Assembly.

It was widely believed that the evidence against the Executive Branch was overwhelming. But with the members of the Lower House on vacation until the second Monday of 2014, the vote of the Senate was only of a symbolic nature. When the Lower House reconvened in January 2014, no mention was made of the president's impeachment.

By his actions and those with whom he surrounded himself, President Martelly indicated that he yearns for the era of the all powerful president, as it was under Papa Doc, and to a lesser extent under Baby Doc. In a light moment on stage during the Carnival of Jacmel in February 2012, the president jokingly uttered what were probably his innermost ambitions: "Martelly, President-for-life!"

The president ridiculed those who opposed the amended—and contested—Constitution, as well as his self-imposed Permanent Electoral Council. He said they fear that "Olivier Martelly could be president in ten years." What President Martelly did not say is that he himself considered circumventing the new Constitution to succeed himself in power. Were he to be successful in his stratagems, he could anoint his son to assume the presidency after he would have ruled for ten years, not unlike what Papa Doc had done for Baby Doc in 1971.

Even another Duvalier could get the nod before Olivier Martelly. The son of Jean-Claude Duvalier, the 30-year-old François-Nicolas, is an adviser to President Martelly. He has an office at the National Palace. On April 19, 2013, François-Nicolas made his first formal entry into the political arena by publishing an opinion piece in *Le Nouvelliste* entitled "In Memoriam Dr. François Duvalier, President-for-Life," it was an insult to those who were commemorating, on April 26, the fifty years of the massacre that was ordered by Duvalier on that date.

François-Nicolas praised his grandfather as one "who used his sharp mind to defend the values and interests of the Republic of Haiti." He asserted that "Dr. François Duvalier, throughout his life, defended the republican values that were his: integrity and steadfastness . . . a Haitian of conviction, a great nationalist." That so-called nationalist, I will add, massacred thousands of citizens and caused the brain drain of Haiti. Thousands departed the hell on earth that had been created under his grandfather's cruel dictatorship.

Although Baby Doc did not have an office at the National Palace, he was also an unpaid adviser to President Martelly, who staunchly defended the former dictator. But any attempt to bring Duvalierism back to power by any means will be strongly contested by those who brought down the dictatorship twenty-five years ago. That would include the *Lavalas* partisans of former President Jean-Bertrand Aristide who, like Jean-Claude Duvalier, also returned to Haiti in 2011 before the presidential election that resulted in Martelly's victory.

Chapter 19

Flaunting Democratic Governance

The Constitution of 1987 was established to curtail the power of the president. To accomplish that, the authors of the Charter introduced the concept of a dual executive. That was the intention of the newly created office of the Prime Minister. He would exercise power as Chief Executive Officer (CEO) of the country, while the president would be like a Chairman of the Board and guarantor of the Constitution.

Since 1988 when the first Prime Minister, Martial Célestin, Esq., held the post, the presidents have always tried to eclipse the prime ministers. The presidents claim that they were elected by the people, not the prime ministers. But the prime ministers gain their legitimacy from Parliament whose members, including 99 in the Lower House and 30 in the Senate, are also elected by the people.

Whereas the presidents since 1988 have pulled the rugs from under their prime ministers in various degrees, President Martelly was more blatant in his crude humiliation of Prime Minister Conille in 2012. First, President Martelly began his presidency without a prime minister. As expected, the first two candidates he had proposed for the post, Gérard Rouzier and Bernard Gousse, were rejected. The president knew, just as most political observers had warned, that Parliament would not approve them. Yet, he was determined to make his will stick. While the choice of a prime minister lingered, during the first four months of his presidency Martelly exercised power alone as a potentate.

Alone in this power, President Martelly took that opportunity to issue an important decree—a tax on money transfers. He imposed a $1.50 tax on every transfer of funds to Haiti to finance his program of free and mandatory universal education. Incoming international telephone calls were also taxed for the project. Most people agree that the education of Haiti's unschooled children is a noble and urgent cause, but President Martelly went about it in a dictatorial manner that resulted in much criticism. There was no transparency regarding the money collected and how it was affected. Neither was there a law regulating the new National Education Fund (French acronym FNE). Three years after the set-up of FNE, the government didn't give an accounting of how much had gone into the Program for Universal Free and Obligatory Education, known by its French acronym PSUGO.

The $1.50 tax on transfers was a lightning rod for demonstrators against President Martelly at Brooklyn College in September 2012. While the President attended the annual General Assembly of the United Nations, he decided to address the Haitian community. He was welcomed by a lively demonstration led by pop singer Raymond Divers, a.k.a. King Kino. On handwritten signs and loud slogans shouted from bullhorns, the message was "What have you done with our $1.50 on the money transfers?"

After his early game of attrition, President Martelly was forced by the international community to accept Dr. Garry Conille as prime minister. However, the president let it be known that he did not need any Dr. Conille. Martelly had an undated resignation letter written for the prime minister even before he was approved by Parliament. Dr. Conille refused to sign.

Dr. Conille was about to withdraw totally from the process when surprisingly President Martelly telephoned him to beg that he refrain from that decision. The President asserted that he knew nothing about the action taken by his subordinates in regard to the pre-written resignation letter; he was on a trip away from the capital. Nonetheless, that initial move of the President's surrogates was generally interpreted as an easy way for Martelly to fire Conille whenever he felt like it.

By standing up to the President's arrogant team which wanted to show him the door even before he had gotten in, Conille became the darling of Parliament. Thus, the Lower House voted unanimously to approve him as Prime Minister. Though the Senate was less sanguine, it also approved him and considered him an ally. The parliamentarians saw Conille as a counterweight to President Martelly and his coterie of friends.

The Prime Minister had only the title, but not the power. Even his choice for Minister of Planning and External Cooperation was turned down by President Martelly at the last minute. On the day that the Prime Minister was to present the general policy of his government together with the members of his cabinet to Parliament, he found out that his choice had been replaced by someone close to President Martelly. Conille swallowed his lumps and hoped for better days. Already, the president was protecting his relative, former Prime Minister Jean Max Bellerive, who also had held the Planning portfolio under President Préval. Eventually that will become clear.

At the outset, Prime Minister Conille was at odds with President Martelly on several issues of national and international importance. Less than two weeks after he assumed his post, the Prime Minister found himself at opposite ends of the President on a political scandal that pitted President Martelly and his team against the Legislative branch. The President was bent on showing that he was the Supreme Chief, thus deserving of full respect. Forget that he must also show others the respect due them.

Following an altercation with Congressman Arnel Bélizaire at the National Palace, in the presence of other legislators, President Martelly told Bélizaire, "You know that some people could find themselves not leaving here alive!" Still fulminating, the President stated that the Parliament is a den of bandits and fugitives from the law. He threatened to go after them all.

Three weeks after that incident, Congressman Bélizaire was arrested. On October 27, 2011, as he landed at the international airport in Port-au-Prince from an official trip to France, he was grabbed on the tarmac. Martelly decided to make an example of Bélizaire, because he dared respond to the President's provocation to his face.

The arrest of Congressman Bélizaire was a major operation that involved several ministries, the Police and even units of the MINUSTAH. The latter were mobilized around the airport to deal with any possible disturbance by supporters of the congressman when he landed. Fortunately, no confrontation occurred, because the Haitian Police had ordered the congressman into an idling vehicle that was waiting on the tarmac at the airport. His supporters never knew when he arrived and how he had left the airport.

Although the Ministry of Justice was responsible for the operation, Minister of Interior Thierry Mayard-Paul took over its execution. Flanked by his bodyguards, he arrived at the airport, and with no regards for the security personnel, he badgered his way onto the tarmac. By shoving aside the security folks as he did, he violated internationally mandated security regulations. But this was the new Haiti where might is right.

The scandal was such that airport security employees denounced the minister publicly and even started a strike the following day. However, Mayard-Paul denied that he had touched any member of the airport security staff. The workers were forced to retract their statements against the minister and to put a quick stop to their work stoppage.

Back to Congressman Bélizaire. From the airport, he was driven to the National Penitentiary, without any court appearance. But the officials at the penitentiary refused to incarcerate him without proper charges brought against him. Thus, the legislator spent the night in the office of the penitentiary, receiving visitors and some amenities, including bedding for the night.

One prominent visitor was Prime Minister Conille who told penitentiary officials to show all the respect due Bélizaire. It should be noted that the Prime Minister had not used his official vehicle when he went to visit the congressman. The next day, he followed up his visit with an official statement deploring the arrest.

The congressmen were on leave and could not meet to deliberate on how to react to the humiliation of their colleague. In solidarity with their fellow legislators of the Lower House, the senators called a meeting and set up a commission to investigate the arrest of Congressman Bélizaire. Those targeted in the investigation included the chief government prosecutor for Port-au-Prince whose office had issued the arrest warrant, the minister of Justice that had oversight over the prosecutor, the secretary of state for foreign affairs who regulates the diplomatic salon at the airport, and the director general of the Police.

Although he was considered among the architects of the plot to arrest the congressman, Minister of Interior Mayard-Paul escaped blame. Against all evidence, he denied having had anything to do with the arrest. Even President Martelly said he had nothing to do, one way or the other ("in black or white," was how he put it) with the arrest of Bélizaire. In the final analysis, an investigation by a commission of the Lower House concluded that the arrest of the congressman had originated with President Martelly.

By the time the Lower House came into session on the second Monday of 2012, nearly three months had elapsed since the arrest of Congressman Bélizaire. Many deals had undoubtedly been reached to squash the scandal. There was no longer the urgency to "do something" to rein in the Executive branch as had been voiced publicly by several congressmen. Even the victim showed little interest in pursuing the Minister of Interior, who was the main target of his colleagues at the beginning of the crisis in October.

Some lessons can be drawn in the aftermath of the scandal surrounding the arrest of Congressman Bélizaire. There is no way to escape the power of intimidation and corruption in their various forms in Haiti, despite the trumpeted promise of change by President Martelly when he was campaigning. The airport employees were threatened with the loss of their jobs if they did not retract their charges against Minister Mayard-Paul who had publicly abused them. Sadly, Haiti has returned to the era of personal power and the abuse thereof by the Executive branch, which also controls the Judiciary.

From President Martelly's point of view, Prime Minister Conille committed the unforgivable sin when he tackled corruption. Allegations were rife about some contracts doled out after the earthquake that didn't adhere to the bidding process. So, Conille set up an audit commission to review $500 million worth of contracts signed by his predecessor, Bellerive. Reportedly a cousin of Martelly, Bellerive continued to have his office at the National Palace as an adviser to the President. Both Bellerive and the President objected to the audit commission. That put the new Prime Minister on a collision course with the President.

Conille was forced out of office before the commission completed its work. However, the commission issued a damaging report about certain of the contracts signed by Bellerive, some literally on the eve of President Martelly's inauguration. Without bids, certain Dominican firms, owned by alleged friends of Bellerive, obtained the lion's share of the contracts, to the detriment of the State. Bellerive disputed that. The firms included those owned by Dominican Senator Felix Bautista who had contributed up to $2.5 million to Martelly's campaign. The last payments to the Haitian president occurred in

November 2011, six months after he had been sworn into office. This year, 2014, events in the Dominican Republic show the relevance of Felix Bautista, a multimillionaire whose properties have been ordered confiscated by the equivalent of Attorney General. There is a bicameral investigation going on concerning the charges of corruption against the powerful senator of the ruling party.

The audit commission's report recommended that some of the contracts be renegotiated and others cancelled outright. The international community followed this saga closely, especially since some of the contracts granted covered areas in the north of Haiti, far from the zones devastated by the earthquake of January 12, 2010. To protect his cousin and adviser Bellerive, President Martelly began to engineer the firing of Prime Minister Conille. Certainly, accountability and transparency in State affairs, as envisaged by Conille, would have put Haiti on the path to development. However, by forcing out a capable and honest prime minister, President Martelly had painted himself in a corner—that of the status quo. The country has suffered the consequences.

The nationality issue caused the final break between the Prime Minister and the President. The Constitution of 1987 forbade a Haitian-born citizen holding another nationality to occupy high elective or executive posts. A few months after Martelly was sworn into office as President, Senator Moïse Jean-Charles (*Inite*, North) accused the President of holding onto two nationalities other than Haitian. Allegedly, Martelly would have been both an American and Italian citizen.

It was the task of the Provisional Electoral Council empowered to supervise the elections to ascertain the true nationality of all the candidates, including Candidate Martelly. It was also its task to have found out that Congressman Bélizaire was a fugitive from jail! Instead of immediately clearing up the matter of his nationality, President Martelly arrogantly said he would not make available his traveling documents. These were the passports he had used over the years. "They will remain where they are—in my pockets," he said arrogantly on television, while putting his right hand below his belt in front of him. "Come and get it," he taunted his accusers.

During four months, Haiti was riveted by the dispute between the President and the investigation of his nationality and that of senior officials of his administration. Martelly's sordid past, including an arrest in New York for unprovoked violence, was repeatedly aired. The national atmosphere was poisoned. Again, then Prime Minister Conille found himself at odds with President Martelly.

In the final analysis, the Office of the President issued a communiqué to formally reject the demand of the Senate commission that all ministers, secretaries of state and the president himself submit their traveling documents for analysis. Citing various articles of law as well as the Constitution, the Palace went through all sorts of contortions to thwart the investigation.

On the day that the members of the Executive were to appear before the commission, only the Prime Minister showed up with his documents. He had encouraged the ministers and secretaries of state to do likewise, but none paid any attention to him. At the last minute, on the date for their appearance, a collective letter from the ministers was sent to the commission requesting an eight-day delay for a review of their position.

Meanwhile, it was carnival time in Haiti. This annual tradition of *Mardi Gras* (Fat Tuesday) is a collective folly when regular business stops and all inhibition disappears. Beginning Friday after work right through the wee hours of Ash Wednesday, it is non-stop revelry.

Their eight-day request for delay to respond to the Senatorial commission fell two days after the official close of the carnival. Somehow, the ministers must have regained their common sense, because the Senate could have voted them out of office for insubordination. Though nominated by the President, the ministers owe their approval to the Senate. So, on the delayed date, the ministers, except for one, and almost all the secretaries of state showed up at the commission. In solidarity with President Martelly, they wore the pink bracelet that is the president's symbol since the electoral campaign.

On leaving the Senate hearing, the ministers thumbed their noses at Prime Minister Conille by not attending a cabinet meeting he had called. The Prime Minister's office was only one block from Parliament House. By their action, the ministers confirmed what was already known in the public. The cabinet no longer recognized the Prime Minister's authority as Chief Executive. The following day, he wrote his resignation letter to President Martelly, with copies delivered to the presidents of the two Houses of Parliament.

After only four months in office, Conille, a dedicated international public servant, was underhandedly forced out. It was very humiliating for an experienced high level cadre of the United Nations like Conille, who had been on the staff of former President Bill Clinton, the special UN envoy to Haiti. Conille was no match for a conniving President Martelly bent on occupying the whole executive space.

The reactions of the international community were swift. They expressed concern about the political void and urged President Martelly to find a speedy solution to the crisis caused by the sudden resignation of Conille.

President Martelly called on the international partners to be calm. He said he had already contacted the heads of Parliament in view of rapidly filling the prime minister's post. Yet, it took nearly three months to have the President's latest choice for Prime Minister approved. Overall, during President Martelly's first twelve months in office, there was a prime minister for only four months. Obviously, the Chief of State was very comfortable with that situation, while the country was literally put on hold.

————

Soon after Martelly was sworn in, he came under pressure to publish the amended Constitution. He would attend to that, he said, when Parliament approves his new prime minister, his former business partner Laurent Salvador Lamothe. The debate for publication resumed soon after Lamothe was approved. The critics against publication of the amended Constitution, including some of the president's advisers, vociferously expressed their opposition. Meanwhile, President Martelly maintained an unusual silence about what he planned to do.

Then on Monday, June 18, 2012, the press was summoned to the Palace for an important announcement by the President concerning the amended Constitution. That Tuesday, President Martelly, flanked by the presidents of the two Chambers of Parliament and the president of the Supreme Court, announced that he was ordering the publication of the amended text.

Among innovations, it stipulates that a quota of 30 percent shall be reserved for women in political organizations as well as in public offices. Individuals born abroad of Haitian parents who never renounced their citizenship are forever Haitian. However, all Haitians are subject to Haitian law once they set foot in the country. They cannot claim protection under their foreign nationality if they infringe Haitian law. Haitians, indistinctly, enjoy all the rights and responsibilities afforded them in the Constitution. This was a muted victory for Haitians in the diaspora who had been ostracized by their country, while their remittances to the country amounted to more than $2 billion annually, or about 25 percent of GNP.

For the first time since he was inaugurated a year earlier, President Martelly had reached unanimity among the three major branches of State. This was considered a good omen for the country which had been deadlocked in discussions on a broad range of issues, from holding of senatorial and local elections to the nationality of high officials of the administration, including the President.

Chapter 20

A New Army and Agents of Repression

During the 2010–2011 presidential campaign, Candidate Michel Martelly promised that, if elected, he would reestablish the *"Forces Armées d'Haiti" (FAd'H)*, as the Haitian Armed Forces was called. As previously mentioned, in retaliation for the Army coup against him in 1991, on his return from his Washington exile, President Aristide disbanded the force by decree in January 1995. Similar to Papa Doc's *Tontons-Macoute*, President Martelly was intent on having a force that would be solely under his control.

Contrary to what his presidency would prove, Martelly made it very clear at his inauguration on May 14, 2011, that he was pleased with the "demobilized soldiers" who had begun training for their spectacular "Coming Out" parade on November 18. On that date in 1803, the Haitian army defeated Napoleon Bonaparte's troops. Considering the effects of the devastating earthquake of 2010, it was ill advised, even pure folly, to spend a reported $95 million to reestablish the Army at that time.

Moreover, the international community, especially France, Canada and the United States, did not ascribe to the resurrection of the corps. They reiterated their commitment to help Haiti in beefing up the National Police.

On November 18, there was a meager parade of the "demobilized soldiers" at the Champ de Mars, near the National Palace. President Martelly didn't show up to receive the honors. Instead, he announced the formation of a commission to study the eventual remobilization of the Armed Forces. That was a departure from his intial comments about setting up the force.

President Martelly was vilified by nationalists who deemed him a traitor for knuckling under pressure of the international community. But he couldn't do otherwise, because foreign aid accounts for 60 percent of Haiti's budget. Attempts to find the money elsewhere came to naught. Nonetheless, through trickery, the Haitian president was moving forward with his plan.

Rumors were rife about a commitment of funds from Venezuela. It was even said that Iran had earmarked $500 million for Haiti, most of which would be for the remobilization of the Army. Haiti's minister of foreign affairs at the time, Laurent Lamothe, was forced to deny reports that Iran's President Mahmoud Ahmadinejad would visit Port-au-Prince on March 9, 2012, at which time he would officially release the funds to Haiti.

What truth existed in the rumors is unknown. But the Iranian president was quoted as saying at an official event in Tehran that a new world order is envisaged, and Haiti will have its place in it. He also said the time had come for the powerful nations to stop bullying the weak States. Apparently President Ahmadinejad was testing to see what would be the response of Washington to his interest in Haiti. And Haiti's foreign minister wanted to show his determination in pushing his trumpeted South-South policy.

Long before the rumors about the Iranian president's visit to Port-au-Prince, eyebrows were raised in some diplomatic circles about a photo of President Martelly with the Washington nemesis. It was taken in Managua at the inauguration of Nicaraguan President

Manuel Ortega, far from being a darling of Washington himself. Anyway, here was President Martelly rubbing shoulders also with such greats as Presidents Hugo Chavez of Venezuela and Raoul Castro of Cuba. That did not go unnoticed in Washington. Haiti's relations with the United States suffered somewhat. Thus, more than two years into his presidency, Michel Martelly was not invited, as expected, to meet his American counterpart. (On February 6, 2014, President Obama finally had a five-minute tête-à-tête with President Martelly at the Oval Office.)

Despite the assurances given by President Martelly that a commission was studying the feasibility of the Army and its eventual deployment, groups of "demobilized soldiers" took over several former Army camps and other government establishments in various parts of the country. They recruited young men and women to grow the army, and in some cases, the new "soldiers" were better armed than the National Police. They did not seem alarmed by communiqués of the ministry of the Interior that ordered them to disband and stop wearing army uniforms.

A deadline of March 18, 2012, to comply with the Ministry of Interior order to disband came and went without any sanction against the embryonic Army. Worse yet, two days after that date, uniformed "soldiers" paraded in the streets of Cap Haïtien, Haiti's second largest city. The crowd welcomed them with great applause. There is no doubt that the new soldiers had official support to operate. They were sharply dressed. They wheeled around proudly in brand new vehicles. The communiqués of the ministries of Interior and Justice to "disband or suffer the consequences" were ignored. The Haitian authorities were doing surreptitiously what they swore they would not allow to ever happen: the establishment of a military force independent from the National Police under the direct control of President Martelly.

While Martelly faked ignorance of what was happening, just as he had done in other cases where he was fully involved, he had encouraged the preparation of a military force intended for his personal use. In that sense, he was copying Papa Doc who instituted the *Tontons-Macoute* to offset the Army. Thus, hiding behind the Constitution, President Martelly was about to reinstate the Army that President Aristide had banned by decree. If Martelly were to have his way, the actual National Police would have become subordinate to his new armed force.

It is revealing that President Martelly publicly praised Duvalierism. On September 7, 2012, while he visited the government's power plant *Electricite D'Haiti* (EDH), or Electricity of Haiti, he exclaimed that "[EDH] shows the progressivism of Duvalierism." The power plant was an accomplishment of the Duvalier regime. In no subtle way, Martelly was proposing going back to the days of the Duvalier dictatorship.

Faced with international resistance to the remobilization of Haiti's Armed Forces under any guise, President Martelly had to take action against the so-called soldiers. On May 18, 2012, Haiti's Flag Day, most of the uniformed "demobilized soldiers" left their camp to parade at the Champ de Mars, near the Palace. Heavily armed policemen, backed by MINUSTAH soldiers, took over their camp. Those parading on the Champ de Mars were overwhelmed and arrested by the Police and MINUSTAH. Several makeshift military camps in the country were soon deserted.

In interviews after the dismantling of their camps, several leaders of the "demobilized soldiers" denounced the "treason" of some officials who had misled them. Although they didn't mention names, the former "soldiers" suggested they had received regular visits from certain dignitaries of the Martelly government. They said they didn't have money to buy new vehicles, uniforms, and weapons. And they were properly provided for their daily upkeep. In other words, as suspected by most, the "demobilized soldiers" were a creation of the Martelly government.

While the President succumbed to international pressure by disbanding the "demobilized soldiers," they were not disarmed. That prompted several parliamentarians to say that a "sword of Damocles" still hangs over the country. At an opportune time, those same "demobilized soldiers" could pop up somewhere as guerrillas.

Despite the official disbanding of the "demobilized soldiers," there still existed a sinister plan for an independent force under the control of the President's men. Three weeks after that action, the Minister of Interior announced recruitment for border patrol guards. Minister Mayard-Paul said a border patrol of about 2,500 individuals would be set up as a distinct force from the National Police. This was a stratagem to recruit among the "demobilized soldiers," including among those too young to have been in the Army when it was disbanded in 1995.

The Minister of Interior tried to buy the silence of the soldiers by offering to pay another installment of their severance pay. Thus was bought the silence of the individuals who had been officially encouraged to set up the illegal army camps.

Those who were arrested on May 18 at the Champs de Mars disappeared quietly. There was no court appearance for disturbing the peace or for disobeying orders to disband. Eventually, Zeke Petrie, one of the Americans arrested along with the "demobilized soldiers, surfaced in the United States and announced on Facebook that he is writing a book about his experience in Haiti.

While a border patrol unit is a commendable decision, it should not be under a leadership separate from the National Police. Otherwise, it will soon turn into a paramilitary group not unlike the *Tontons-Macoute*. From a border patrol unit, the authorities plan to branch out to local and rural units, still independent from the National Police. As much as these local forces would fill a void, they should not escape the oversight of the National Police. Certainly, they will eventually replace the old disbanded Rural Police with its all-powerful *Chefs de Section* (Section Chiefs) who were the actual rulers in Haiti's countryside. At the same time, there is no guarantee that the central power will not use them as in the past for its own purpose.

In August 2013, President Martelly welcomed back to Haiti forty-one young Haitians who had been studying in Ecuador and declared that they were "Army engineer officers." They were deployed with the Ecuadorean unit of the MINUSTAH in the Artibonite Department in north-central Haiti. At their inaugural ceremony, President Martelly said he had finally accomplished a campaign promise to re-establish the Army. The leader of the Haitian unit was Youri Lator-tue, the President's adviser and a former Army officer who had been senator of the Artibonite.

The Ecuadorean-trained officers are said to be the embryo for the future military force. Meanwhile, the senior senator of the Artibonite, François Annick Joseph, said he was not aware of the deployment of the new Haitian Army officers. "They haven't been provided for in the current budget," he noted. In other words, President Martelly was surreptitiously introducing the new armed force for his own purpose.

I believe that Haiti cannot remain forever dependent on an international force for the security of the land and the safety of its citizens. I have proposed beefing up the National Police to about 20,000. I agree with a border patrol of about 2,500 individuals and a much larger Forest Rangers unit, whose main purpose would be to accompany and protect the reforestation of the country. The Rangers could easily assume some of the duties and responsibilities of the old *Police Rurale*. Essential to the new Defense Force would be a beefed up naval unit to oversee the nearly 1,700 miles (2,700 kilometers) of Haiti's coastline. A small air unit, using mainly helicopters, should complete that force. Given the mountainous landscape of the country, with its deep gorges and valleys, the use of helicopters will greatly reduce the distances. Above all, community policing should be an integral part of the training of these specialized units of the National Police.

Some dangerous and distasteful practices of the past have come back. Those who are close aides of the President or agents working for the First Lady seem to have unlimited power. At times these free roaming agents use their power indiscriminately, even causing death in murky circumstances. The number of vehicles with tinted glass and strobe lights has increased alarmingly. Going often against traffic and at high speed, they represent a real menace.

Some new potentates demand respect in the most unusual ways. Ronald "Roro" Nelson, a close aide of President Martelly, with no clearly defined title, was the most often cited example of lawlessness. A photographer snapped a photo of Nelson's black tinted vehicle. The photographer was in trouble, because he did not know that Roro was in the vehicle with one of his lady friends.

The photographer's car was blocked by Nelson's vehicle and ordered to follow the black car to a police station. The photographer had to explain his insolent act. But before Nelson arrived at the station, he switched into a back-up vehicle and left his lady friend in charge of matters. Although the lady asserted that she was a police officer, she had no badge to prove it. Neither would she give the photographer her name.

When the officers at the police station said they could not proceed with the case, the photographer was taken to a second police post where the alleged female police officer had some friends. As she waited for the arrival of her friends who were absent, she became impatient and ordered her aides to drive the photographer to the airport holding cell, which was less than a mile away.

As they were about to leave, the lady's friends arrived and took matters in hand. The whole incident was rehashed. The police seized the photographer's film. Fortunately, he had already deleted all the photos he had taken. Although the photographer mentioned that Roro Nelson had been in the vehicle when the photo incident occurred, his name did not appear in the report. Neither was that of the alleged female police officer. However, the photographer was fully identified. He had to give his address and telephone number. Then, he was let go, but told he must remain at the disposal of the Police for further investigation.

In jest, the photographer asked, "Would you have done the same thing to a White foreign photographer?" After a mysterious break-in where he lived, the photographer moved to an undisclosed location.

Obviously, this incident shows that the intimidation techniques once in vogue in the days of the Duvalier dictatorship are making a surprising comeback.

Other egregious acts have been attributed to Roro Nelson. He made national news when, for no reason, he violently slapped a woman on both sides of her face. She had only asked him to move his vehicle which had blocked the entry to her garage. The evening of the incident, the woman's husband went on radio to announce that his wife had been kidnapped. But the scandal was quickly muffled, probably in the usual manner that such scandals are made to disappear in Haiti—by increased intimidation coupled with monetary payment to buy silence.

Roro Nelson is a recidivist. He was blocked from leaving the United States in 2011 in a case involving violence against a female friend in Boston. His lawyers finally convinced the judge handling the case that Nelson was not a flight risk and that his travel restrictions should be lifted. Soon afterward, he rejoined President Martelly's team in Haiti. Thus, Ronald Nelson, on probation in a Massachusetts court case, was causing major trouble in Haiti where he apparently enjoyed a strange presidential immunity. Roro reminds us of Ti Bobo, Boss Peintre, Zacharie Delva, Luc Désir and other infamous official thugs who exercised lawlessness under the Duvalier dictatorship.

The behavior of the unofficial agents of the Martelly regime flies in the face of the law and justice. The case of Calixte Valentin, who publicly murdered a 32-year-old businessman, was the most troubling. Valentin, according to concordant testimonies by several

witnesses, had gunned down Octanol Dérissaint at Fonds Paris-
ien, a locality near the Dominican border town of Malpasse. The
government prosecutor for the district had ordered the arrest and
incarceration of Valentin, who was said to be "on mission" for the
government.

The prosecutor, Mario Beauvoir, came under heavy pressure to
release Valentin. He said he was first threatened by Jean Renel Sanon,
who was secretary general to the president, equivalent to cabinet
chief. Sanon had called him to ask whether he knew who Dérissaint
was. "Were I in your place, I would not have jailed him," Sanon said.

Two weeks later, Jean Renel Sanon replaced Justice Minister
Pierre Michel Brunache at that sensitive post. Mario Beauvoir,
the prosecutor in the Calixte Valentin murder case, was dismissed.
Though officially jailed, Valentin went home every evening. As if the
jail had become his new place of work! Six months later, the government stopped playing hide-and-seek with Valentin. He was officially
released, without facing trial. This caused a major uproar in society.
The leading human rights organization, *Réseau National des Droits
Humains* (RNDDH), or National Network of Human Rights, as
well as several leaders of political parties denounced the injustice
perpetrated against the family of Octanol Dérissaint—to no avail.

After the fact, it became known that Calixte Valentin's "mission"
at the Malpasse customs was to control every day's receipts and to
physically transport the cash to the Palace to the First Lady after
closing time. Thus, Valentin, who had no official title, was considered among the most powerful in the presidential entourage. The
arrogance of power had pushed him to the ultimate limit, meting
out death to a citizen, knowing that he would be covered by presidential immunity.

A gruesome murder scene further confirmed that criminality is
condoned by the Martelly administration, not unlike what happened under previous regimes since the fall of the Duvalier dictatorship. On the evening of September 27, 2012, Manès Monchéry and

his family were shot dead at their home in the Thomassin suburb of Pétionville. The house was set afire. Only Cindy, the 25-year-old daughter of the Monchéry couple, escaped. A nurse, she had been held up at work.

Manès Monchéry happened to have been the accountant at the ministry of Interior. A scrutiny of the ministry was under way for suspicious disbursements made to certain programs that were managed by President Martelly's wife. The compromising documents that he had taken from the office disappeared. No investigation was undertaken in this salacious murder of a whole family, a crime which had the imprint of an official execution.

The arrogance and boorishness of the associates of President Martelly reached a new plateau when a senator closely tied to the President insulted a judge and the representative of a political party that he felt were out of line. Senator Edwin "Edo" Zenny, of the Southeastern Department (Jacmel), spat in the face of Justice of the Peace Bob Simonis and threatened him and Professor Pierre Lucien of the MOCHRENAH political party.

The senator was incensed about an unflattering remark they had made about him in an interview and their criticism of the Martelly administration. The senator burst into the studio of *Radio Bellevue International* (103.9 FM) in Jacmel to confront his victims while they were still in the studio. He called them derogatory names, such as "dirty niggers," and warned that next time they would face the worst.

Edo Zenny happens to be a mulatto, one of many such individuals around President Martelly who have injected skin color into the explosive political mix. In an interview, Judge Simonis said, after Senator Zenny spat in his face, he yelled out, "You must respect a mulatto. Edo Zenny knows you, but not Senator Zenny. I am white, and you are a Negro!"*

Haïti Lberté, September 10, 2012

Chapter 21

The Official Power versus the Free Press

President Martelly had some high level criminals in his entourage. Their actions were a blot on the presidency. Due to their powerful connections, the criminals were often shielded. But eventually they ran out of options, ending up in jail or in thin air. Thanks to a relatively free press since the fall of the Duvalier dictatorship, the dirty linen is washed in public, and even the most powerful come under scrutiny.

When Clifford Brandt was arrested on October 22, 2012, he was in possession of a special card making him an adviser of President Martelly. Brandt, a member of Haiti's economic elite and scion of a wealthy family, was involved in the kidnapping of two adult children of Robert Moscoso, the chief executive officer of the major banking establishment Sogebank. He had demanded a ransom of $2.5 million. Brandt confessed to the kidnapping of the Moscoso children and led the Police to the house where they were held hostage.

Brandt's arrest revealed the involvement of Haiti's economic elite in a criminal enterprise and the structure of a sophisticated system of extortion. Bank tellers and Police officials were connected to the network which extended even to the Palace. The intelligence chief of the Palace happened to be in charge of security for the Brandt family operations. That probably explains why the kidnapping of the victims could be carried out in broad daylight and on a major thoroughfare by individuals circulating in official vehicles. Moreover, Brandt had named Olivier Martelly, the President's son, as a member of his organization. Brandt was jailed, awaiting a trial that never came. He probably knew too much. Were he to be tried publicly, he could be an embarrassment for many.

Denying any participation in Brandt's criminal enterprise, in January 2013, Olivier, a musician like his father, released a video in Creole entitled *Veye Yo* (Watch them). He sang away: *"Some people don't see your strength, but your weakness. They will not encourage you. . . . Some say I am a kidnapper. Some believe. Some don't. We need to watch all those people, friends who do not like you. Watch them!"*

An incident in Port Salut also raised the curtain on another sordid operation. Two days after the President left Dan's Creek, the luxury resort of his frequent host Evinx Daniel, the latter was arrested with a drug shipment. Nabbed September 12, 2013, Daniel was released twenty-four hours later on orders of a judge in Cayes, the administrative capital of the Southern Department. From his jail cell, Daniel was allowed to give interviews. He explained the circumstances surrounding the drug found at his place. He said he had been at sea in his yacht when he discovered the packages floating. He picked them up to prevent any harm to the youth. He said he was about to call the Police to recuperate the loot at his house.

Few people believed the convoluted explanation of Evinx Daniel, who was well known as a major drug dealer in the region. His operation would have gone smoothly except for an accident. His boat had run out of fuel and he called for help. Indiscreet eyes had seen the merchandise and someone snitched to the Police.

The release of Evinx Daniel caused a huge uproar in Cayes, especially when the prosecutor who ordered his arrest, Jean-Marie

Salomon, was demoted. The population protested and obtained his reinstatement. But it wasn't for long, because Salomon was eventually fired. On leaving office, the prosecutor issued a public warning in which he said his life was at the mercy of Evinx Daniel.

When a Senate delegation visited Washingon on September 20, Senator Steven Benoit referred to the drug incident at Port Salut, including the sacking of the prosecutor, as one of the most egregious and illegal acts of President Martelly's administration. Evinx Daniel disappeared on January 6, 2014, leaving no trace. His disappearance was not commented on by the government. Neither did his friend, the President, say anything about it.

Another close ally of the Chief of State involved in kidnapping was Woodly Ethéart, owner of the restaurant *La Souvenance* in Pétionville, a favorite of President Martelly. Ethéart, nicknamed Sonson LaFamilia, headed the "Galil Gang," named after the Israeli-made rifle they use. On February 17, 2014, businessman Sami El Azi was kidnapped for ransom of $1.2 million. The Police traced the order for his kidnapping to Ethéart, who quickly disappeared.

President Martelly was accused of hiding the fugitive in one of his plush apartments, thereby putting him out of Police reach. Eventually, Sonson LaFamilia turned himself in, but not before he gave a radio interview to denounce the Prime Minister as his persecutor. Apparently, his friend, the President, was not able to protect him.

Meanwhile, a judge ordered the closing of his restaurant and the arrest of his wife, Marie Taïssa Mazile Ethéart, as an accomplice. Two days later, on March 29, without the judge being advised, the Port-au-Prince prosecutor released her from jail. The scandal was such that the prosecutor resigned. But Mrs. Ethéart never went back to jail. The restaurant remained closed.

With so many scandals swirling around him, President Martelly decried the poisoned political atmosphere and declared that the people needed some form of relaxation. He would give them "rara every weekend." The fun-loving crowds were offered the mini festivals, beginning with the weekend when the President should have been at the UN General Assembly in New York. He dispatched Prime Minister Lamothe to represent him.

During the first three years of his presidency, Martelly concentrated on making the people dance. In February 2012, for the first time the National Carnival was organized in Cayes, the capital of the Southern Department. Evoking the theme of decentralization in vogue since the earthquake, President Martelly ordered that Cayes be the beneficiary of the event. The four-day affair swallowed up $2.3 million. In staging the first National Carnival outside of Port-au-Prince, the president was paying a political debt. For his election in 2011, the South gave him the highest margin of victory.

He followed through with the "Carnival of Flowers" in July of that year, which is homage to the Jean-Claude Duvalier era because that was the last time that carnival was produced. Before those two extravagant fiestas, he had participated in the regional carnival of Jacmel in February 2012.

In a prelude to the 2013 National Carnival, the president was again in Jacmel for the regional fiesta, although he didn't exhibit himself as he did the previous year. The official Carnival, in Cap Haïtien, was staged February 10, 11, and 12. But the festivities really began on Saturday, February 8. An elaborate "Royal Ball" took place in the renovated ruins of King Christophe's "Sans Souci Palace" in the town of Milot. "King Martelly" and his "Queen Sophia" were very impressive in their outfits, reminiscent of the days in the 1800s when King Christophe, surrounded by dukes and barons, led the lavish life of Haiti's unique royalty. Various government sites displayed photos and videos of the event and declared the Carnival a major success.

The Sunday following the Cap Haïtien extravaganza, Louis Kébreau, Archbishop of Haiti's second city, castigated the leadership of the country which he found wanting. The change promised at the inauguration of President Martelly, he said, was nowhere to be seen, especially by the poor.

The criticism of that prelate came as a surprise, because he was considered a friend of the president. At Martelly's inauguration on May 14, 2011, the prelate had pronounced the homily. Blessing the new Chief of State, Archbishop Kébreau had called on President Martelly to "gird yourself with your Sweet Micky pants" to undertake the task at hand. Certainly, he did not mean wasting millions for dancing in the streets.

Soon after the affair in Cap-Haïtien, the word was out that the "Carnival of Flowers" will again take place in Port-au-Prince in the summer. And it did on July 27, 28, and 29. But the president could not wait for the summer to keep the party going. Thus, on May 14, to celebrate his second anniversary in power, he threw a big bash whose cost was not divulged. Estimates ran from $900,000 to $1.2 million, in a country where people eke out a living on less than two dollars a day.

The two official carnivals and the May 14 bash became a tradition, despite bitter criticism about the waste of financial resources.

In the summer of 2014, judges staged a weeklong national strike to bring attention to their plight. They had not been paid for eight months. At the beginning of the school year in September 2014, public school teachers threatened to strike for nearly a year of arrears. The Minister of Education, Nesmy Manigat, promised to meet obligations for 1,000 teachers. But Josué Mérilien, speaking for a teachers' union, said that this would still leave 6,000 teachers in the lurch.

By their actions, the Haitian authorities clearly indicated what their priority was. That brings to mind the insensitivity of Marie-Antoinette, the wife of Louis XVI. When told that there was no bread to give to the people, she allegedly said, "Let them eat cake!" In Haiti, however, the cost of dancing is less expensive than that for cake.

No amount of dancing had brought any change to a deteriorating situation. Long before the denunciation by Archbishop Kébreau,

Guire Poulard, the Archbishop of Port-au-Prince, had raised his voice against the waste of resources by the authorities. In his January 1, 2013, national homily, he denounced leaders who fail to lead while helping themselves at the expense of the people mired in abject poverty. He pointed to "per diems of $20,000, as they multiply their travel abroad."

No one could have mistaken the allusions of the highest authority of the Catholic Church at the time. President Martelly was criticized for his incessant trips abroad, ostensibly to sell the image of the country. He collected $20,000 for his daily expenses. And when the authorities travel, they have a delegation of officials and a coterie of friends accompanying them, who also collect per diems. Those trips drained the Treasury without tangible results for Haiti.

The Justice and Peace Commission of the Archdiocese of Port-au-Prince (JILAP) organized a weekend of reflection the last days of August under the theme: "Let us reflect together where we are to better plan the future of our country." After four days of review, the commission concluded that the country had gone from bad to worse. It was worried for the future of the poorer citizens. In a harsh statement, JILAP condemned the regime: "The only visible change that can be pointed to is that the government has succeeded in gathering in its bosom all the enemies of the people – the Duvalierists who are threatening essential freedoms."[1*]

On August 21, 2013, the Protestant Federation of Haiti organized its own retreat in Torbeck, in the Southern Department, to reflect on what stand to take. At the end of three days of reflection, the leadership of the major Protestant organization released a lengthy analysis condemning actions of the government.

The Federation denounced political and judicial scandals. It pointed to ostentatious living displayed by our leaders.

(1*) *Le Nouvelliste, September 3, 2013*

It was evident that a broad moral consensus had been reached against the elected President of Haiti. Given the gravity of the situation, there was no certainty as to the future of Haitian democracy more than a quarter century after the overthrow of the oppressive dictatorship of the Duvaliers.

━━━━

President Martelly had one major obstacle in his plan for total control of the society. He must rein in the press. When Haitians rose up against the Duvalier dictatorship in 1986, the press, including the *Haitian Observateur*, played a major role and had set the stage for a new reality. Freedom of the press, earned on the battlefield, ranked high among the prerogatives that have been forcefully defended ever since. Despite attempts at controlling the press, or intimidating it into silence, no president since 1986 has ever succeeded in fighting this genie that got out of the bottle.

Early after his inauguration in May 2011, President Martelly began to intimidate the press. He started by telling reporters what subjects were important to cover. He publicly ignored and disrespected news people whose questions he did not like. To defuse a tense situation that was evolving for about a year, President Martelly chose International World Freedom Press Day to bring about reconciliation. On May 3, 2012, he invited some senior press stalwarts to the Palace for a tête-à-tête. Speaking like a father upbraiding his wayward children, the President said he no longer listened to the radio. For, he was in daily contact with the people. A slap in the face to the oral press in a country where illiteracy is about 60 percent, and radio is the most common news medium.

━━━━

At the outset of his regime, President Martelly and his team were bent on curbing the press. Whether the First Lady was assigned the job by her husband or whether she decided to tackle it on her own, she had begun discussions with trusted government employees on how to bring the press under control. The information leaked out to the press which immediately went on the warpath. The government was challenged to come clean on the subject.

The consultations came to a halt. When a new ministerial cabinet was formed in May 2012, the Minister of Information, the journalist Pierre Raymond Dumas, lost his post to Ady Jeangardy, another journalist. I had learned that Dumas was a dissenting voice among the early consultants to muzzle the press. Following his ouster, Dumas again picked up his pen. He didn't mince words in his criticism of the government. In the third cabinet reshuffle, in January 2013, Ady Jeangardy was himself replaced by Régine Godefroy, who resigned after three months. In three years, the government had gone through five ministers of Information. The management of the free press proved to be unmanageable for the government.

Obviously, the arrogance of power has put the government on a collision course with most independent news people. Undoubtedly, the Martelly government yearns for a former era when it was much easier to deal with the press. During the dictatorship of the Duvaliers, dissenting journalists were either dead, in jail or in exile.

The new regime uses other techniques. When Guyler Cius Delva, the spokesman of the union-like Association of Haitian Journalists, began investigating the case of a journalist who was beaten by a government official in the town of Thomonde, he was simply co-opted. Delva was bought out. He was named secretary of state at the Ministry of Information. He became a forceful defender of the government. Meanwhile, he found himself under attack by his former colleagues who decried the power of corruption as it reaches into the inner sanctum of the press. In another cabinet reshuffle in January 2013, Delva lost his post. He continued, however, to be a defender of President Martelly's administration.

Notwithstanding intimidation or corruption from on high, Haiti's honest and fearless journalists, who tasted freedom after the fall of the Duvalier dictatorship, remain a major impediment to a project, still being refined, of how to return Haiti to the old days when the "President-for-life" was the law and the fount of all virtues.

Nevertheless, the Martelly administration tried by all means to impose restrictions on the press. During the 2013 National Carnival in Cap Haïtien, Minister of Justice Jean Renel Sanon issued a communiqué reminding all about the law against defamation of officials. He pointed to a decree of 1985 which censures such acts by individuals as well as the press.

The government was reacting to the popular song *Aloral* of Don Kato and his Brother's Posse group who hail from Cap Haïtien. As previously mentioned, President Martelly personally had banned Don Kato from participating in the official carnival. There was a general outcry against Minister Sanon's attempt to muzzle the press. Parliament denounced the veiled threat against the press and summoned the minister to explain his action. He was reminded that the decree he mentioned was issued under Jean-Claude Duvalier's dictatorship. It had no effect on the 1987 Constitution which guarantees freedom of speech.

On April 8, 2014, CONATEL, the government's National Council of Telecommunications, threatened press organs, especially radio and television, which "disrespect the norms." Citing a communiqué of 1977, the government agency said it would withdraw the license to operate and slap a monetary penalty on those that failed to show "respect for public order [and for] national security." Although CONATEL didn't mention any organ by name, this was interpreted as a threat against *Radio TéléZénith*, a Port-au-Prince station that the government previously accused of "defaming the authorities" in its broadcasts. "SOS Journalists," a local association for the defense of newspeople, immediately came to the support of the station and reminded the government that its communiqué is a relic of the Jean-Claude Duvalier dictatorship which was ousted in a popular uprising in 1986.

To curry favor with the press, the Martelly administration egged on his Judiciary to resurrect a famous case regarding the assassination of a leading news icon. On May 8, 2013, former President Jean-Bertrand Aristide was summoned to court by the Port-au-Prince chief prosecutor in the case of Jean Dominique, the late owner of *Radio Haïti Inter*. Aristide was being queried about the aforementioned double assassination in 2000 of the eminent radio personality and Jean-Claude Louissaint, the guardian of his station. Unlike his reaction to a previous summons two months earlier when he failed to appear, Aristide decided to show up this time.

Ignoring a Police ban on demonstrations, thousands of his followers accompanied him to court. Suddenly, Jean-Bertrand Aristide became the crowd pleaser of times past. Commentators unanimously noted that President Martelly's team had resurrected Aristide, who had been in seclusion since he came back to Haiti two years earlier from a seven-year exile in South Africa.

The *Lavalas* leader took advantage of the moment to express criticism of President Martelly.

Aristide sounded less strident and more conciliatory than in the past. He took the opportunity to visit one of his popular bastions in the Bel-Air section of Port-au-Prince where he threw kisses to energized onlookers. Whatever plan President Martelly had against the former president had backfired. However, a bloody attack on a journalist of pro-government *Radio Télé Ginen* (RTG) by Aristide followers revived a past that Aristide would have liked to forget. During his rule, he was also hostile to the independent press. Now at his first major public event since he returned from exile, the press was being attacked by his followers.

The National Association of Haitian Media (French acronym ANMH) forcefully condemned the attempt against free expression, and reminded *Lavalas* about the fight that had been waged for freedom, including freedom of speech. "By no means will we accept to go back to the old days," said ANMH Liliane Pierre-Paul. I was not the only one fighting for democracy.

Chapter 22

No Elections, No Democracy

Although Michel Martelly assumed the presidency through an election, he is not devoted to elections. After nearly four years in power and six major carnivals under his belt, he failed to organize even one election. He gave the impression that he won't attend to the mandated elections if he doesn't fully control the electoral process. Although elections are supposed to be held periodically, President Martelly failed to follow the calendar. He has not called for the elections, as constitutionally mandated. Instead he's resorted to nominations, thereby placing his own partisans in charge of all the municipalities and other local bodies that should be the emanation of the popular will.

For the first time since the 1987 Constitution called for an independent electoral council, President Martelly set up the *Conseil Electoral Permanent* (CEP), or Permanent Electoral Council.

He swore in six members named by himself and the Superior Council of Justice (French acronym CSPJ) and named a director general for the CEP, signaling that he would be in control of its deliberations. Gabrielle Hyacinthe, the director, had been named Mayor of Port-au-Prince two months earlier when the President replaced elected mayors with his nominees. Considering that the cards were stacked up in favor of President Martelly, Parliament balked at naming its three members.

As another slap to the legislators, the President named Josué Pierre-Louis to preside over his partisan CEP. Pierre-Louis was the minister of Justice who had ordered the illegal arrest of Congressman Arnel Bélizaire in October 2011 and who had resigned before being censured by the Senate. President Martelly should have known that Pierre-Louis was anathema to the legislators. By naming him to that sensitive post, the President was following his own agenda to delay the elections.

Influential personalities in civil society, leading religious voices, and several of the most representative political parties called on the the President to scrap his Electoral Council as constituted. Instead of a Permanent Council, some legislators proposed another Provisional Electoral Council, whose composition would be more representative of society at large. Such a council would inspire confidence.

After six months of resistance, President Martelly turned to *Réligions Pour La Paix* (Religions for Peace), an ecumenical group, which proposed a solution on Christmas Eve. Their proposal called for an interim council called *Conseil Transitoire du Conseil Electoral Permanent* (CT-CEP), or Transitional Council of the Permanent Electoral Coucil. It took an additional four months to finally set up the CT-CEP. Trying to dictate to the new organization, President Martelly ran into resistance from its most independent members.

Without an apparatus that he could totally control, President Martelly failed to hold the elections he had promised, including for one-third of the Upper Chamber, governance in local communities, and 120 mayoralties. Since the 2010 earthquake the electoral calendar had been disrupted. The local representatives should have been elected in November 2010. When President Martelly was inaugurated in May 2011, he said elections would be held soon.

Most political observers thought he would not be able to hold them by the end of the year. So, there were no elections in 2011.

Instead of elections, early in 2012 the Minister of Interior and the Collectivities (equivalent to Homeland Security) named mayors in several localities to replace those who had been elected but whose mandate had run out since 2010. The Executive power grab began in February with the dismissal of thirteen mayors. By July, the central government formalized the total takeover. The Executive had replaced all but a few mayors, who were then designated "interim executive agents." In so doing, the president could be preparing to rig the elections whenever they are held in favor of his own partisans, both for local and national offices.

The bizarre loss of election equipment at the CEP's warehouse was considered part of that plan. Several pieces of equipment disappeared, including 460 laptop computers, 207 extended computer memory cards, 88 portable batteries and 160 solar panels. Since there was no break-in, it was generally believed that the alleged robbery was an inside job. Six unnamed individuals who worked at the CEP warehouse supposedly were arrested. The CEP never gave an explanation of what really happened. This was treated as a nonevent. It's unbelievable that all that equipment disappeared in Haiti without leaving a trace.

Two individuals, experts in past election shenanigans, were suspected in the heist. Both were working for President Martelly at the time. One was former Senator Joseph Lambert who had helped manipulate the vote to put Jude Célestin, President Préval's candidate, on top at the November 2010 elections. The other, Gayot Dorcinvil, the former president of the Electoral Council, had consented to those illegalities. As disgraceful as he was, Dorcinvil was not replaced as president of the Council.

By their actions in behalf of Célestin in the 2010 fall elections, those two men caused a major upheaval in the country. Angry at the unfair elections, the people rioted in several cities. Scores were killed and several government offices were torched in Cayes. The headquarters of *Inite,* the government's party in Port-au-Prince, was destroyed.

As previously noted, the international community had to step in to force the annulment of the fraudulent tabulation of the vote that had placed Célestin in first position. The revised tabulation benefitted Martelly in the second round against Manigat.

Again, in 2012, Messrs. Lambert and Dorcinvil were trying to pull strings to give President Martelly a majority in the Senate and ensure him control of the countryside through a majority of mayors and other local officials who would have been fraudulently elected. In case their plan failed, the president could hide behind the lack of equipment to conduct the elections on time.

Martelly's fear of holding elections may result from his doubt of winning. Although he had won nearly two-thirds of the popular vote for the presidency in 2011, he had no parliamentary constituency. Only two congressmen (and no senator) were elected under the banner of *Repons Peyizan* (Peasants' Response), the party which lent him the legal hat to run. Uncertain that his frayed popularity would serve as coattails for local officials under his banner, President Martelly apparently chose the easy path of fraud, not unlike his predecessor. In trying to fashion an undemocratic and fraudulent new majority for himself, the president ran into major problems. Demonstrations began to take place against him in several cities.

President Martelly increased the ranks of his critics and malcontents. The case of Mayor Muscadin Jean Yves Jason of Port-au-Prince is an example. During the last presidential election, he had mounted a spirited campaign in favor of Michel Martelly. Soon after the candidate's victory, Mayor Jason was considered as a possible prime minister or minister of Interior. Subsequently, he was not only ousted from power, but threatened with arrest and worse.

The threat against Jason became ominous when he was considered a suspect in a fire that destroyed a public marketplace in

Port-au-Prince. However, he denounced a political plot to tarnish his reputation and to arbitrarily have him arrested. He went underground, not unlike what used to happen under the Duvaliers.

Considering Martelly's penchant for Papa Doc's tactics, he may delay local elections for years. If successful, he could pull a surprise à *la Duvalier*. It could be something similar to the 1961 vote when the dictator gave himself a second mandate before the expiration of his six-year term.

On June 21, 2013, the president of the Senate, Senator Dieuseul Simon Desras, denounced a plan of the Executive to dissolve Parliament and create a constitutional assembly whose role would be to rewrite parts of the Constitution to allow President Martelly to succeed himself. In effect, that would not be much different from what Papa Doc did in 1964 when he declared himself President-for-life. In that light, it was understandable that elections promised for 2013 did not occur.

In January 2014, the Senate was poised to lose another third of its constituency, if President Martelly were to have his way. That would make for a dysfunctional Senate with only ten remaining members. As noted, since May 2012 the Senate had been operating with only twenty senators, or two-thirds of its membership. By the second Monday of 2014, President Martelly could have evoked an exceptional situation requiring him to rule by decree. That would have given him the pretext to abolish the whole Parliament and call for the constitutional assembly mentioned by Senator Desras.

From several political quarters, President Martelly was warned about the dire consequences he would face if he were to fail in holding the elections before the end of 2013. At a conference July 25, 2013, at the Center for Strategic and International Studies in Washington, Mark Schneider, vice president of the prestigious International Crisis Group, asserted that if President Martelly were to "cross the red line" and were to begin ruling by decree the second week of

January 2014, he would lose the support of donors and diplomats. A "financial crisis will be added to a political one," he said.

Then on the weekend of August 3, 2013, Senator Bill Nelson (Democrat of Florida) arrived in Port-au-Prince where he met separately with various political leaders and President Martelly. The elections will be held this year, Martelly assured him. At the same time, the presidential commission which was reviewing the electoral law said its work had been completed. The group released its amendments and additions to the law to the press and sent them to Parliament for approval before publication in *Le Moniteur*, the official State gazette.

Before the Legislative session was closed on September 9, the congressmen voted the electoral law. They approved a director general for the CT-CEP, as the president wanted, thus giving him oversight of the supposedly independent institution. At the same time, they voted to keep the ten senators in place until January 2015, thereby maintaining the equilibrium of Parliament. Some congressmen close to President Martelly accused the president of the Lower House for depriving the Chief of State his wish of getting rid of ten additional senators. But a majority of the congressmen was not about to commit *hara-kiri*. For, once the Senate became dysfunctional, the Lower House couldn't be operational in a bicameral system.

The electoral law voted by the Lower House caused a major friction within the ranks of the Executive. From Paris, France, where he was on official visit, Prime Minister Lamothe praised the work of the congressmen and rejoiced in the fact that the long awaited elections would be held. Asked when that would be, he declined to specify, adding that this was the prerogative of the electoral commission. Elections experts have repeatedly said that after the adoption of an electoral law, six months are required to organize credible elections. President Martelly had given Senator Nelson full assurance that the elections would be held before the end of 2013. December came and went, and no elections were held.

The country would not have reached that crisis stage had President Martelly played fairly. In July 2013 when he received the electoral law prepared by the independent CT-CEP, he had turned it over to his in-house presidential commission for review. He rejected the revision of his own commission which had agreed with some decisions of the Electoral Council. A key point concerned the executive director to oversee operations, as appeared in the CT-CEP version of the law. But the President imposed a general director.

By having an executive director, named internally by the Electoral Council, the organization would have been totally independent. On the other hand, insisting on a general director, President Martelly endeavored to keep oversight of the Electoral Council's work. As previously mentioned, long before the members of the CT-CEP were named, the President had sworn in Gabrielle Hyacinthe, his close aide, to the post of director general.

As things stood, Martelly had staged a coup d'état against the CT-CEP. On August 9, 2013, he summoned the members of the Electoral Council to the Palace to read them the Riot Act. Seven of the nine members attended the meeting when the president told them to set aside their electoral law and organize the elections under the aegis of the 2008 electoral law. But that law was in conflict with the revised Constitution of 2011. The president also told them they had no recourse but to accept his director general. And they should immediately address him a letter asking the "President of the Republic" to call for elections before the end of the year.

On August 12, *Le Nouvelliste* published an editorial entitled "Orders to the CT-CEP or intimidations?" The editorial went on to say, "The meeting of last Friday could contribute to poisoning the electoral process instead of facilitating the necessary understanding between the councilors and the political power." In an accompanying article, Léopold Berlanger, a council member in attendance at the meeting, said President Martelly read his statement as if he were dictating to the councilors. Moreover, he concluded by saying he would be sending his decision to the Council as a presidential decree.

Berlanger, general director of Radio Vision 2000, is not a man to be cowed. So, he insisted on talking. The President finally relented and allowed him to speak. Berlanger told him that his propositions "are unacceptable and unconstitutional and, according to me, incoherent with the independent [nature] of the Council."

It was obvious that President Martelly had superseded his authority by imposing his decisions on the CT-CEP, supposedly an independent institution. By his actions, the President behaved as his predecessor who, through his control of the Provisional Electoral Council, had derailed the elections of November 2010, causing widespread violence.

The political atmosphere was indeed poisoned. Almost all the major political parties declined an invitation to meet with President Martelly on August 15 to discuss the upcoming elections. Some of the parties were harsh in their refusal.

Lavalas accused the President of "lying to the people, persecuting leaders of the opposition and not respecting individual rights."

In an open letter to the President, the OPL (Organization of the People Struggling) said, "It's no time for a simple dialogue on the elections. The hour is grave. . . . To use the language of Shakespeare, soon time will be over."

Also issuing an open letter was *Fusion*, the party of the Social Democrats, which asserted that it would not participate in any meeting with President Martelly. It pointed to "crisis upon crisis confronting us, threatening even the stability of the country." *Fusion* even pulled the alarm switch by stating that the situation "risks becoming antagonistic, even violent."

As for the *Patriotic Movement of the Democratic Opposition* (French acronym MOPOD), a consortium of about fifteen political parties and organizations, President Martelly was no longer a credible partner for dialogue. He wants "to substitute himself" to the Transitory Electoral Council, said MOPOD, which also accused the President of "lying" in the suspicious death of Judge Jean Serge Joseph. Anyway, there can't be any dialogue with a president who should be "impeached," based on the recommendations of a Senate commission.

———

President Martelly had become quite adept at defusing explosive situations. By the end of 2013, he pulled a rabbit out of his hat. Just as he had done in December 2012, when he turned to the ecumenical group *Religions for Peace* for an 11th hour solution, he reached out this time to an eminent religious figure. He called on Bishop Chibly Langlois of Cayes to calm the waters.

By this action, the President angered some among the ecumenical group which had a broader representation, including Catholic, Protestant, and Voodoo. But his decision proved to be strategic. One month later, Bishop Langlois was named cardinal, the first Haitian to be so distinguished. That strengthened the hand of the bishop, who became the authoritative voice of the Catholic Church in a country where Catholicism is the official religion.

Despite his new status, Cardinal-designate Langlois could not convince several major political parties to attend the deliberations, far less approve the El Rancho Accord, named for the hotel in Pétionville where the talks were held. The accord called for a new Provisional Electoral Commission to replace the year-old CT-CEP, and for long delayed elections to be held throughout the country. Due to wrangling between President Martelly and the Senate, the cardinal failed to have the accord signed before he departed for Rome for his consecration by Pope Francis on February 22, 2014.

President Martelly and Senate President Desras were in Rome on that day for the historic event. President Martelly was received by the Pope. During that trip he had the opportunity to meet some high dignitaries, including French President François Hollande at the Elysée Palace and King Philippe of Belgium.

Apparently, Rome had a salutary effect on the Haitian politicians. On his return home, President Martelly approved all the members of *La Cour Supérieure des Comptes,* the independent Government Audit Commission that he had held up for five months. That was a bone of contention with the Senate whose prerogative it is to name the members of that commission. President Martelly had only ten days to express any objection to the names he had received since September.

Senate President Desras authorized Senator Steven Benoit to sign the El Rancho Accord. Article 12 of that agreement foresaw that the pact could face opposition in Parliament. Thus, it provided for organizing the election with the old CT-CEP, which is anathema to the Senate and to various political parties, as well as to influential sectors of civil society.

As expected, the Lower House approved the Accord, but the Senate never passed it. It could not surmount the opposition of six senators who vowed to defeat any vote intended to approve the El Rancho Accord. President Martelly was experiencing the negative effect of his own making. Had he organized the election for the ten vacant seats of the Senate, he possibly could have gotten a quorum to pass the electoral law. Although the Senate had been reduced to twenty members since the summer of 2012, its rules still required the positive vote of seventeen to approve a law. President Martelly and Prime Minister Lamothe had used the vote of four senators favorable to the Executive to block certain actions of the Senate against the Executive branch. Now six anti-Martelly senators vowed to block what they termed an unconstitutional agreement.

Suddenly, President Martelly became a champion of elections. Usurping the right of a yet-to-be-named independent Electoral Council, he declared that elections will be held on October 26, 2014. He confirmed this to a bipartisan Congressional delegation from Florida that met him at the end of March. Democrat Frederica Wilson had traveled to Haiti with her Republican colleagues Ileana Ross Lehtinen and Mario Diaz-Balart on a special mission.

In an interview to *Miami Herald* correspondent Jacqueline Charles (March 23), Congresswoman Wilson said, "There are certain things a democracy must do: they must have annual elections; no ifs, ands or buts about it. Let's hope that they do, because the consequences will not be kind." It was a direct message to President Martelly who had not held the mandated elections for three years.

Notwithstanding President Martelly's assurance to the Congressional delegation, there was no certainty that the elections would be held by the end of the year. But that would not be the first time that the Haitian president made similar promises. In 2013, he had assured Florida's Senator Nelson that the elections would be held before the end of that year. December came and went, but no elections were held. Neither did he keep his promise to the international community in 2012 when he affirmed that the elections would be held that year. Obviously, democracy was put on hold during most of President Martelly's term.

In the first half of 2014, the Haitian elections became the major topic even beyond Haiti's borders. The leaders of the international community, beginning with the United States, put their weight in the balance as they pushed the Haitian authorities toward the long awaited elections. In February 2014 when President Obama first met with President Martelly at the White House, President Obama advised him to organize the elections. The US Congress had threatened to withhold $300 million in aid to Haiti if the elections were not held on time.

Now the new pro-election President Martelly pointed his fingers at the Haitian Senate which impeded the formation of an electoral commission to move the process forward. So, on May 6, he issued a decree creating the Provisional Electoral Council with seven members, instead of the nine called for by the Constitution. On May 12, the Minister of Justice swore in the Council in the presence of the Diplomatic Corps, including representatives of the United States, Canada, France and the civilian head of MINUSTAH.

In what appeared to be a coordinated action, on the same day that President Martelly was announcing, in Port-au-Prince, the formation of his Provisional Electoral Council, in Washington, Secretary of State John F. Kerry was certifying to Congress the democratic nature of the Haitian government.

He filed the following statement to appear in the Federal Register: *"I hereby certify that Haiti is taking steps to hold free and fair elections and to seat a new Haitian Parliament; the Government of Haiti is respecting the independence of the judiciary; and the Government of Haiti is combating corruption and improving governance, including passage of the anti-corruption law to enable prosecution of corrupt officials and implementing financial transparency and accountability requirements for government institutions."*

Such a certification was required for Congress to approve any disbursement of funds to Haiti.

But the declaration of Secretary Kerry did not match the reality in Haiti. Although the Haitian Government readily applauded that declaration, several political and civil society leaders criticized Secretary Kerry for having been misled on the existing situation. Thus, the heavyweights of the international community, the United States, France, Canada and MINUSTAH, allied to an increasingly repressive government, found themselves at odds with a large sector of the political opposition and Haitian society at large.

On May 27, Desras, the president of the Haitian Senate, declared that the "El Rancho Accord [is] dead and buried." The seven-member Provisional Electoral Commission, he continued, "lacks credibility, because it is fully under the control of President Martelly."

The international community apparently had failed to gauge the level of resentment against President Martelly's administration. A declaration asking for a "credible" and "equilibrated" council that all sectors can trust obtained the approval of a broad cross-section of the country's leadership. The signers included major religious leaders, such as the Catholic Archbishop of Port-au-Prince, the head of the Episcopal Church, the president of the Protestant Federation and the *Ati*, as the highest Voodoo official is called. Moreover, several civil society personalities, including the president of a leading human rights organization, added their signatures to the text. Following in their steps, independently, the Haitian Chamber of Commerce and Industry made a similar demand.

Time was of the essence if elections were to be held by October 26, as President Martelly had unilaterally declared. Elections experts concur that credible elections require at least six months after an electoral law is voted. Thus, on May 28, Fritzo Canton, the lawyer that President Martelly had named to preside over the council, issued a statement about the elections. He informed all political parties that the first round would be held October 26, with the second to take place December 15.

I wondered about the level of participation in those contested elections. In comparison to President Aristide's election in 2000, several major political parties had shunned the exercise, because the process was heavily controlled by Aristide's followers. The level of participation was under 10 percent. That revealed the whittled popularity of President Aristide and, in part, resulted in a chaotic situation which eventually led to his ouster before the completion of his second five-year term.

In late July 2014, the Electoral Council was revamped again, the fourth such Council since President Martelly assumed power in May 2011. Two members of the old Council were replaced and two former members who had chosen not to be sworn in earlier joined the completed nine-member organization. In an internal vote, Fritzo Canton, the president of the Council imposed by President Martelly, lost the leadership to Max Mathurin, who had led the organization in the 2006 elections.

But the six previously mentioned senators held up the vote by the Senate of the electoral law already approved by the Lower House. They contended that the Council failed to be representative, because it ignored the spirit of Article 289 of the 1987 Constitution in the formation of the Electoral Council. That article requires a Council based on a representation of the wider society and not only of the three branches of government: The Executive, the Judiciary and the Legislative.

Meanwhile, the specter of Haiti without elected institutions in the beginning of 2015 haunted all. The mandate of all 99 Lower House members will elapse on the second week of 2015. The thirty-member Senate will also lose another third of its members by that time, leaving it with only ten senators. In other words, there will not be a working Parliament. Only President Martelly will still have a valid Constitutional mandate until February 7, 2016. The specter of a one-man rule was a distinct possibility.

As most analysts foresaw, no election was possible at the end of October. On August 11, the president of the newly reconstituted Electoral Council wrote to President Martelly to tell him of the impossibility to hold the elections on October 26. In the absence of a legal framework, there is no way to conduct the elections. The Council advised President Martelly to undertake consultations with various sectors of society, with the political establishment, the two Houses of the Legislature as well as with the Judiciary to reach a decision on "a legal framework" to hold the elections before the end of the year. The President didn't respond.

It was doubtful that elections could be held at all in the remainder of 2014. In mid-August, influential members of civil society called for prolonging the mandates of the legislators until May 2015 to allow time for their reelection. In no way should the country remain without a working Parliament. But on August 27, the Permanent Council of the OAS in Washington met to urge the three branches of the Haitian government to abide by the "El Rancho

Accord" to hold the elections before the end of the year. The OAS pointed fingers at the six senators who blocked passage of the electoral law. Sandra Honoré, the civilian head of MINUSTAH, concurred.

The response of the legislators was swift. They said the OAS, which botched the 2010 elections in Haiti, had no credibility to dictate what they should do. Instead, the OAS should show respect for the Haitian Constitution by supporting a credible Electoral Council. As for MINUSTAH, her representative in Haiti had not objected when, for three years, President Martelly didn't hold any elections.

If the country reached that crisis point, it is the fault of President Martelly who had failed to hold mandated elections in the past three years. During that time the OAS said not a word to bring the Haitian President to his democratic senses. With that sort of partiality on its part, the OAS contributed to the current electoral crisis and flawed governance in Haiti.

Two events in August 2014 contributed to the uncertainty of the elections. There was a massive jailbreak at the maximum security prison of Croix-des-Bouquets, about eight miles from Port-au-Prince. The government admitted that on August 10, 320 from a total of 899 detainees had escaped. It warned that there were hard core criminals among them. Then on August 13, an arrest warrant was issued for President Jean-Bertrand Aristide. Although there was no connection between the jailbreak and the arrest warrant, their occurrence in such close proximity raised tensions at a time when the government should have been preparing for the elections.

The jailbreak drew attention to two illustrious prisoners. Among the escapees was Clifford Brandt, the scion of a rich family who had plotted the kidnapping of two adult children of a rival businessman for ransom of $2.5 million. The other, who chose not to escape, was Woodly "Sonson LaFamilia" Ethéart, a restaurateur who was held also for the kidnapping of a businessman for ransom of $1.5 million. Both happened to be friends of President Martelly. Thus, the jailbreak was thought to be an attempt to free them. But it was the work of Colombian drug dealers who had been incarcerated at the Croix-des-Bouquets jail. Six of them, as well as an undetermined number of Jamaicans, were gone.

Two days later, Brandt was caught in the Dominican Republic and helicoptered to the Haitian Police in Port-au-Prince. Two months later, only fifty of the fugitives were caught, including some in the Dominican Republic and on a boat on their way to the Bahamas. With so many hardened criminals on the loose, most Haitians, especially around the capital, lived in fear. The jailbreak had put a damper on the elections.

It was in this context of confusion that Judge Lamarre Bélizaire, reputed close to President Martelly, had brought charges against Aristide and thirty of his close associates and members of his *Lavalas Family* party. Among other things, they were accused of embezzlement and laundering of drug money between 2001 and 2004. The charges stemmed from a 2005 investigation by UCREF, the anticorruption Central Financial Enquiry Unit set up in 2004 by the interim government of Boniface-Latortue.

Whereas the jailbreak was unpredictable, the judicial action against Aristide was deliberate. At a time when a peaceful atmosphere was needed for the elections, the government decided to roil the waters with a warrant for Aristide's arrest. As expected, the followers of the former president took to the streets with their favorite arm—the flaming tire. MINUSTAH soldiers had to disperse them with tear gas and water cannons. Although Aristide was not arrested, he was declared under house arrest with units of the Police surrounding his compound.

By the end of September no one believed the elections would be held in the remaining months of 2014. Whatever happens, President Martelly was poised to rule by decree on the second week of January

2015. Prime Minister Lamothe so declared to the press in New York in late September 2014 when President Martelly addressed the UN General Assembly. He said by January 12, 2014, the mandate of the senators who blocked the electoral process will run out. Then, President Martelly will organize the elections.

Considering his antipathy toward elections since he assumed power in 2011, the scenario of ruling by decree fits the President's character. In the morning of October 26, 2014, President Martelly's office issued a communiqué to announce that the elections announced for that date had been delayed. Meanwhile, thousands of citizens took to the streets of the capital, calling for the resignation of the President who had failed to hold the elections as he himself had dictated.

In the process, Haiti was ruled undemocratically during nearly four years of President Martelly's five-year term. He succeeded, if only partially, in reviving the era of the strongman-president—with the support of the international community.

CONCLUSION

When I experienced the irresponsibility of our Haitian leadership during the earthquake, I felt the urge to explain what I think ails Haitian society. After more than two centuries of independence, Haiti shouldn't have to find itself at the bottom of the pit. I refused to accept the concept that God was punishing the country for a so-called pact with the Devil to win its independence. As if God condoned slavery!

The surprise return of Jean-Claude Duvalier on January 16, 2011, after a twenty-five-year exile in France was an added impetus to tell my story of the past fifty years and the struggle to usher in an era of democracy. As I have shown in *For Whom the Dogs Spy*, the return of Baby Doc in the midst of Martelly's presidential campaign was not that innocent and the president protected the dictator to the end.

Former President Préval revived old charges against Baby Doc and also the victims of his dictatorship joined forces to organize a class action suit against him. They accused Baby Doc of crimes against humanity and embezzlement of State funds. Appearing in court once, he denied the charges.

A judge ruled that due to statute of limitations, most of the charges against Duvalier were not valid. Protected by the Martelly administration, Baby Doc led a normal life in Haiti after his return. He was often spotted dining in fancy restaurants in Pétionville. He had revived his political *Parti Unité Nationale* (PUN) or National Unity Party. He even became an unpaid adviser to President Martelly, while his son François Nicolas officially worked at the Palace for the Haitian President.

Surprisingly, Jean-Claude Duvalier died on October 4, 2014, escaping justice and leaving President Martelly in a dilemma. Soon after the dictator's death was announced, President Martelly issued a statement. "On behalf of the entire government and people of Haiti," he said, "I take advantage of this sad occasion to extend my sincere sympathies to his family, his relatives and his supporters across the country. Despite our quarrels and our differences, let's salute the departure of an authentic son of Haiti. Love and reconciliation must always overcome our quarrels. May your soul rest in peace."

I joined the majority of the citizens in disagreeing with that effusive statement. Martelly had not spoken in our behalf. In fact, this must be considered an insult to the victims of the Duvalier regimes, both father and son. To make matters worse, President Martelly was planning to honor the son of his mentor with a national funeral. A general outcry made him refrain from further damage. He left Haiti three days before Jean-Claude Duvalier's funeral to attend a CARICOM meeting in Port of Spain, Trinidad. On the same day, Prime Minister Lamothe left on official business in Washington.

On October 11, the Duvalier family and their supporters proceeded with a grandiose funeral for Baby Doc. On that same day I received an honorary doctorate in anthropology in Brooklyn from the Private United Universities of Haiti. I outlived both father Duvalier, who condemned me to death in 1968, and his son who maintained that condemnation when he assumed power in 1971. The Duvalier family had not been seen in public together or set foot in Haiti since 1986 when he was overthrown. In the front row sat: his divorced wife Michèle Bennett, his son François Nicolas and daughter Anya; sisters Marie-Denise and Simone Duvalier. A third sister, Nicole, was absent. There is division in the Duvalier family. Véronique Roy, his girlfriend and companion, was relegated to a spot by herself. A sister of Baby Doc's mother Simone Ovide Duvalier joined her.

———

On the day before the funeral Judge Lamarre Bélizaire ordered that Aristide be "extracted" from his house where he was kept prisoner during a full month and brought to his court to answer questions about the charges brought against him: embezzlement of millions of dollars of State funds and laundering of drug money while he was in power from 2001 to 2004. The same thing people accused Baby Doc. I am quite sure Judge Bélizaire did not order this action without consulting with President Martelly first. I find it strange that Martelly's administration provided protection to Baby Doc but wanted to further penalize Aristide. However, there was no "extraction" and it was never done.

The deference shown Duvalier until his death and the aggressiveness demonstrated toward Aristide revealed the arbitrary nature of the Michel Martelly administration. Yet, there are similarities between President Martelly and former President Aristide. Both surrounded themselves with unsavory characters who were involved in drug dealing and kidnapping. Some of Aristide's collaborators served time in US federal prisons. Some of Martelly's cohorts are jailed in Haiti or have disappeared without leaving a trace.

By reviving old charges against Aristide, President Martelly may be creating a precedent. If Aristide cannot be above the law, others like President Martelly cannot be above the law. When he is no longer president and enjoying immunity from prosecution, he could face the same fate as Aristide. Thus, the relevance of the Creole proverb: *Baton ki bat chen nwa a se li ki bat chen blan an.* (The stick used to beat the black dog is the same that beats the white dog.)

AFTERWORD

Haiti, an Ecological Disaster

While Haitian politicians fight over the spoils that power provides, Haiti has turned into an ecological disaster. If deforestation of the land isn't forcefully addressed, Haiti will increasingly become a burden for its Caribbean neighbors and even for the United States, as its desperate citizens continue to flee in search of a better life.

The environmental degradation of Haiti brought tears to my eyes in 2004 when I returned home after a 13-year absence. Flying into Port-au-Prince, I was struck by the flimsy abodes hanging at the sides of ravines. The mountain serving as backdrop to the capital was denuded. I foresaw a hurricane turning the city into a house of cards.

Flying in from the Dominican Republic, one faces a stark reality. As one crosses the border delineating the two nations that share the second largest island of the Caribbean chain, the green disappears as one leaves the Dominican Republic. Bare and brown mountains welcome one to the Republic of Haiti.

Haiti's tree coverage stands at 2 percent. The process of desertification must be reversed. Otherwise, all the laudable projects announced since the earthquake to "build [Haiti] back better" will come to naught. For the country will have become a giant desert.

The process of desertification of the land began more than five centuries ago and the culprits for this situation are legion. When Christopher Columbus came ashore on December 12, 1492, at the bay he surnamed St. Nicolas for the Catholic patron saint of that day, he had exclaimed, *Española* (Little Spain). He had "discovered" a jewel to which he laid claim for the Spanish crown. It was a lush land, with tropical trees and birds of all sorts. Soon, however, some of Haiti's precious wood, like mahogany, began to find their way to Europe, where they adorned palaces, cathedrals, and the homes of the rich and powerful.

The Treaty of Ryswick (Netherlands), signed in 1697, ended the nine-year war between France and the Grand Alliance (England, Spain, the Holy Roman Empire, and the United Provinces). Following that treaty, Hispaniola was divided between France and Spain, with the French in control of the more mountainous western third which they called St. Domingue.

The French colonists began a vast deforestation program to prepare the fields for sugar cane, cotton and other commercial plantations which turned Haiti into the richest colony of France. It is reported that Haiti provided more than 50 percent of the sugar, cocoa, cotton and the indigo consumed in all of Europe at the time. In the 17th and 18th centuries, Haiti's forests, especially in the lowlands, were depleted for the benefit of Europe.

A mere twenty-one years after the January 1st, 1804, declaration of independence, the deforestation of the country began in earnest. Supported by slave owning States, including the United States of America, France had imposed an embargo on Haiti, ostensibly for property lost when the French were defeated on the battlefield. In 1825, Haitian President Jean-Pierre Boyer acquiesced to pay indemnity equivalent to about $21 billion in today's dollars. The French asked that part of the payment be in precious wood.

When the United States marines invaded Haiti in 1915 for an occupation that lasted nineteen years, the country was reportedly 30 percent wooded. The Americans contributed to the deforestation when they discovered Haitian hardwood, like *Campêche* and *Gaiac*, which found their way to North American railroad tracks as tresses.

With a population of about half a million at independence, Haiti's population grew rapidly, reaching approximately ten million in 2014. In the process, the forests came under the onslaught of an ever growing population in search of energy for cooking, for their bakeries, dry cleaners and their guildives, as the indigenous distilleries are called. Charcoal made from wood became big business, to the detriment of the environment.

With government support, the Catholic Church contributed to the deforestation of the land. As previously mentioned, the *Rejete* movement of the 1940s set out to destroy the huge *Mapou trees* because they were considered homes for the *loas*, or Voodoo spirits.

In 1954, Hazel, one of the most devastating hurricanes to hit Haiti, wiped out some forests in the twinkling of an eye. A few years after Hazel, a human hurricane added to the plight of Haiti's forests. In the 1960s, François Duvalier ordered the clearing of a large swath of land on the Haiti side of the 160-mile Haitian-Dominican border. That was his method to thwart the guerrillas who were crossing from the Dominican Republic and hiding in the forested border regions, while preparing their war of liberation.

President Jean-Bertrand Aristide unwittingly aggravated the situation when, in 1995, he disbanded the Haitian Armed Forces together with their rural auxiliaries, the *Chefs de sections* (Section chiefs). Those chiefs also acted as forest rangers.

The abolition of the rural police, with their auxiliaries also allowed the emergence of gangs and thieves that have created havoc everywhere, including in the countryside. That situation discouraged peasant farmers who neglected the land. Too often they had lost their crops to the nightriders who became the law. Cultivation of all sorts suffered greatly as farming families left the arid soil to find non-existing jobs in the cities. In great part, this movement away from the rural areas has resulted in the proliferation of the shantytowns that have disfigured the major agglomerations.

The deforestation of the land has resulted in a host of problems for the country. Without tree protection, land erosion has set in. Instead of being a blessing, each downpour is accompanied with avalanches that wash away the topsoil to the sea, contaminating sea fauna and flora which eventually die. Reportedly, 15,000 acres of top soil are washed down to the sea each year.

During the annual hurricane season that begins June 1st and lasts till November 30, Haiti braces for the worst. Most of the other islands, covered with trees, suffer much less. In Haiti, the flimsy abodes hanging precariously at the sides of dry river beds are washed away.

Hurricane Sandy, in late October 2012, provided an illuminating example. The eye of the giant storm passed about 100 miles to the west of Haiti, over Jamaica and Cuba. While Jamaica, Cuba, and the Dominican Republic combined registered thirteen deaths, Haiti reported at least fifty-four, and 200,000 were left homeless. About 60 percent of the peasants' harvest was destroyed. Due to Sandy, Haiti suffered a famine in 2013.

Since 2010 when I returned to live in Haiti, I have observed, with much sadness, the slide of the country toward a state of total desertification. I became hopeful, however, when I participated in a project undertaken by Pastor André Gustave Louis, who was also the congressman for the district of Kenscoff.

On May 1st, Agriculture Day 2011, the congressman began a tree planting program in the mountainous region of Kikwa, high above the town of Kenscoff. With participation of the community, some 14,000 saplings were planted in one week. The program continued with school students involved in tree planting activities on a regular basis. Maintenance, in the form of watering, is carried out by the community. Community ownership is the key to success of any reforestation program.

The Reverend Homer Altidore in Rivera Beach, Florida, mobilized his congregation to help the tree planting activity in the mountains of Kenscoff. Since the initial May 1st debut, Pastor Altidore and members of his congregation returned regularly on tree-planting missions.

On the other hand, the folks at a village in Haiti's central highlands called Tilori cut the trees of the Sabana Clara Forest Reserve on the Dominican side of the Haitian-Dominican border. That is where the Artibonite River originates. The Artibonite, the largest river in Haiti, is a source of life for the citizens of the Artibonite region. It is also the original source of the cholera outbreak in October 2010. Unrestrained, the action of the inhabitants of Tilori eventually would dry up the Artibonite River and adversely affect the vast Artibonite valley, which is a rice basket for the nation.

The Dominican Ministry of Environment and Natural Resources mobilized its *Fondo Pro Naturaleza* (Pro nature Fund) to bring a solution to the critical problem. The Dominican Churches Social Service, an ecumenical organization, also came to the rescue. With financial support from the US-based Nature Conservancy organization, the partners launched a "family forestry garden project" in Tilori. Their aim was to provide Tilori residents free, fast growing fuel and fruit trees that will mature in five years.

Meanwhile, alternative cooking methods have been introduced at Tilori. Energy-efficient stoves and solar ovens, paid for by Nature Conservancy, have been manufactured by Solar Household Energy (SHE), a 501(c)(3) non-profit concern based in Maryland.

Women in Tilori have been trained on the use of the alternative cooking ovens with great success. Nature Conservancy delighted in the fact that 136 families were nurturing 136,000 trees in private gardens.

Another encouraging experiment is the work that Hugh Locke and Timoté Georges began in 2011 with a group of farmers in the Gonaïves area. Within three years the Small Farmers Alliance grew to a membership of 2,000 in food producing cooperatives both for their own use and for commerce. Now, the Gonaïves model is being replicated in the St. Michel de l'Attalaye area, still in the Artibonite region.

I have raised funds for the reforestation of the land through my organization "A Dollar a Tree for Haiti." My young Haitian-American colleagues Frantz Kénol, Albert Decady, and André Jean work together to hopefully get more than four million Haitians and citizens of Haitian descent abroad to adopt this noble cause as their own. Many who feel disconnected to Haiti or have been active in helping Haiti but now suffer from "Haiti fatigue" should be re-energized as they undertake a rescue operation of the land of their birth or that of their parents and forefathers.

On May 1st, 2013, A Dollar a Tree officially planted our first tree in conjunction with congressman Louis. We planted more than 20,000 saplings in five communities over a two-week period. We are concentrating on a pilot reforestation project in the Cabaret area on thirty acres of private land put at the disposal of the organization. With that project, we will get the experience to replicate it in other communities in need.

Haiti's President Michel Joseph Martelly declared 2013 "The Year of the Environment." The 2013 National Carnival, held in Cap Haïtien, was called "The Carnival of the Environment." A catchy slogan was devised to go along with the President's vision: *Yon Ayisyen, Yon Pye Bwa* (One Haitian, One Tree).

The movement for reforestation has caught the attention of the presidents of both Haiti and the Dominican Republic. In 2013, President Martelly met with Dominican President Danilo Medina to launch a joint reforestation project for the two countries.

Members of my immediate family have wondered about this latest passion of mine. My son Pierre voiced his concern this way: "Dad, at your age and after two stints at the Embassy [of Haiti] in Washington, I thought you would have retired."

"Pierre, the day I retire that's the day I die," I said.

A few months later, I received an email from Pierre who had found a Greek proverb that he wanted to share with me. For my birthday on August 31, 2013, he framed it and gave it to me. It reads: *"A society grows great when old men plant trees under whose shade they shall not sit."*

ACKNOWLEDGMENTS

Before the 2010 earthquake, I had sketched what I thought would be my memoirs and began some writing. But Lola, my wife, said that the memoirs can wait. "You should tell about your struggle for democracy," she added. Thus, I set aside much of what I had already written to concentrate on the half century since the 1960s when I became involved in Haitian politics, first as an outsider, and later as an insider.

I thank Lola for her understanding during the months when I had to be somewhat in seclusion in the mountains of Fermathe and Kenscoff, totally immersed in writing. She volunteered to be my reader and critic. An excellent one, I would say. Without her advice and full support I wouldn't have succeeded in this task. Again, thanks, Lola.

When the first draft was ready, my friend Seth Lipsky, Editor of the *New York Sun,* introduced me to Carol Mann, of the Carol Mann Agency in New York, who accepted to represent me. I owe Seth a load of gratitude. A colleague from our days at the *Wall Street Journal,* Seth is a wise adviser who has always been kind to me. When he revived the *Sun* in 2002, he offered me a platform for a weekly column in his newspaper. Thanks, Seth, for all your help. I also thank Carol, who spent time reading my manuscript, and told me: "You have made a contribution to Haitian history with your work."

When Ms. Mann introduced me to Krishan Trotman, my editor at Skyhorse Publishing Inc., I discovered a reader who is very interested in Haiti. "The new generation of Haitian-Americans needs your perspective," she said. At times she prodded me to be more specific regarding some matters, and less voluble about others. She greatly helped with the flow of the story for a readership that may not be familiar with Haitian history. Thank you, Krishan.

Margaret "Maguie" Tanéus was right when she told me "I have the perfect place for you to write." Margaret and Roger, my friends from Maryland own the *Auberge sur la Montagne,* a bed-and-breakfast in the mountains of Fermathe, Haiti, which became my pied-à-terre for months. The mountaintop *Auberge,* away from the beaten path, provided me the serene atmosphere that stimulated my thinking. Thanks, dear friends.

Having been living in the United States for half a century, I have depended on trusted friends to reconnect with the country and to settle in. I don't know how I would have done it without the help and support of Eric Saint Louis, Jean Occelvio Armand, better known as Sergo, Etzer Dépestre and my cousins Dumel Joseph and Pastor Jude Valéry. Thanks, fellows, for all you've done.

Frantz Kénol has been egging me on to write the book for the past six years. He told me that he's in awe when he hears how people of my generation, including his father, operated in dangerous circumstances under the dictatorship of the Duvaliers. "You have to write the book," he kept saying. "Our generation needs to know what happened. I can't wait to read it." He's read snippets of it and has made some comments which I have taken into consideration in revising certain sections. Frantz and his wife Cynthia have helped me in numerous ways. Special thanks to Cynthia who has been very generous with her hospitality.

My children and stepchildren have been very supportive and have become my advance team in preparing for the coming out of the book. Their questions have helped me remember certain things that should have been included in the book. Thus, indirectly, they have contributed to making the book. Thanks, Jacqueline Andrée and Casey Patrick, Paul and Velma Joseph, Pierre-Emile and Tracy Joseph, Gigi Ndiaye, Patrick Poisson and André Ernest Forsberg Joseph. Without the help of André, it would have been difficult to finish the book on time. The computer expert that he is, he not only provided me with the laptop for my work, but was always available whenever I ran into technical problems. In the process, I've gained some technological experience that will serve me well as I work on the next book.

INDEX